One Hundred Years Ago in Burrillville
(RHODE ISLAND)

The PASCOAG HERALD
BURRILLVILLE NEWS-GAZETTE

Selected Stories from the Local Newspapers

Patricia A. Mehrtens

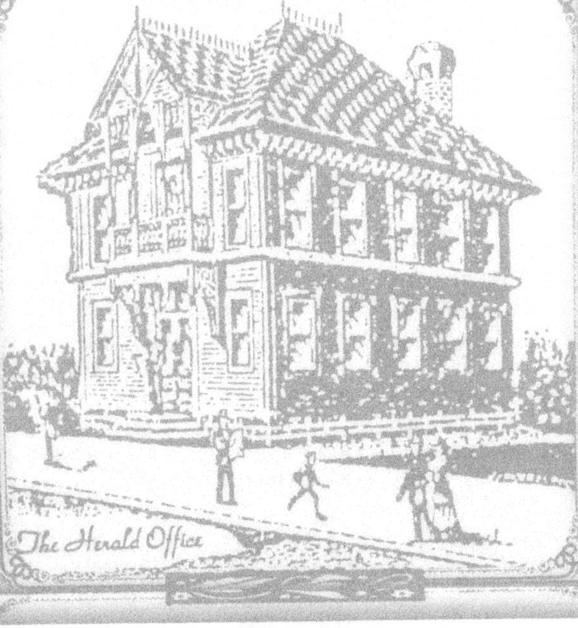

HERITAGE BOOKS
2016

HERITAGE BOOKS
AN IMPRINT OF HERITAGE BOOKS, INC.

Books, CDs, and more—Worldwide

For our listing of thousands of titles see our website at
www.HeritageBooks.com

Published 2016 by
HERITAGE BOOKS, INC.
Publishing Division
5810 Ruatan Street
Berwyn Heights, Md. 20740

Copyright © 1992 Patricia A. Mehrtens

Heritage Books by the author:

*One Hundred Years Ago in Burrillville (Rhode Island):
Selected Stories from the Local Newspapers*

*The Elusive Booths of Burrillville (Rhode Island):
An Investigation of John Wilkes Booth's Alleged Wife and Daughter*
Joyce G. Knibb and Patricia A. Mehrtens

CD: *The Elusive Booths of Burrillville (Rhode Island):
An Investigation of John Wilkes Booth's Alleged Wife and Daughter*
Joyce G. Knibb and Patricia A. Mehrtens

All rights reserved. No part of this book may be reproduced or transmitted in any form or by any means, electronic or mechanical, including photocopying, recording or by any information storage and retrieval system without written permission from the author, except for the inclusion of brief quotations in a review.

International Standard Book Numbers
Paperbound: 978-1-55613-716-7
Clothbound: 978-0-7884-6419-5

One Hundred Years Ago in Burrillville by Patricia A. Mehrtens

CONTENTS

Introduction vii

Newspapers & Editorials 1
Newspapers in Burrillville. Communication. A Stranger's Impression of Burrillville. Outlook in the Future for Burrillville. Business Outlook in Town. Newspaper Complaints. Young Men's Bad Habits. A Painting of Pascoag. Free Pictures from the *Pascoag Herald*. Vacancy Filled by Arthur Fitz. Democrats Criticize Town. Newspaper Man Mathewson Dead. Our Oldest Subscriber.

Weather Stories & Farms 16
Large Potatoes. The Yellow Day. Burrillville Cackler. Sherman's Stock Farm. Flood in Burrillville. Heaviest Snowstorm of the Season. Thunder Shower Does Damage. Steam Engine at Tarkiln Farm. Visit to the Poor Farm. Handsome Home for Gallant Steeds. Enjoying the Heavy Snowstorm. Echoes of the Blizzard. Mammoth Ice Plant at Wallum Lake. A Card about Burrillville. Sumner Sherman Obituary. The Ice Men Cometh. Smith's Large Barn Burned. Storm Knocks Out Trolleys. Runaways from State Home.

Fires 32
Narrow Escape in the Harrisville Mill. One Less Saloon. Wood's Barn Struck by Lightning. Mill at Gazza Destroyed. Pascoag Fire District Meeting. Immense Forest Fire. Pascoag Swept by Flames. Daring Rescue from Flames. Fire Destroys Laurel Hill Yarn Mill. Up in Smoke. Tenement Block Destroyed in Gazza. New Fire Alarm Installed. Big Fire at Mohegan. Midnight Fire Menaces Pascoag's Center.

Around Town. 45
Manufacturers Hotel's New Landlord. Brooks' New Store in Harrisville. Glimpses in Shop and Store. Post Office for Tarkiln? Change Name of Post Office? The Burrillville Post Office Question. Improvements in Harrisville. Fountain in Post Office Square. Building Our Fountain. New Post Office in Laurel Hill. Will of Mary E. Smith. Questions about Mrs. Smith's Will. Bridgeton Square Has New Fountain. Father of 41 Children. Burrillville Memorial Library. Odd Fellows Block. Post Office Burglarized. The New "Wet Wash" Laundry. First Mail Service. Free Mail Delivery for Pascoag.

One Hundred Years Ago in Burrillville by Patricia A. Mehrtens

Mills 65
    Riot at Gazzaville. J.T. Fiske's New Mill. Stone Drain and Steps. White Mill & Privilege. How Turkeyville Got Its Name. Great Activity at the White Mill. Boiler at Inman Mill Explodes. Happenings at Random. Disappearance of Herbert M. Wilson. Harrisville's Big Woolen Mill Destroyed. Prospects of New Mills. Magner Bros. Mill Destroyed by Fire. Wm. Sheldon's Obituary. Mapleville Mill Sold. Bridgeton Knife Co. Stone Worsted Mill Destroyed. Fly-Wheel Burst. New Harrisville Mill. Stonemason Francis Sprague.

Railroads & Trolleys 82
    Trains Collide. A Trip Along the Railroad. The New Railroad Extension. Oakland Station Accident. Laurel Hill to the Front. Andrew Hubbard Killed by Train. Fast Train through Burrillville. Columbian Street Railway. Pleasant Trolley Trip. Providence & Springfield RR History.

Summer Resorts & Parties 96
    Shore Resorts in Burrillville. Picnics on July Fourth. Sunday at Herring Pond. The Last & Best Excursion. Drum and Fife Band of Pascoag. One for Dixie. Wallum Lake House. What "Quiet" Girls Did. Arrested for Taking a Bath. New Year's Party at Overlook. Camp Notes on Wallum's Shore. Man Found in a Cabin. Ballou Reunion. Oakland Whist.

Churches. 110
    Baptist Church Dedicated at Harrisville. Life by Mrs. Edwin S. Bates. Catholic Excursion to Oakland Beach. Friends Meeting House Celebration. Soliloquizing. Laurel Hill Methodist Episcopal Church. The Advent Church. Mysterious Ringing of Bells in Glendale. Mapleville News. Mapleville Catholic Church Dedicated. Many Listen to "Shang" Bailey. Glendale Clambake. Confirmation at St. Joseph's. Dedication at Mapleville of M. E. Church. Free Baptist Church of Pascoag.

Schools 125
    Unprovoked Attack on a School. Troubles at the Schools. School District #11. Rumpus in the Nasonville School District. School Committee Meeting. Changes Needed in the Schools. Tarkiln School. Meeting in District #7. Valuation of School Property. Flag Raising. The Schoolhouse Gone. Dedication of New Pascoag School House. History of Burrillville Schools at Pascoag Dedication. School Census Figures. Round Top School Celebration. Recollections by Manning Wood.

One Hundred Years Ago in Burrillville by Patricia A. Mehrtens

Town Business 141
        Burrillville Census of 1880. Political Communications. Letter from Horace Kimball. Communication from a Taxpayer. Burrillville Voting List. Feeding of Tramps. Liquor Licenses Granted. Burrillville Senators since 1843. Board of Canvasser's Meeting. Saturday Night's Rally. Alvah Mowry, Ex-Town Clerk. Electric Lights for Harrisville. Sanatorium Inspected. June Town Meeting. State Census for 1905.

Sports 158
        Rooster Fighting on a Sunday. Pascoag Trotting Park. Local Baseball Teams. Grand Regatta. Petition Found on Highway. Cockfight Near Joe Mowry's. Horse Racing at the Trotting Park. Complaint About Baseball Players. Pascoag Driving Park. Allum Pond Cockfight. Baseball Meeting. July Fourth Amusements. That Fish. Excitement in Burrillville. Pugilistic Contest at Herring Pond. Sunday Baseball Playing. Old Time Fishing.

Saloons, etc. 172
        Gazza Bipeds. Liquor Seizure in Harrisville. Arrest of Itinerants. Saloons Raided Tuesday Last. Havoc Raised in Pascoag. Buck Hill Raid by RI and CT. Cowboy Dupes Townspeople. Terrible Fright of Two Women. Savage Assault at Round Top. Advertisement for Round Top. Tramps in Town. Two Questionable Women Visit Town. Great Little Invention. Flutter in a Dove Cote. Buck Hill Tavern Fire. Fatality at Saloon in Pascoag.

Horses, Stealing, & Robberies 185
        Excitement in Harrisville. More Horse Thefts in Town. Runaway Horses in Pascoag. Horse Trader Arrested. Beware of Tramps. Burglaries at Harrisville & Pascoag. Horse Thief Caught. Wars and Rumors of War. Mad Dog Bites Horse. Eldridge's Mad Cow. Attempted Robbery. Elopement in Pascoag. Bold Daylight Robbery. Sedgwick's Store Robbed. Triple Burglary.

Accidents & Deaths 199
        Lifeless Body of Woman Found. Dead in a Well in Mapleville. Frozen to Death. Sleigh Accident in Mapleville. Drowning in White Mill Pond. Accident in Pascoag. Death of Lydia Phetteplace. Body of Baby Found in Mill Trench. Lost Four Days in Woods of Douglas. Sudden Death in Glendale. Who Shot the Man? Martin Mowry Sentenced. Dynamite Explosion Near Box Turtle. Wagon Accident on Buck Hill.

One Hundred Years Ago in Burrillville by Patricia A. Mehrtens

Accidents & Deaths, continued.
Charles A. Stoddard Suicide. Discovery of Injured Man. Bridgeton Fountain Accident. Fatal Shooting at Graniteville. Sad Fate of Annie Trask. Depot Square Accident. Accident at Wilson's. Snake Hill's Mystery.

Memories 223
William Rhodes & Rhodesville. Old Town House. Two New Houses in Pascoag. Blowing-Out Ball of 1852. Memories of Central Pascoag. More Central Pascoag by L. D. S. Mapleville & Daniel Cooper's House. Retrospective & Prospective. How to Pat the Juba. Pascoag in 1872. Remarkable Caves in Pascoag.

100 Years Ago in Burrillville by Patricia A. Mehrtens

Introduction

It appears the old saying is true:—That one thing leads to another. While researching information for a previous book on Burrillville's history, I located bound and unbound copies of the *Pascoag Herald* and the *Burrillville News-Gazette* dating from 1880 through 1917. The stories were so well written and amusing that I xeroxed the more interesting ones for a potential future book. Approximately 600 articles were discovered, copied, indexed by category, and saved. When the time came to use this collection, I selected the following 234 stories, which seemed to give a pretty good overview of that period in the history of Burrillville. These had to be typeset, a major editing job done, hopefully without losing the gist of the stories, then the contents retyped into their final form.

Both major papers were in print simultaneously between 1892 and 1895, but the majority of the stories used from that time frame came from the *Burrillville News-Gazette*. The writers for the *Gazette* had a better sense of humor about happenings in our town. The *Pascoag Herald* stories dealt more with facts and figures, including histories of the various churches, mills, and other points of interest. My choice went to the *Gazette* version of the local news for the obvious reasons. It was time something like this was accomplished, because nothing new had been written on the history of Burrillville since Keach's book, *"Burrillville As It Was and As It Is"* in 1856. (Reprinted by Heritage Press this year.)

A large thank you goes to the brave newspapermen and women—the editors, writers, and printers—who took the time and effort to report and to print the news, and then to save the product of their writings so that we, who live in their future, can reap the benefits of their thoughts and ideas.

Many thanks also go to my family, and particularly to my husband, Don, for his understanding when things that seemed important didn't get done and, that priorities are in the mind of the beholder. My sincere hope is that all of you enjoy reading these bits and pieces of information as much as I enjoyed gathering them.

Patricia A. Mehrtens
Burrillville, RI 1992

One Hundred Years Ago in Burrillville by Patricia A. Mehrtens

NEWSPAPERS & EDITORIALS

Newspapers in Burrillville
April 5, 1895

The *Pascoag Herald* and *Burrillville News-Gazette* which appears the first time in consolidated form this week is the result of several attempts in the newspaper business in Burrillville. Mr. Keach, Mr. E. A. Mathewson and Whittemore Brothers were the first to establish weekly papers published in the interest of this section with the *Burrillville Gazette* and *Burrillville News*. The *Gazette* was printed by Whittemore Brothers in the attic over the blacksmith shop on Sayles Avenue. It was started in February, 1880, and in a few short months succeeded to the control of the entire field. Mr. E. A. Mathewson's *Burrillville News* which started soon after the *Gazette* did not prove to be a paying measure and was sold out for a small sum to the *Gazette* publishers. The *Gazette* continued to be printed at Pascoag for some months. The printing and newspaper plant was then moved to Providence and has been located at 54 North Main Street.

In March, 1892 at the request of several influential citizens of the town the present editor of this paper, Mr. A. S. Fitz, was asked to look over the field and see what could be done towards starting a newspaper that would be located with its printing plant within the town. Mr. Fitz agreed to start if proper encouragement was given. He ordered his printing machinery and made due preparations to begin business April 1st. Upon Mr. Mathewson hearing of this he went to Woonsocket and contracted with the *Reporter* people for the printing of a five-column, eight-page paper which appeared the last of March some two weeks earlier than the *Herald*, naturally dampening its prospects. The *Herald* made its first appearance on April 2, 1892, and from its first start has tried to have every em of its type set in Burrillville and distribute its earnings where they would be spent among the merchants of the town. This plan has proved profitable, and one by one the businessmen have fallen into line and attested their appreciation by placing their advertisements in the *Herald* columns.

After about nine short months of life, the *Burrillville News* No. 2 was obliged because of a lack of advertising support to consolidate with the *Burrillville Gazette* in January, 1893. The name of the paper has since been the *Burrillville News-Gazette* with Messrs. Whittemore & Colburn owning one-half interest and Mr. E. A. Mathewson the other. This arrangement lasted until about the first of January when we are told that Mr. Mathewson was obliged to surrender his interest to his partners in order to pay his proportion of the expenses of printing the paper. Mr. Mathewson was retained as editor until last week's issue.

The *Herald* publishers were approached by Lawyer Harris attorney for Messrs. Whittemore & Colburn nearly a month ago and asked if they would consider the purchase of the *News-Gazette* if the price was right. They began to consider negotiations which resulted in their buying that paper last week Wednesday with its good will, subscription list, advertising contracts, etc. at a price just about one-quarter of that asked us some year and a half ago. The consolidated *Pascoag Herald* and *Burrillville News-Gazette* now appears under one heading and with one management, its circulation increased, its news columns expanded and many other departures. The advertiser can find no stronger medium of its class and none reaching a more enterprising and intelligent class of people. All advertising contracts will be fulfilled with either paper at their agreed on rates, and those running from week to week will be charged the regular rates of the combined paper and continued until forbidden by the advertiser. All correspondence should be addressed—*Herald*, Pascoag, R. I. Those desiring to furnish news or special articles to the paper should make known their wants and always sign their articles with their full name.

As we have in the past we shall continue with malice toward none. Blackmail articles, petty spite, or jealousies will not appear in our columns with our approval. No true newspaperman ever indulges in them. It is field enough to furnish the news (not manufactured but reliable news), and to work for the advancement of the town and the prosperity of its citizens. To this end we ask your assistance in the future while we thank you for past favors received. The *Herald-News-Gazette* will be published every Friday morning. All news matter and advertisements should be in our hands by Wednesday morning of each week in order to secure a prompt insertion. We have neglected to recite the history of the *Burrillville Democrat* which started early in the year 1893 and lived seven short weeks, Mr. I. H. Mesick was its editor.

Communication
June 13, 1884

Dear Gazette - Some weeks ago the Hon. L. Prendergast informed us through your columns that we would find plenty of Democrats round the Town House. If they existed they must have been round the house for they did not come in. One of those western zephyrs called cyclones struck them, caught them and has scattered them so you cannot find one with a fine tooth comb.

What caused the earthquake? One word will explain and that word is "dishonesty." Take the case of Peter Corcoran. The late president of the Town Council, late Moderator and late Assessor of Taxes knew him for years and knew that the property upon which Corcoran lived was owned by the wife and that it could not qualify Peter to vote. Yet knowing all this, the late president thought a great deal of Peter and would take especial pains to see that he attended Town Meeting. Well a few days since he discovered Peter was in the same condition of the boy's puppies. Another boy wanted to see them and they went to the shed and the owner of the pups says, "see my Democrats." A fortnight later the boy made another visit and the owner of the pups said, "see my Republicans." "But," says the other boy, "when I was here before, you called them Democrats." "Oh yes, that was before they got their eyes open." When Peter got his eyes open and declared himself a Republican then the late president discovered that Peter was an illegal voter and had always been. So he caused Peter's name to disappear from the voting list although he had allowed him to vote previously. Not only that, but had accepted him as bondsman for liquor sellers.

One more trick last year in the Democratic caucus. No nomination for Town Clerk was made, but when we arrived at Town Meeting we found that Willaby Nason had been run in. The Democratic party could never have elected him against Alvah Mowry with their own votes had a ballot been taken and had every Republican stayed at home. It was not the objection to the man (for he has made an excellent Town Clerk, very accommodating, indeed, whenever he happened to be at the office) but it was the mode of electing him. - Taxpayer

One Hundred Years Ago in Burrillville by Patricia A. Mehrtens

A Stranger's Impression of Burrillville
August 8, 1884

He states: I found the people very civil, cordial, and courteous, without any attempt at elaborate politeness. I did not think the people to be as curious and inquisitive as they are in many places, although perhaps on a longer stay I might possibly change my mind. One thing, however, I was sorry to see and that was a lack of public interest in keeping the village roads, sidewalks and bridges in good repair. It reminded me of what a little girl asked her mother when visiting in a village similar to Pascoag: "Mother, where are the sidewalks?" The mother replied: "I guess they are too poor to have any my child." The roads are as bad if not worse than any I ever saw and it will be a wonder if the town is not called upon to pay damages to some person injured by their defects. The pump in the middle of the street in front of the Manufacturers Hotel should be removed, the iron railing down near the post office should be taken away, the telegraph poles are not set in a handsome way—and in some places are exactly in the middle of what footpath there is. In Harrisville nice sidewalks could be made without much expense and they are needed. Finally it seems to me there must be something wrong in regard to the management of the place or there would be more system and uniformity in the appearance of its villages. I have been told that there is money enough spent to insure good roads. If that is the case, where is the trouble? With a little bracing up in some directions, the town of Burrillville will compare favorably with any town in New England.

Outlook in the Future for Burrillville
July 20, 1888

The outlook in the future for Burrillville is quite encouraging notwithstanding the croaking of some that are everlastingly looking on the dark side of everything. We believe many changes will take place affecting the town's interest and within but a few years. The past two years although disastrous in several respects, particularly as regards fires, has been more than offset in building. Two new houses costing nearly $20,000 have been erected in Pascoag within two years. A neat cottage on Sayles Hill has reared its head and the foundation for another building is already in next to it. Several houses are now in process of construction and others are soon to follow.

The new addition to the Harrisville mill has been a move

towards prosperity. At that place tenements were scarce and although Miss Emilie Clarke invested some of her spare cash in building several houses for letting purposes, a two-tenement house coming into the market built by Mr. R. F. Brooks and also one by Mr. John M. Smith and others, the scarcity continues. A fine addition to the mill of J. T. Fiske, Jr. has been fully utilized within a year. The mill formerly occupied by Sayles & Nichols partially burned and owned by Horace A. Kimball of Manton has been rebuilt and is ready for some enterprising persons to buy or hire for manufacturing uses. The new mill built by Sayles & Nichols is just ready for occupancy by that firm. At Oakland the silk mill is running full blast furnishing employment to many, thus filling the cottages that were vacant so long. At Gazza it is reported that better times are in prospect as two able businessmen have leased the mill for a term of years.

A cursory view of the town as a whole shows fairly well for the future. It is safe to say no step has been taken backward. But to insure rapid financial growth several things should be done in the shape of improvement and comfort of the people that are as yet hardly talked or thought of except by the most wide awake and thoughtful citizens. Glendale surely has been coming into more prominence of late and several new buildings erected. The new addition to this mill brought more people to this place and more business. By such an increase in business the necessity of quicker and better mail facilities became very evident and absolutely necessary. The Postmaster General granted a commission as postmaster to J. Henry Carpenter who keeps the popular general merchandise store at which place Glendalites can hereafter get their mail twice each day if desired.

Nasonville is prospering under the mill management of Joshua Perkins who has kept things moving, earning an honest dollar for himself and giving employment to others that they might also earn their portion of the filthy lucre. Harrisville is nearer the center of the town but Pascoag is the center of trade from the surrounding country. It must show enterprise to hold and increase this vantage. It must have gas, it must have water, it must have better streets.

The streets of Pascoag are in a terrible condition, and the impression a stranger receives in passing from the depot to the square along the Main Street is anything but reassuring and pleasant after passing the beautiful grounds of Mr. Fiske. There is no sidewalk, and many of the houses look untidy and ill kept. A zephyr from the direction of the water causes one to hurry along to get away from the beautiful aroma arising from the mud hole. On the left is a row of liquor saloons which give everyone a fine impression, especially as they hear swearing, loud talk and see streams of half intoxicated persons emerge from the doors of the window-darkened rooms. Oh! yes, many improvements are needed. A little further along the right, beautifully bedecked damsels cover the stoop of the door and seem to exist with no apparent means of support. Yes, improvements are needed in many directions, not only in Pascoag but also in Oakland, Harrisville and each village in the town. Reform is called for in everything where reform is needed.

Business Outlook in Town
August 22, 1890

    The general business outlook in town looks considerably more encouraging at the present time than two months ago. It is hoped our manufacturers may secure enough orders for goods to make the fall business very brisk. The summer months have been exceedingly quiet and several of the mills idle. This was the case to a certain extent when the enumerators took the census. It was taken in the worst time it could have been to show the correct population. We believe that had it been taken earlier or even at the present time, the town would have shown no decrease in population, but on the contrary, a gain instead. To be sure that the mill at Gazza has been burned, and the Kimball Mill burned several years ago has never been rebuilt, but there have been extensive additions to some of the mills and in some instances, you might say, entirely new mills.

    Since Joshua Perkins took hold of the mill at Nasonville he has dug out the bank and enlarged the capacity of the mill quite a little. The Mohegan Mill took a new lease of life when the Glendale Company took it in charge. The mill at Oakland idle four years ago has been put in operation as a silk mill and all the tenements in that village formerly vacant are filled at the present time. A very large extension has been built within three years to the already large mill at Harrisville. John T. Fiske, Jr. has much increased his plant and employs more help. Fred L. Sayles & Co. has built a new wing or weave shed besides raising the roof of the old mill and increasing the capacity for production. Sayles & Nichols at Laurel Hill built a fine new mill which was idle when the census was taken and which is being rapidly started up.

    Taking it all in all we are unable to see how the population can be less than it was in 1880. We believe if it was to be taken two months hence, this town would show an increase of population. We would like to see the town take the matter in hand and verify the facts, which we believe we have stated correctly, and not allow such a report to go out without any attempt whatever to place the town in its true colors.

Newspaper Complaints
July 24, 1891

It was once said that a schoolmaster who whipped the scholars considerably would whip them if they did and whip them if they didn't. There is a class of people who are whipped today for the same thing—journalists and newspaper men. If news comes out in our paper that the Town Council has made a mistake, or our roads are bad, some Reverend gone wrong, a deacon of the church a little crooked, a saloon has broken the law—any or all of the misdemeanors of life—someone will say why does he trouble himself about that, it is none of his business. If he doesn't make mention of them, he is blamed for not letting the public know. I send a letter to have my paper stopped, it does not stop. I write my name and post office but forget to put on the state or put on the state but forget to notice the post office—who is to blame? There is so much advertising there is no room for news—there is too much fun and nonsense—there is no fun in it, I think I will stop it. There is too much baseball news—there is no baseball news. They have spelled somebody's name wrong—advertising too much out of town—my paper did not come last week—they charged me for a card of thanks and I'm a regular subscriber. These are not half the complaints that the publisher receives weekly. The editor is human, the reporter more than human—if not he would not live through it. Editors, journalists, reporters, all live and that is about all—many are poor, few get rich, and all for being a public benefactor—trying to promote the most good for the least pay. The knowledge the press throws out and scatters broadcast up and down the world is read by those who could not afford to do without it. There is no amount of satisfaction one gets so cheap and which is so profitable as what one pays for reading matter.

Young Men's Bad Habits
February 5, 1892

It is entirely natural for people to form habits so that if bad habits be avoided the good ones will generally take care of themselves. I take the liberty of suggesting to those who are interested in this kind of thing that if there be anything that demonstrated total depravity it is the readiness with which young men imbibe bad habits. I have seen original sin in the shape of "a short six" sticking out of the mouth of a lad of ten years. It is strange what particular pains boys and young men will take to learn to do that which will make them miserable, ruin their health, render them disgusting to their friends, and damage their reputation.

Some of the bad habits of the day are connected with the use of tobacco. Here is a drug a young man is obliged to become accustomed to before he can tolerate either the taste or the effect of it. It is a rank vegetable poison and in the unaccustomed animal, produces vertigo, faintness, and horrible sickness. Yet young men persevere in the use of it until they can endure it, and then until they love it. They go about the streets with a pipe or cigar in their mouths or into society with breath sufficiently offensive to drive all unperverted nostrils before them. They chew tobacco—roll up huge wads of the vile drug and stuff their cheeks with them. They ejaculate their saliva upon the sidewalk, in the store, in spittoons which become incorporate stenches, in dark corners of railroad cars to stain the white skirts of unsuspecting women, in lecture rooms and churches, upon fences and into stoves that hiss with anger at the insult. And the quids after they are ejected! They are to be found in odd corners, in out of the way places—great boulders, boluses, bulbs! Horses stumble over them, dogs bark at them. They poison young shade trees, and break down the constitutions of sweepers. This may be an exaggeration of the facts but not of the disgust which one writes of them.

Now young men just think of this thing! You are born into this world with a sweet breath. At a proper age you acquire a good set of teeth. Why will you make them a set of yellow pigs? A proper description of the habit of chewing tobacco would exhaust the filthy adjectives themselves for further use. Yet you will acquire the habit and persist in it after it is acquired. It is very singular that young men will adopt a habit of which every man who is its victim is ashamed. There is probably no tobacco chewer in the world who would advise a young man to commence this habit. I have never seen a slave of tobacco who did not regret his bondage. Yet against all advice, against nausea and disgust, against cleanliness, against every consideration of health and comfort, thousands every year bow the neck to this drug and consent to wear its repulsive yoke. They chew it, they will smoke it in cigars and pipes until their bedrooms and shops cannot be breathed in and until their breath is as rank as the breath of a foul beast and their clothes have the odor of a sewer.

Some of them take snuff, cram the fiery weed up their nostrils to irritate that subtle sense which rarest flowers were made to feel. In all, this is working against God, abusing nature, perverting sense, injuring health, planting the seeds of disease, and insulting the decencies of life and the noses of the world. A clean mouth, a sweet breath, unstained teeth, and inoffensive clothing, are not these treasures worth preserving? Then throw away tobacco and all thoughts of it once and forever, be a man. Be decent, and be thankful to me for talking so plainly to you.

A Painting of Pascoag
November 9, 1894

It is said that history sometimes repeats itself, and in the instance in question this is true. Several months ago Joseph Bevin achieved much notoriety by a painting exhibited in Gross's art store and noticed in the *Herald*. The same artist has this week completed another painting, entitled "An Evening View of Fountain Square." It is twenty-four by thirty-six inches in size. To view the work in a critical view is beyond the ability of the writer as is also the power to give a perfect description of its many features. On the canvas is depicted the post office, bank, a part of Granite Mills, etc. At the left of the bank the slopes of South Main Street arise to a dizzy height, and shaded as it is by a thrifty mulberry tree, has an inviting appearance to the weary traveler.

The north side of Granite Mills is shown and is perfect in every detail even to the escaping steam from the engine and the towering smoke stack and chimney in the background. Nearby the limpid waters of the mill pond are seen flowing into the fountain from which a dashing black charger is abstracting a cooling draught. Around the fountain a group of merry bicyclists are disporting themselves. The scene is one from which the artist turns at last, sighing because it is not real. The electric light gleams brightly as if to awe the effulgent beams of fair lunar who floats silently along on the fleecy clouds of the starlit sky. But we are done. To attempt further description would but belittle the painter and his masterpiece and bring down upon us the scorn of an art-loving public. Suffice it to say that so highly does the present owner value the picture that he has refused an offer of $75 for it.

One Hundred Years Ago in Burrillville by Patricia A. Mehrtens

Free Pictures from the *Pascoag Herald*
May 17, 1895

Every citizen of this town has an idea that they would like to see how its villages look on paper. Views have been taken of mills and private dwellings time and time again but in no case have they done more than represent the particular object taken. Not until the coming to town of Mr. Bailey some two months ago was the idea conceived of sketching the villages and reproducing them on paper exactly as they would appear if we were elevated above them and could look down on streets and homes. The scenes of our childhood, manhood, and in some cases mature years, how familiar they are but how the changes and improvements about town are altering them.

Everyone wants a copy of this beautifully lithographed view of Burrillville as it is today. Mr. Bailey has come to town, sold his work to a select few he could reach without a general canvass and departed. The birdseye view is 25x38 inches, printed on the best of plate paper, and sold at one dollar per copy. The *Herald* publishers were able to secure a few thousand copies of the view in full size and exact duplicates of the dollar copies before the stone was destroyed. We propose to give each of our subscribers one FREE, to all who call at our office provided that they are not in arrears on the paper. All who are in arrears can secure the view by calling at the *Herald* office, Pascoag and paying up their arrearages. New subscribers will also be entitled to a free copy if they call at our office and pay a subscription in advance. This is absolutely the only way to secure a copy of this valuable work which will be a source of pleasure both today and in after years when time and her changes have wrought a multitude of improvements in our town.

Vacancy Filled by Arthur Fitz
September 26, 1902

His Excellency Charles Dean Kimball, Governor of Rhode Island, last Saturday appointed Arthur S. Fitz of this town a member of the State Returning Board to fill the vacancy caused by the death of the late Addison S. Hopkins. This appointment is very pleasing to Mr. Fitz's friends who have earnestly urged his candidacy for the position.

Arthur S. Fitz was born in Hartford, Conn., March 24th, 1860 and is the son of the Rev. William and Ellen L. Fitz. On his father's side, he is a descendent of Jeremiah Fitz who was with

One Hundred Years Ago in Burrillville by Patricia A. Mehrtens

Perry's famous squadron at the battle of Lake Erie. On his mother's side he is the great-great grandson of Edward Salisbury, who was one of the prominent men in this section in the days before the Revolution. Edward Salisbury was born in Smithfield and when a young man was engaged in the French and Indian War and in King Philip's War, after which he returned to Rhode Island and settled in Burrillville in 1734. He was an ardent patriot, and when the news of the gathering of the Minute Men at Lexington came, he started for the front. Afterwards, although long past the age when men were required to take part in warfare, he secured a commission and marched to New York state and was engaged in service until after the close of the Revolution.

William Fitz, the father of the subject of this sketch, was a Baptist minister and held pastorates in a number of places in New England. He was a man of prominence in every community where he settled. In the days of the Civil War Rev. Mr. Fitz was pastor of a church in Westerly and was anxious to enter the army and go to the front. Three times he attempted to enlist and thrice he was rejected on account of physical disability. Finally he was given a commission as chaplain in the 23rd Rhode Island regiment and went to the front, reaching there just before the fall of Richmond. Mr. Fitz has lived in Burrillville the greater part of his life and his education was secured in the public schools of this and other towns.

In 1892 Mr. Fitz came to Pascoag and established the Pascoag *Herald*. At the time there were two other newspapers in the field but the energetic manner in which the *Herald* pressed its campaign for supremacy enabled it to soon outdistance its competitors. He later purchased the rival papers and consolidated them with the *Herald*. A job printing plant was also established at the same time and has been constantly added to, until today it is one of the best equipped plants in the state outside of large cities, and numbers among its customers firms and corporations in various sections of New England. The business is owned by the *Pascoag Herald Company* of which Mr. Fitz is the treasurer and manager.

Democrats Criticize Town
July 31, 1903

It has been the misfortune of the State of Rhode Island to have had a Democrat for Governor the past year, and he has used that high office to aid in spreading the impression throughout the land that the men of this State are corrupt and venal. The

One Hundred Years Ago in Burrillville by Patricia A. Mehrtens

average voter would almost hesitate to believe that high State officials could be found spreading such calumnies, yet the proof is abundant. Within the past few days from Democratic sources has gone forth a circular containing articles reprinted from a New York publication making charges that are plainly false and casting reflections on our homes and private character. The voters of Rhode Island should rebuke this sort of treatment of its good name.

To bring to your attention more forcibly the nature of the charges made by these Democrats, a few quotations are submitted. Burrillville - "The double admixture of farmers and mill workers and a large foreign element with the degenerate native stock has combined with environment to make Burrillville one of the most corrupt towns in the State. It is in the so-called "Crime Belt," and its morals (social and political) are low. The topmost of the western tier of towns comprising the "heathen" district, it has better railroad facilities than its notorious neighbors. The mills are responsible for these outlets to civilization. The wagon roads that wind drearily over the broken, stony, uneven countryside are poor and unkept."

"It was usually found that where a manufacturing community adjoined a farming country, immorality was the rule rather than the exception. This is true of certain sections of Burrillville. Women were pointed out who divided their time impartially, living as 'housekeeper' for first one man and then another. Stories of sexual immorality and crimes of decadence unprintably vile were told."

"The farms are not well kept as a rule, many of the houses being unpainted and some of them dilapidated. A prosperous-looking farm is the exception. The people seem to have become deadened to many virtues by the sordid circumstances in which they live. Because of its manufacturing industries the town has gained steadily in population. The newcomers are nearly all of foreign birth and earn a livelihood in the twenty mills at Bridgeton, Glendale, Harrisville, Mapleville, Nasonville, Oakland, Pascoag, Tarkiln, and Whipple. The mills at the two last-named villages are possibly in the poorest condition. They are rated as 'fair' by the factory inspectors."

"Burrillville is not one of the twenty small controlling towns, but it is one of the fourteen notoriously corrupt ones. It is counted upon as Democratic. Bribery is an open and regular feature of every election. When the Republicans make a strong contest, money is spent even more freely. At the last election, Joslin the Democratic candidate for Senator was elected by only forty plurality. The eight churches and twenty-four schools in the town are in part counterbalanced by its twenty-three saloons and unknown number of illegal resorts and disorderly houses. In any campaign for the regeneration of the State, Burrillville will offer a virgin field."

Newspaper Man Mathewson Dead
June 26, 1908

At 7 o'clock Wednesday morning Edgar A. Mathewson passed away of heart trouble at the residence of William Burlingame, Main Street, Harrisville where he had been boarding for some time. Edgar A. Mathewson was born in Harrisville fifty-eight years ago the son of the late Sterry and Eliza (Steere) Mathewson. After attending the public schools in his native town, he took a course in the Eastman Business College in Poughkeepsie, N. Y. He was an exceptionally fine penman and soon developed into an expert accountant and his services as such were in ready demand. For many years he was head bookkeeper for Jerome Salisbury & Co. in Providence and held similar positions of like nature in other places.

Among the many newspapers with which he was connected are the following: *St. Louis Globe Democrat, New Orleans Picayune, Atlanta Constitution, Providence Journal, Providence Star, Providence Sunday Dispatch*, of which later he was the city editor. About thirty years ago he established the *Burrillville News*, the first newspaper published in Burrillville. After a few issues the *News* passed into other hands and after a brief existence, it suspended. In 1892 he again published the *News*, which a year or two later was consolidated with the *Burrillville Gazette*, and in 1895 the *News-Gazette* was purchased by the *Pascoag Herald*. Mr. Mathewson afterwards published the *Burrillville Star* for a year or two or until about the time when his official duties required his entire attention.

His services were in great demand locally as a bookkeeper and writer. He was frequently engaged by the late Alvah Mowry to do copying on the town records. His beautiful and perfect handwriting may be found on the record books from time to time for many years back. Mr. Mathewson entered active politics in 1897 when he was elected tax assessor and a member of the school committee. In 1898 he was reelected tax assessor and town clerk in a warmly contested election to fill the vacancy in the office caused by the death of Job Steere. Mr. Mathewson's knowledge of town affairs gained through his work for Town

Clerk Mowry, and the familiarity with the work which a long newspaper career brought, were important factors in securing for him the large vote.

Everybody liked Edgar Mathewson and was ready to give him a vote, as his ability was unquestioned. Year after year he was elected town clerk by large majorities. In 1905 he declined further nomination to that office and was succeeded by the present incumbent, John H. McCabe. In 1905, 1906 and 1907 he was elected town councilman by old-time majorities and would have had the nomination again this year had he not positively refused to be a candidate. Mr. Mathewson served continuously on the school committee from 1897 until the time of his death, his last public act being to attend the special meeting of the school committee on Wednesday evening of last week.

Mr. Mathewson was a man of remarkable and striking personality, and there were indeed few persons in the town who were not known to him and with whom he was not acquainted. His comprehensive knowledge of the contents of the town records and his excellent memory, made him an authority in town affairs, and his thorough knowledge of probate matters made the labors of the council members and administrators far less difficult than otherwise would have been. As town clerk he was painstaking, and the records and papers under his charge were kept in model form.

At the time of his death he was engaged in the arduous task of preparing a general index of the land records of the town from 1806 up to the present time. This work is not only difficult but it requires the utmost care. He had completed the task of drawing off the names of grantors and grantees from the numerous books and was engaged in arranging them in alphabetical form preparatory to indexing them. The funeral services will be held from the Universalist Church this afternoon at 2:15 o'clock and will be conducted by Rev. Frederic T. Nelson, pastor, assisted by Rev. J. A. Mitchell, pastor of the Berean Baptist Church. There will be a large attendance at the services. Interment will be in the family lot in Pascoag Cemetery.

Our Oldest Subscriber
June 28, 1912

In a pleasantly situated cottage in the beautiful village of Hopedale, Mass., dwells the *Herald's* oldest subscriber Francis H. Buxton. The *Herald* man called upon the venerable reader of these columns the other day and found him to be in excellent health aside from slight infirmities of elderly life. Mr. Buxton, who has rounded out 96 full years of life and is close upon the 97th, is as keenly alive to happenings of the present day as is many a younger man. After greetings had been extended, Mr. Buxton said, "I was thinking the other day that I would send you a list of the buildings as they were 78 or 79 years ago in 'Monkey-town' which you know is what Pascoag was once called. I can remember every one of them and just where they were located. I worked in the mills there at that time."

"That was before the Free Baptist Church was built," remarked the *Herald* man. "Yes, that is so," replied Mr. Buxton. "I can remember when that was built and I used to sing in the choir in that church and play the organ," he replied. "Where the big Union Mill now stands there was a little wooden mill containing one set of machinery. I used to spin there. I also worked for Peter Place in his mill lower down the stream." Mr. Buxton described with zest the then famed turkey supper which led up to the transfer of the mill privilege where now stands the mill owned by William H. Prendergast. It was the outcome of this supper which gave the name "Turkeyville" to that locality, a name which clung to it for long years afterwards. "There was a mill at 'Alum Pond' where they made cotton goods, and I worked there a few days once," he further informed the scribe. Coming down to matters of the present day, Mr. Buxton showed that he is a faithful follower of the current news by remarking, "I see you are having some new sidewalks in Pascoag."

Mr. Buxton lived in Chepachet more recently than in Burrillville and he is now a member of Friendship Lodge A. F. & A. M., and its oldest member, too. "Tell the boys I am coming down to the Lodge one of these fine days," was the message he gave the scribe to take to his brethren in the Lodge. Truly, Mr. Buxton is not 96 years old, he is 96 years young, and bids fair to round out a full century of life—and more. He resides with his daughter and is in the best of health. His only complaint is regarding his strength and consequent inability to get about as in the days of yore, yet he stood firmly erect and waved a genial farewell as the scribe took his departure.

One Hundred Years Ago in Burrillville by Patricia A. Mehrtens

WEATHER STORIES & FARMS

Large Potatoes
July 2, 1881

    Mowry Salisbury, the boss farmer for Fiske & Sayles, raised on about one half acre of land this present year, 152 bushels of potatoes of the early rose variety. He had potatoes as large as a common man's fist. When you find men that have so much push to them as not to be afraid to lay out a great amount of money and labor on their land, the earth must bring forth her increase. 102 bushels of these potatoes were large ones, one or two of them were weighed and tipped the scales at one pound and thirteen ounces. Now ye farmers of Burrillville go thou and do likewise and you will be rewarded with the same blessing for your labor and expense. I will say that the new way of perfecting a surety of preservation of potatoes through the winter is to dig and store them early. The old way was to wait until just before the late frost comes. The new way is to dig and house them the last of August. - L. D. S.

The "Yellow Day"
September 12, 1881

    Tuesday, September 6, 1881, will long be remembered as presenting to the people not an entirely new phenomena, but a longer continuance of what may have been seen before for a half hour or so. The sun arose red as blood but soon disappeared. The sky assumed a dark and smoky appearance commencing in the northwest which soon covered the entire heavens. Everything assumed a yellowish look except the grass which took a very dark green hue. Between 12 and 1 o'clock it was so dark that a light was needed to "stick type" within two feet of a window. The light wasn't of much account being almost killed by the yellow ether waves which flooded space. All the afternoon this state of affairs continued with slight modifications from time to time, 6:30 p.m. being the lightest portion of the day since 10 a.m. The condition of things produced considerable consternation among some of the women, many of the children, and some of the lords of creation.

The causes which led to the remarkable phenomenon are involved in obscurity. The various reasons given by local philosophers are as follows: 1. Smoke from the forest fires in Canada. 2. Heavy yellow fog some distance from the earth. 3. Evidence of wind storms not far distant. 4. Some effect produced by the Northern Lights. 5. The earth passing through the tail of a comet. 6. A comet coming between the earth and the sun.

Of the above everyone is at liberty to accept one, all or neither, and perhaps the genuine philosophers will give some explanation satisfactory to all. The idea that the last day had come prevailed to a certain extent and considerable excitement was caused thereby. The *Gazette* thought they had a satisfactory theory to account for the "yellow day" but at this writing are somewhat uncertain whether to charge it to smoke from distant fires or to a heavy fog or a combination of both. The pressure on the lungs and difficulty in breathing experienced by some would indicate that gasses were present in the air not usually found there. This fact may point towards the comet theory. Of the domestic animals, horses and dogs seemed to pay no attention to the atmospheric disturbance but cows were much excited and the chickens in some places went to roost between 12 and 1. The "Yellow Day" adds one more to the list of wonderful events in the year 1881.

Burrillville "Cackler"
May 9, 1884

We have gained some additional particulars in reference to the aged hen, the property of Alonzo A. S. Mills of Burrillville. Said hen is not only old, it is older than we said it was, having seen 22 summers. Moreover, it was a native of Providence and has always shown a decided inclination to put on city airs and never has quite forgiven her owner for removing her to Burrillville in the spring of 1862. We trust this "fowl article" will attract the notice of some of the "roosters" who air their talents and do their "crowing" in some of the numerous country papers. If they can produce anything so remarkable they will "pullet" out before the public so that all may know "eggsactly" how much exclusive honor is due to the Burrillville "cackler."

One Hundred Years Ago in Burrillville by Patricia A. Mehrtens

Sherman's Stock Farm
August 7, 1885

A visit to Sherman's stock farm found everything in apple pie order, and the help busily at work haying. The site of this place is very good and pleasant. A fine view of Pascoag can be obtained from the grassy dooryard by the house and a still finer one from the cupola of the barn which is elevated some forty feet from the ground. An addition has been built on the south side of the elegant large barn for the purpose of covering a new silo recently constructed. This silo is 28 feet long, 12 feet wide, and 14 feet deep built in a most substantial manner of stone and cement and capable of holding nearly 100 tons of fodder. Timbers have been arranged above the stone work so that plank can be placed around it if necessary, increasing the depth eight feet and adding one-third to its present capacity. This new silo is the outgrowth of happy results obtained last winter in experimenting with fodder put into a smaller silo under the barn, Mr. Sherman finding that the bovines thrived and kept sleek on ensilage.

A new Knowles patent two horse power with an ensilage cutter made by W. E. Ross & Co., Fulton, N.Y. has been purchased and will be placed so the fodder as cut will fall directly into the silo. The horse power is of the most recent pattern, having a patent speed regulator attached which governs its movements completely. Knives are attached to a revolving shaft or drum which makes 600 revolutions per minute. It is calculated this cutter will chop up corn fodder fast enough to require two men to feed it.

In passing through the capacious barn, several fine looking calves of Ayshire blood were seen, of which breed Mr. Sherman makes a specialty. The two silos have the capacity of 175 tons. If the results this winter prove as favorable as before, a large crop of fodder will be in order. We found six acres of land covered with a good growth of corn which will soon be ready for its winter home. All carriages, rakes and machines were properly housed, a thing that too many farmers neglect. The barn (and it is a large one) is built so that no posts of any kind are needed to support the timbers in the center thus leaving the cellar perfectly free from all obstructions. This cellar is open on one side making it very convenient to drive in and turn around, etc. In many things, this barn is a model of convenience and everything connected with the farm indicates thrift, which is only attainable by hard and persevering labor.

Flood in Burrillville
February 19, 1886

The town seems to have been favored in the recent flood, for not a bridge or dam was carried away. The roads in some sections were washed to some extent, but in this direction the town still did not suffer to the amount of $300 all told. Near Caterell's, a causeway required some fixing to insure the safe passage of horses. The nearest approach to a flood scene was near W. A. Inman's Mill. Here the river makes a bend, the road laying alongside. The river overflowed its banks and a current began running under the gate in the fence to the mill dry yard. This was checked so that no great damage was done. The water was three feet deep at this point over the road bed, and here was where the trouble in the flood of 1876 occurred when two houses were carried away. A further occurrence of trouble here could be easily obviated by raising the road, which is quite low at this point, about four feet.

Just below beyond the bridge the water again overflowed the bank taking a short-cut between the house occupied by Mr. Irons and Hickey, and Owen Creighton's dwelling and blacksmith shop, finding its way into the river again. Many cartloads of sand were washed out and deposited on the bank of the river at this point, and the road and bank gullied out about two feet in depth. Mr. Creighton worked hard to keep the current from undermining his house, the water being at one time up to the sills of the house filling his cellar full of water. The road near the river at this point is closed to travel for the present. The Reservoir in Pascoag was not nearly full, and the only effect on it was to rise the water in it about four feet. No large streams empty into this reservoir, which accounts for the water in this large basin not rising more rapidly.

The Providence and Springfield Railroad Company experienced the least damage of any road leading out of Providence. The bridge at Oakland, reported in the city papers as carried away, was incorrect. The stringers and ties placed on the piers were knocked out of line about one and one-half feet by the ice and the rails somewhat bent, but this was fixed without much trouble. The greatest difficulty to surmount was at Dyerville, and this bridge would have remained intact if the Dyerville dam had not succumbed to the raging torrent. The rails settled down when the props were knocked from under and hung suspended from each side of the chasm. The first train making a through trip was Wednesday morning. Tuesday trains were run on schedule time from Pascoag down to the break, the passengers using "shanks mare," crossing over the water on planks placed on the ties which had been shored up Monday by workmen, taking the cars again on the other side.

Our mail agent, getting shut out from Providence by rail Saturday, secured a team and worked his way into the city with the mail. He was the only mail agent getting into Providence from any of the surrounding roads. Mr. Fiske returned Sunday and reported a rough passage. At or below the White Mill the water rose so as to run over the bank into the trench making a breach, filling the trench a foot or so with sand which caused probably $100 damage to the owner of the property, Edwin Sayles. The water came even with the top of the earth dam at the mill of J. O. Inman & Son, the rollway not carrying it away fast enough. Saturday the water began to run over on to the land belonging to Mr. Taft, but was quickly stopped by bags and gravel, thus preventing a serious washout.

Heaviest Snowstorm of the Season
March 16, 1888

The heaviest snowstorm of the season begun early Monday morning and continued throughout the day and following night. More snow fell here than in the city, although the latter was more solid by moisture. Since the storm some of the roads are impassable because of their drifted condition. Part of Sayles Avenue in Pascoag was not broken out, and Inmansville was reached either through the Flats or around by Church Street. Some trees were broken down by the weight of the accumulated white mantle upon their branches, and shrubbery in some of the gardens was crushed to the earth. The average depth is estimated to be two feet, but many drifts of impassable depths are noticeable in various localities both in and outside our villages. The train men found it rather a trying time and by far the worst storm this winter.

The train, due in Pascoag at 5:30 and leaving Providence station at 4:15, made time about halfway when the snow which was deeper at this part of the road causing slower time, reached Pascoag about 30 minutes late amid the blinding storm. The 6:20 train from Providence was not so lucky. It left the city on time and worked its way as far as Stillwater without any serious difficulty, but after passing this station, the drifts blocked the way to such an extent that the train was brought to a standstill several times. Backing up and then going ahead became the order of the night and each time it carried the train nearer to its destination only to stop again. Finally, just this side of Oakland station, the train plunged into a drift and could not be moved, the engine becoming entirely helpless in the snow bank.

All efforts to proceed further were unavailing, and Bartlett started about nine o'clock at night up the track to Pascoag to notify F. F. Arnold where the train was to get help. The way was hard and dark and Mr. Bartlett wallowed along in the blinding storm not being able to keep the track. Several times he ran against the fence by the track, which with the telegraph poles, prevented him from getting lost. Pascoag was reached at twelve o'clock after three hours of exhausting travel. The distance traveled was nearly four miles. There were few passengers on the train at this time but they were well taken care of by Conductor Ballou who traveled to the Oakland store and secured crackers and cheese. The night was spent here, and at daybreak beefsteak and coffee was furnished the passengers from the residence of Arnold W. Clark.

Workmen began early at the Pascoag end and also where the train was stalled to shovel through and meet. This was accomplished Tuesday afternoon at 2 o'clock. A train with shovels was then started for Providence and shoveling was most continuous as far as Stillwater when progress became less difficult and the city was reached a little past six o'clock. Wednesday morning the trains ran nearly on time but encountered some difficulty. No freight was moved either Tuesday or Wednesday and but little on Thursday.

Thunder Shower Does Damage
June 22, 1888

Is Pascoag wicked that lightning should visit it? The thunder shower last Friday evening was severe. Mrs. Coyle's house on Cemetery Hill was damaged $30 worth. The bolt struck and went through the roof near the chimney, rattled the shingles and broke some glass. No one was in the upper tenement at the time, the family happening to be away. The lightning also visited the resident of Whipple Walling, doing damage of $300 or more. One chimney was wrecked, shingles thrown from the roof, tin ware and closets visited, gilt on the picture frames and cornices blackened and it cut up generally. The shock was severe but no one was hurt. The telephone wire at the depot was burned off, and one of the engineers at the round house was thrown down while looking over his engine, but no ill effects resulted.

One Hundred Years Ago in Burrillville by Patricia A. Mehrtens

Steam Engine at Tarkiln Farm
December 13, 1889

J. D. Nichols' men are teaming boards from the woods in the rear of the John A. Wood estate to the cars at Tarkiln. Steam has come into so general use that it is no longer looked upon as mysterious and dangerous. By observing a few rules in its management, it can be utilized with great benefit and advantage. This was more fully impressed by a call upon Mr. Henry S. Nichols in the east part of the town. This gentleman has a boiler and engine with which he gets power to saw wood and cut fodder. Also, he has pipes arranged so that the swill is cooked and warmed for his swine. He recently bought a new circular saw and frame for sawing cord wood. The saw is patented, the patent consisting in the arrangement of its teeth. The saw has a speed of 1500 revolutions per minute and will go through a stick of wood like a flash. Mr. Nichols sawed a cord of wood three cuts in thirty-six minutes. A tornado feed cutter is run by steam and a large quantity of work can be done in a short time. Every farmer having much of a farm and stock should have an engine of his own, for by a little care in keeping it in trim, he can save many hours of hard work and when not in use, it is not eating anything.

Visit to the Poor Farm
June 16, 1891

The visit at the Town Farm last week by the Ladies Societies of Pascoag and Laurel Hill churches was a perfect success. Those not availing themselves of the opportunity can but regret the fact they were left this time. John Moore was the driver chosen and was glad to be with so merry a company. He carried twenty-nine, which was quite a pull for three horses, "over the hills to the Poor House." They were equal to the emergency, landing their precious freight at the farm about 2:30 with abundant provisions for each and all consisting of delicious baked beans, white and brown bread, choice variety of cake, bananas, oranges, sugar and lemons which some thoughtful one had brought to quench the thirsty, which was immediately made into drink.

The good order of things at the farm met the general approval of all, and the four inmates seemed to be very much pleased to see such a company to change the monotony of their life. Everything passed off splendidly. Just before supper all were called to come out-of-doors and arrange for a photo to be taken by Rev. W. P. Stoddard. Quite a time was spent in quieting so many ladies' tongues and getting them straightened out for business. After supper some of the ladies sang a few pieces to the inmates, then the time came for separation. Revs. Mr. Dennett and Stoddard took the foot train, while the others went same as they came, all agreeing that this visit at the Town Farm was one of the pleasantest visits which has been made this season and hoping it might not be the last but may be renewed another year.

Handsome Home for Gallant Steeds
June 25, 1892

For some months carpenters have been at work on the barn of J. T. Fiske, Jr., and as the *Herald* reporter had heard much of the inside beauties of the new stable and had seen only the outside, he took the liberty of an inspection under the guidance of its hospitable owner on Thursday afternoon. As the doors to the stable proper slid backward, a row of neat stalls in which four well groomed steeds stood anxiously awaiting bit and saddle were exposed to view. The stalls were on the east side of the barn proper and were well fitted with feed boxes and hay racks, beyond was the ever flowing water with a large trough full to tempt both horse and rider. An alley way nearby leads to the new part of the barn, where downstairs is a large harness room fitted up with steam radiators, closets, set-bowls and a new harness case. The paper on this room is of the latest style and would well become a handsome library. It is not out of place. Mr. Fiske most studiously studies shade and effect and all other arrangements are in full accord.

We climb an easy flight of stairs and enter a well-lighted room which Mr. Fiske well calls his. Here also we find the same lavished elegance, hot and cold water, easy chairs, books and cupboard for rod and gun, with ample dressing cases which will make this indeed a model room for either the quiet smoker or impatient sportsman. On the walls are pictures of America's finest horses that lead one to think of the famous blooded span below and give a faint hint of trotters yet to come. As we pass on through hall and hayloft into the more northern part, we see more signs of convenience. Upstairs are the sleigh rooms, a place for piazza chairs in winter, while down is the granary, washroom and on the northwest, two large and well arranged carriage rooms that bid defiance to the entrance of dust or spider's webs. Down cellar are the apartments for Madam Molly Cow, here in clean apartments with straw well up to her eyes, she eats her hay and grain and diffuses sweet milk that supplies the household needs. Outside she has her yard. Beyond is a thick wall where all the manure is kept well ventilated and apart from other rooms. Outside, the green lawn with walls, stone posts, and flowering shrubs and well-filled vases, all lend their rich effect to the mansion house beneath the mammoth elms, the tall windmill tower, and this most elegant stable that is not to be outdone by those of our city millionaires.

Enjoying the Heavy Snowstorm
January 13, 1893

The heavy snowstorm last week brought glum looks to the faces of the older ones of the community, but stars above! how the young ones did enjoy it. Last Sunday everything that could slide was brought into service and the streets were alive with merry sleighing parties. Of course every fellow wanted the liveryman's best horse to do honor to the occasion and his best girl. Consequently, the liveryman's best was soon out. Then in rapid succession the balance of his stock went on the road. Horses that had performed six days honest toil were pressed into extra service, and finally everything that could "get a gait" of any kind on was wearing sleighbells and the fun was at its height. The roads were what are colloquially known as "bumpy" and when the swift gliding runners struck one of these mounds, it was pretty difficult to tell whether the fellow wore an Ulster or a fur-trimmed jacket. But these little haps served only to brighten the smile on the lips and the color in the cheeks of the fair one, while the look of quiet enjoyment on the face of the driver deepened into positive ecstasy at these episodes. The carnival was kept up until well into the evening, and all Burrillville was satisfied that 1893 had yielded one good sleigh ride even if never another came along.

Echoes of the Blizzard
February 24, 1893

Just as we, encouraged by the fine weather of the preceding few days, had come to think that spring had comfortably seated herself in the lap of winter, a snowstorm set in last Friday that beat the record. Saturday night found the snow piled to the depth of 18 inches, but fortunately not drifted much. The weather Sunday settled the snow somewhat, but on Sunday evening the flakes commenced falling again, and by midnight three inches more was added to the accumulation. When the snow ceased falling the wind took up the cause of battle, and at daylight Monday morning a regular hurricane was in active operation. The light snow of the previous night was whirled, piled and banked in every conceivable manner. The roads soon became almost impassible and, excepting in the main streets in the villages, all travel was stopped. The weather on Monday was extremely cold, and the sifting, shifting, blinding snow, driven by a wind tornado-like in its power, made out-of-door life almost unendurable.

    The railroads came in for their share of trouble, and the culmination was reached Monday night when a coal dump in the local freight broke down near Carson's Grove. This accident upset everything, as the morning trains on Tuesday could not leave Pascoag Station and the tracks at Harrisville were choked with blockaded freight cars. The wrecking train came from Providence about nine o'clock and the line was reopened. The passengers and freight trains ran on wildcat time Tuesday forenoon but were back on schedule in the evening. Tuesday morning the outside highways were broken out, and the council next Saturday will have a chance to see the cost in dollars and cents of the worst snow and wind blizzard of the winter. Everybody is hoping this is the last snowstorm of the season, but it is a long time yet to the first of April.

    The above was written under the warm sun of Tuesday morning. A change came o'er the landscape again Tuesday night when another howling snow blizzard broke out, continuing all night, all day Wednesday, and up to ten o'clock Wednesday night. The second storm was many degrees worse than the first, and railroad and all other traffic was knocked out again. The snow plows, heavy sleds, shovels and other tools were placed in active service, and by noon on Thursday the main highways were barely passable once more. The back roads are still completely blocked with drifts in many places being higher than the boundary fences. This (Thursday) afternoon a bright sun is lending its welcome aid to the snow shovelers, and once more we fervently hope we have seen the last snowfall of the season.

Mammoth Ice Plant at Wallum Lake
February 23, 1894

    The past week Wallum Pond has presented a busy scene of ice harvesting. Earlier the north shore, usually deserted and desolate in the winter season, has resounded with the voices of teamsters, masons, blacksmiths, and carpenters, all doing their part towards erecting houses for storing ice. All this is due to the Wallum Pond Ice Company, a corporation composed of fourteen capitalists representing millions of dollars, and in one sense successor to a Providence company which found it necessary to procure better quality ice for customers. Three Pascoag men are members of the syndicate. The purpose is not only to supply Providence people with ice but to harvest in such quantities as to be able to supply dealers and ship direct from the houses to any point desired. Money will not be lacking to make the undertaking a great success. The pond's inaccessibility, until the railroad was built along its shore, precluded previous development. No better place could have been selected for the purposes of the company.

  The pond itself is one and a half miles long, north and south, and from one-fourth to one-half a mile in width. The north half lies in Massachusetts and the south half in Rhode Island. Its altitude is high, and nine inch ice has been known here, when because of an open winter none was cut in Rhode Island. Fed entirely by bubbling springs at its gravel bottom and absence of all decaying substance insures purity. Tests by expert chemists show unexcelled drinking qualities and, consequently, its ice must be superior and much sought for.

A Card about Burrillville
October 8, 1897

  Our summer sojourn is at an end and we now return to our Philadelphia home leaving our good wishes for all. The experience of three or four years at Hill farm has been very pleasant, and Mrs. Westbrook has greatly enjoyed life on her "native heath." Old Burrillville is shaking herself and I trust is preparing for greater improvements. Our macadamized roads give the hope of better roads throughout the whole town. But we must be more careful in the selection of our supervisors. Indeed it seems that these gentlemen need supervising. They too often regard their position as a prerequisite rather than a trust. Very little if any of the road money should be paid in advance and the work should be examined and approved by competent and disinterested persons before payment is made. Honest and competent men do not fear full inspection. I am told by an old and respectable citizen that one-half of the money raised for highways is seldom expended on the roads.

  Our Town Hall is in a deplorable condition, emblematic

of the public spirit of old Burrillville. I am ashamed to tell strangers when I pass it—that is our town hall! Why not pull it down or repair it? Notwithstanding this general growl, I am in love with our people and desire to see them more prosperous. Our Pascoag editor did much to make our recent Grange Fair a success. Our treasurer who is the faithful custodian of our public money can run a national bank alone! Few places can boast of such an able and careful officer.

Our dentist has no equal this side of Philadelphia, and no superior in that city of dental colleges as I have learned by experience. Our postmaster is most polite and obliging, and many persons will be sorry that the office cannot be permanent. Our physicians are skillful and sufficiently numerous to look well after the public health, and our lawyers have little to do and seem obliged to seek business in Providence. Our businessmen are generally prompt and energetic, and our mills are showing signs of greater activity. Our ministers are eloquent and efficient and it is a cause of wonder that so few of our prominent citizens are seen in church on Sunday morning. The teamsters are polite and always cheerfully give "the right of way" to those who desire to drive faster. We may not be entirely ready for prohibition in the sale of liquors but why should we not go for a higher license fee and thus diminish the number of drinking saloons! In conclusion I must mention the beautiful new schoolhouse and new fountain in Bridgeton. Let Pascoag and Harrisville make a note of the improvements there and take warning. R. B. Westbrook Oct. 3, 1897.

Sumner Sherman Obituary
September 29, 1899

Early last Sunday morning at his home Sumner Sherman passed quietly from sleep to death. In his death the community loses one of its most enterprising citizens and the state one of its most progressive farmers, and his family a kind and loving husband and father.

Sumner Sherman was a man who began at the bottom of life's ladder and by untiring efforts pushed his way to the top. He was born in Burrillville April 18, 1840, and was a son of Syra and Maria (Wood) Sherman. In early childhood he obtained the rudiments of his education in the schools of his native town. At the age of 15 years he began to learn stone cutting with his father who was an expert in that trade. After serving his apprenticeship he entered into partnership with his father, and together they bought the large farm where Graniteville is now located. Here they erected the Graniteville mill. Mr. Sherman became quite prominent in mill construction and built several in Pascoag. Ever on the watch for opportunities, the farmer boy perceived in the busy city of Providence an opportunity for betterment, and he entered into the clothing business with his uncle on South Main Street. The Graniteville mill was burned and he returned, rebuilt the mill, and purchased the farm where he has since resided.

Frequently in speaking of a man of his stamp, it is said he made two blades of grass grow where one had grown before. Mr. Sherman did better than this. When he purchased the farm, which is today one of the finest pieces of property in northern Rhode Island, it was covered in a large measure with wooded land and underbrush. By patient labor and continuous additions, the farm was brought under a high state of cultivation. This is stocked with upwards of 100 head of cattle and comprises 1,000 acres. Stock from this farm have taken prizes at the Rhode Island State Fair, Woonsocket Fair, and in other localities. It is shipped to all points in the country, going as far south as Texas.

Mr. Sherman married Lucinda, daughter of Col. Ezekiel Mowry of Burrillville. Two children, a son and daughter, were born. The latter died about twenty years ago and the son, Everett B., still resides on and superintends the farm. In politics Sumner Sherman did not take an active part. He was frequently urged to take office but firmly refused. He was a Republican, but not a partisan in town affairs believing the best man should be put in office. He was plain and outspoken, but kind and tender-hearted. For about a year he has been in failing health from a complication of diseases incidental to old age. A short time ago he became worse and went to a Boston hospital for treatment. August 26th an operation was performed. He returned home and appeared much improved in health and ate heartily. He died Sunday morning at 4:40 o'clock. The funeral took place from his late home Wednesday morning at 11 o'clock, Rev. B. F. Eaton of the Universalist Church officiating. A large number of friends were present from all parts of town.

The Ice Men Cometh
January 23, 1903

Tuesday a crew of forty-nine men arrived in Pascoag on the morning train from Providence on their way to Wallum Pond where they were to harvest ice. Not content to await operations until they arrived at the beautiful lake in the northernmost limits of the town they commenced (figuratively) to cut up some ice in Pascoag by attempting to drink up the village stock of strong water, a task which while pleasing to them was a more herculean task than a body of forty-nine men could well cope with. As the result, the village people had the unusual sight of a street full of men in almost all stages of intoxication. The crowd was for the most part undemonstrative and attended to its own affairs without troubling outsiders. A little friendly altercation between two of the crowd resulted in one of the men having a shoulder dislocated.

After a while most of the crowd was rounded up and conveyed by teams to the pond. A carload of camp supplies was sent up to the pond by a special. When one of the wagons carrying the men to Wallum Pond came to the foot of Wilson's Hill, one of the occupants either tumbled out or was pushed out of the wagon and fell head first to the ground which, being considerably harder than the man's head, caused a severe scalp wound. He was attended by Dr. Henry J. Bruce and was sent to Providence on the afternoon train. His injuries were not so serious as the load he was carrying.

Smith's Large Barn Burned
August 2, 1907

Shortly after 11 o'clock Monday night, Daniel A. Smith was aroused from his slumbers by the barking of dogs to find that his barn was on fire and such headway gained as to make it utterly impossible to check it. As Mr. Smith rushed from the house, he met his hired man who sleeps in the barn coming to arouse him. The other hired men were quickly summoned and the work of rescuing the animals was commenced. There were 71 head of cattle in the barn, seven horses, five hogs and six pigs. As the doors were opened on the main floor, smoke was rolling through the structure. It was with difficulty that the men reached the horses. Four of the animals were loosened from their fastenings and got into the open air. Three of the horses perished. After the horses had been taken from the barn it was necessary to station a man at the door to prevent the frightened animals from rushing back into the flames. On the floor below were the cattle, and 41 of these were gotten out in safety, 30 perishing. Several of the hogs were driven from their pens, but at least two caught fire before they got from the barn and, staggering to the open air, died. In the barn was stored about 75 tons of hay, a carload or more of grain, harnesses, farming tools, etc. all of which were consumed. Across the lane a tool house and shed was also burned.

The bright blaze soon attracted neighbors to the scene, and valuable assistance was rendered by them. As nearly as could be determined, the fire originated near the mows on the rear part of the main floor. The fire burned briskly, and by one o'clock the structure had fallen in and glowing embers were all that remained of the barn and contents. The exact origin of the fire has not been determined, but a man who was formerly employed on the farm was seen in the vicinity that night. The following morning in an intoxicated condition he was heard to make some threats. The barn was one of the largest in Northern Rhode Island. It was 108 feet long and 50 feet wide. A portion of it was constructed in 1862 and in 1894 its size was doubled. Mr. Smith estimates the loss at $8000, which is considered a very conservative estimate. The farm of Daniel A. Smith & Son is located about one mile from Tarkiln Station and is noted for miles around for the number of cattle kept.

Storm Knocks Out Trolleys
September 27, 1907

Last Saturday night this section of Rhode Island was visited by a thunderstorm which was by far the most severe of the season. The flashes of lightning were almost incessant and the thunder was unusually heavy. High winds and a deluge of rain accompanied the lightning and thunder. Street car traffic was delayed for nearly two hours, the lightning playing so vigorously on the trolley wire as to make it unsafe to attempt to run the cars. The cars left the Harrisville switch at 7:10 just as the storm was breaking. The Pascoag car proceeded to "trench bridge" on the way to Pascoag. When it had reached that point, a stray bit of lightning ran along the wire and threw out the "circuit breaker" on the car. The trolley pole was pulled down, and the passengers sat in darkness until the fury of the first section of the storm had passed. The car was then started up and went as far as the car barn in Bridgeton, where another bit of lightning burned out a fuse, and again the trolley pole was pulled down.

After the worst of the storm had passed, it was found there was no current in the trolley wire. The storm evidently reached Woonsocket and caused the current to be shut off at the power station. The car finally reached the terminus on Main Street a few minutes before 9 o'clock. The Woonsocket bound car proceeded as far as Herring Pond Brook on the Oakland

Road, and there the antics of the electrical fluid made it prudent to pull down the trolley pole. When the storm has passed, it was found the controller on the car had burned out. The lightning also strayed into the electric light station in such quantities as to place the dynamos in danger. The machines were shut down until the fury of the storm was spent. It was then found that the incandescent dynamo was damaged sufficiently to put it out of commission temporarily.

Runaways from State Home
September 12, 1913

Hungry, dirty, and exhausted after traveling 25 miles over dusty country roads, Willie Cartier, 10, and his 6 year old brother, Eddie, limped into the yard of the Burrillville Town Farm late Tuesday afternoon. Several hours before, they had run away from the State Home and School in Providence and had covered the entire distance on foot, they said. While the two youngsters were resting weary feet and eating a welcome supper at the Town Farm, Mrs. McCormick, wife of the keeper of the institution, was returning from a visit to the school in Providence where she had gone to take one of the brothers away.

Several weeks ago the two brothers with their sister Ethel, 12 years old, were deserted by their father and were taken into custody by Overseer of the Poor Gilbert S. Taft. He gave them lodging temporarily at the Town Farm, but on Monday, under orders from the Town Council, took them to the State Home and School on Smith Street, Providence. Apparently, the brothers became homesick almost as soon as they reached the school and laid plans that same night for an escape the next morning. Tuesday after eating their breakfast, they stole away from the school and took the road toward Burrillville.

While the youngsters were trudging along toward the Town Farm, Mrs. McCormick and relatives of the children made their trip to Providence to take back one of the boys and his sister. On learning the brothers had disappeared, she returned home where she found a very tired, very dusty pair of children awaiting her. Eddie and Willie declared that they had gone back because they liked the place. They said that during their long walk, they had passed the home of an aunt but they were unwilling to stop. They have been taken back to the Smith Street home.

One Hundred Years Ago in Burrillville by Patricia A. Mehrtens

FIRES

Narrow Escape in the Harrisville Mill
March 16, 1880

    The extensive woolen mill of Messrs. Tinkham & Farwell in Harrisville was badly damaged by fire on Friday night of last week, and but for the splendid system of fire extinguishing apparatus connected with the establishment and the prompt and efficient action of some of the employees would have speedily succumbed to the flames.

    Just before nine o'clock as they were on the point of shutting down for the night, a boy employed in the carding room on the third floor was set to work brushing down the light flox from the pulleys. A small particle of it caught in a gas jet and falling to the floor instantly ignited a lot of loose material lying there. The boy shouted to Mr. Thomas Kingsley the boss carder who ran to the spot and attempted with a pail of water and by stamping to put out the flames. He was unsuccessful, and before he could seize a second pail full, the fire darted with astonishing rapidity along the floor. Other occupants of the room made their escape at the first sign of danger, but Mr. Kingsley was speedily hemmed in by a line of fire. Making a bold push through the flames, he reached the door of the dressing room and then fell prostrate, overcome by the heat and smoke. He had the presence of mind to close the door behind him with his feet, and in a moment or two was able to crawl through that room to the stairway beyond and thence make his exit. As it was, his hair and beard were singed and his hands somewhat burned.

    After reaching the yard, Mr. Kingsley and the watchman threw the pumping machinery into gear and turned on the "sprinklers" in the carding room. This is a system of water pipes thickly punctured with holes ranged along the ceiling of each apartment. When a sufficient number of hands had arrived to man the hose, the force pump was put in operation and a heavy stream poured in upon the fire from the outside. These did their work in fine style, and every spark of fire was quickly extinguished. The drenching, however, left an immense quantity of water to drip through into the lower rooms, and the damage from this cause far exceeded that done by the fire. All the nine sets of cards were more or less injured and much stock was destroyed. The damage by water in the weavers' room was considerable, and ten cases of goods ready for shipment were drenched. The estimated total damage done is $32,000 of which only about $300 was to the building. Work in the mill has been suspended except partially until the repairs are finished. This mill gave employment to about 175 hands and was about to be increased in size by the addition of a five-story wing, which would have made it the largest woolen mill in the State.

One Less Saloon
November 11, 1887

About fifteen minutes past one o'clock Wednesday morning as James Lacy of Pascoag was going to his barn across the street from his house, he noticed a bright light down the road on the flats. He concluded at once that it was a fire and rushed in the direction of the blaze to find a two-story house owned by the late Martin Quinn ablaze. The fire seemed to be in the upper northwest corner and had made considerable headway. He routed out those whose houses were in imminent danger of destruction by calling Fire! and pounding vigorously on the doors.

The building was unoccupied save the basement, which was used by Jack Welsh as a liquor saloon. Those living in the neighborhood came forth, and the basement door was smashed in. No fire was visible here, but some of the men began to tumble out the furniture inside. It consisted of a stove, a few chairs, the bar, and a few other articles; also five barrels, some containing beer, two racks of beer, and three jugs of hard stuff. The bells in the towers of John Fiske, Jr. and J. O. Inman & Sons' mills began to peal forth notes of warning at about 2 o'clock, which awoke many more people, although a great many in the village slept right through the whole and did not know of the fire until morning.

Seeing that the building could not be saved, the efforts of all were directed to saving the houses close by. The one occupied by John Callahan was the nearest and in the most danger. Ladders were brought and placed against the house and blankets hung on the side next the fire and kept wet with water brought in buckets from wells in the vicinity, that being the only supply available. Women worked like heroines and carried water, helping materially in keeping the sparks which fell thick and fast upon the roofs of the houses from setting them ablaze. One well was drawn dry and another from which a supply was taken nearly so. By united and vigorous exertion, the fire was confined entirely to the house in which it originated, although a shed between the burned house and Callahan's was considerably scorched.

A good sized party of young men were at the saloon in the evening, and being election night, were pretty well corned by treating around. Inquiry in the vicinity failed to bring to light any disturbance of any kind, and by the fire starting where it did, it is thought it must have been incendiary. Rumors have it that some did not wish the saloon there and took this means to get it out of the way. Those living the nearest stated that Welsh kept a good place of the kind, and they had never been disturbed by the saloon's being there.

Wednesday afternoon, some sawed cord wood that was in the basement was blazing and smoldering away, the only remnant of the building and what it contained. The beer that was rolled into the street also departed, and quite a number took advantage of the occasion to get drunk.

Wood's Barn Struck by Lightning
July 13, 1888

The barn of Hon. Francis M. Wood was struck by lightning during the thunder shower Wednesday night and set on fire. Everything worked favorably so that the flames did not get from under control, and the fire was extinguished with slight damage. The bolt struck the ridge pole of the east end of the barn, throwing the saddle boards off. The fiery liquid seemed to split, part running down a rafter splitting it all the way from the ridge pole to the eaves tearing off a few shingles, and disappearing in the ground down the side of the barn. The other part took a course down the boarding down the end of the barn, setting the hay next the boarding on fire. The instant the fire caught it was seen from the house across the road, and prompt action was quickly taken by Mr. Wood and his help.

Many of the neighbors were also quickly on hand with plenty of ladders, pails and cans, water and people. An intermittent stream of water was soon put where it did the work.

A hole was burned in the end of the barn about as large as a man's head. The hay in this end of the barn, several tons, was pretty well wet up and was taken out of the barn and dried in the dooryard. Tubs of water were kept in the barn all night as a precaution against the fire starting up in the hay again, but the work first done was sufficient. The wind was blowing heavily towards the house, and it is extremely fortunate that the fire was discovered in its incipient state, as otherwise much damage would have been done.

Mill at Gazza Destroyed
August 24, 1888

This section of Burrillville of late years seems to be doomed to bad luck and disappointment, the latest hard luck being the destruction by fire of the mill and several buildings in and near the mill yard. The watchman says that about fifteen minutes past eleven Tuesday night lightning struck the roof of the mill and seemed to go all through it, setting it on fire. He immediately opened the valves to the sprinklers and started the pumps, but for some reason they failed to work properly. The fire spread with great rapidity, and in a short time nothing was left but blackened walls and smoking ruins. The machinery in the mill, although not all of modern make, is totally destroyed and will be only fit for old iron. The property was owned by Fred Whipple and was insured for about forty thousand dollars, thirty thousand of which is held as security for a loan by the Greenville Bank of Smithfield. The mill was about to be started up making yarn, and its ruin thus depresses those having hopes of getting work here.

Pascoag Fire District Meeting
September 11, 1891

A called meeting of the Pascoag Fire District was held Saturday afternoon in Music Hall. The meeting was called to order about 3:30 by the moderator, Manning Wood. Between 40 and 50 were present. The clerk, G. F. Whitford, read the call and also the records of the last meeting. The moderator stated they were ready to hear the report of the special committee appointed to ascertain the cost of lighting the district. The president and clerk looked at it and neither one wished to read it. Henry M. Chase finally ascended the platform and waded through its contents. Frank Fagan moved that the report be accepted. There was a long wait before Addison C. Sayles seconded the motion. It was accepted after Dr. J. J. Lace was assured that accepting it bound the district to nothing.

Thomas H. Fagan said he was very much disappointed at the short report given by the committee. He had expected quite a lengthy report would have been made and figures given on various plans more explicit. He believed most present were disappointed the same as himself or the report would have been more readily accepted. Remarks were made in a similar vein by Dr. Lace who questioned as to the power of making light after the plant was in. He thought it was a good deal like a man buying a carriage and no horse. J. H. Smith, of the committee, said they had been to several places and seen the different parties in the electrical light business. He thought the quicker they got to work the better, for the poles would now skin readily whereas they would not later. A. C. Sayles moved that the district put in an electric plant, and it was seconded by Thomas H. Fagan. J. G. Colburn thought the motion rather indefinite. Dr. Lace thought it was all right. The motion unanimously carried. A babble of voices now was heard and confusion reigned. Rev. Lovejoy asked if there was any more business, and the chair said there was considerable. An expert—name not given—made a talk about direct currents, magnets, care of lamps, burning out of lamps and armatures, which was nearly all Greek to those present. Of course he claimed, as all the rest do that have something they wish to push, that his system was the best.

Elisha D. Sayles said that to have electric lights was unanimous, and he would move that the committee which has been investigating the matter be continued and empowered to put in a plant and furnish light for the district. P. O. Hawkins moved they vote a tax the extreme limit of three mills on a dollar, but according to the charter it could not be done at this meeting not being in the call. It was contended it was germain to the subject but the matter was dropped. The charter also only allows the district to issue bonds to a certain limit for building water works and for no other purpose. This snag was cleared by voting to empower the committee to hire $10,000 at once at the lowest rates obtainable. The meeting was very pleasant and harmonious.

Immense Forest Fire
May 19, 1894

Never in the history of this section has there been a more disastrous or wide spread forest fire than raged in the vicinity of

Wallum Pond the early part of this week. The fire started at the "Brass Balls" near East Thompson, Saturday, and burned over a triangular territory extending east to Douglas Junction and south to "Grassy Cove," estimated to comprise about 1,500 acres. On the east side of the railroad about 500 acres of woodland and meadows were covered by the flames.

    The central point of interest was the immense building of the Wallum Pond Ice Co. The fire did not come dangerously near the ice houses until about one p.m. Tuesday when it approached within about 200 feet. Head fires were set and almost heroic work kept the flames at bay. At that time, the East Douglas Fire Company had been telegraphed for and arrived about four o'clock fifty men strong with engine and hose cart. Their services were not required and they returned home about sunset after partaking a bounteous supper from the larder of the boarding house.

    Wednesday morning the brush and leaves at the north of the boardinghouse were cleared away. It was well this precaution was taken, for about noon the wind drove the flames south and again placed the building in imminent danger of destruction. The barn caught fire twice, and the dense smoke almost overpowered the dozen men who were at work. That evening the fire had "burned itself out" and the weary watchers at last had rest. The buildings belonging to O. A. Inman and H. F. Bellows near the water tank escaped damage from the flames. At one time the flames were running at a speed of a dozen miles an hour and blazing 50 to 75 feet above the treetops. Considering the condition of the forests the wind and the small force of men, it seems almost miraculous that the damage was no greater.

Pascoag Swept by Flames
July 13, 1896

    The most disastrous fire that has visited the village of Pascoag for years occurred early last Sunday morning, entirely destroying E. C. Griffith's hotel and stable, a tenement house, the Commercial Hotel, P. S. Fagan's block and gutting M. H. Lacey's building. The absence of wind alone saved the greater portion of Main Street from destruction. The night was calm, hardly a breath of air stirring, and although the flames were burning briskly when discovered, the heroic work done by the village folk confined the fire to comparatively small limits. The fire was discovered just before 2 a.m. It was confined to the end of the stable towards the hotel and was just breaking through the clapboards. The alarm was quickly spread and nearby residents as quickly appeared. When they arrived, the barn was enveloped in flames and the hotel was beginning to blaze.

The wooden buildings burned like tinder, and the intense heat set fire to the tenement house owned by the Black heirs on the opposite side of the street. By this time, hose had been laid from Fred L. Sayles & Co. Mill and from the Union Mill, and torrents of water were poured on the adjoining buildings, all hope of saving the burning buildings abandoned. The house occupied by James Hoey a few feet north of the tenement house caught fire several times, but was saved by the hosemen from No. 1 mill who were fighting the flames from that side. From the Black tenement house the flames spread to the Commercial Hotel burning it to the ground in a few moments, and from there to the building owned by P. S. Fagan and occupied by John Black. A two story building owned by M.H. Lacy almost touching Fagan's building was partially destroyed, but was saved from being entirely consumed by the hose from the Union Mill.

At 4 o'clock, just two hours after the fire was discovered, nothing but smoking embers remained of the burned buildings. The need of an organized fire department was never more apparent than on that morning. Most excellent work was done, however, by the lines of hose laid from the mills. Too much praise cannot be bestowed upon the willingness of the manufacturers to use their apparatus at such times as these. The spirit displayed by citizens in rendering assistance is also commendable.

Daring Rescue from Flames
January 1, 1897

Again has Pascoag been visited with a disastrous fire on Main Street and, as in preceding instances, had it not been for prompt assistance from mill apparatus the loss would have been far greater. The fire occurred last Saturday afternoon, and as a result there are now two less buildings on Main Street. The fire originated in the building occupied by D. J. Larochelle as a meat market and was caused by the overheating or explosion of an oil stove. About 2 o'clock Mr. Larochelle left the market and went to the barn to care for his horse. When he returned, the room was filled with smoke and his office a mass of flames. He rushed into the office grasped the oil stove, and threw it out, but it was too late, the fire had gained headway and his efforts to subdue it were powerless.

Over the market lived Arthur Carter and family, and Mr. Larochelle, thinking of the imminent danger to the woman and child above him, rushed up and warned them. The stairway was then blazing, but he performed his mission. Warning the mother, he seized the babe and jumped from the window, none too soon either, for the entire building was then enveloped in flames. Next to the meat market was a two story building occupied in the lower story by Altman's clothing store and by a tenement in the upper story. The buildings were but a few feet apart, and before the fire could be checked, it had enveloped this structure. A portion of Altman's stock was saved, and some of the furniture in the tenement above, but aside from this, the entire contents of both buildings were a total loss.

Fire Destroys Laurel Hill Yarn Mill
January 27, 1899

A flood and fire had both laid the mill in ruins, and now a more disastrous flame leaves but a blackened chimney and spectral smokestack where once stood the shapely buildings of the Laurel Hill Yarn Co. It was some five or ten minutes after 2 o'clock last Saturday morning that the editor of the *Herald* was roused from his slumbers by a vigilant wife who saw a lurid glare o'erspreading the heavens. It was as bright as day, and a hasty look about located Bridgeton as the scene of a conflagration that has been unequaled in its history. Hastily dressing, it was but the work of a few moments to reach the hilltop that overlooks the privilege of the Laurel Hill Yarn Co. whose buildings were in flames. Roaring fire and crackling timber told that doom had already been pronounced upon it. Discovered but a few minutes before by an adjacent neighbor and the vigilant watchman at the Clear River Mill, it had been but the work of a few minutes to arouse Supt. Fairbrother and the owners, Messrs. O. T. and F. A. Inman. They were rushing for the pump as the scribe came upon the scene. The main building was 100 x 54 feet and two stories high, and it seemed all aflame. It was impossible to be anywhere near it on account of the awful heat and great tongues of flame that shot out all about building, tower and boiler house.

Scarce a moment had flown when the burning cinders ignited the shingles on the roof of the tenement across the river and were sweeping madly on toward the handsome residences of the Inman brothers on top of the hill. But the wind changed, and the two-tenement house on the Ridge in the rear of the mill caught fire. Almost at the same instant, the shingles on the stock house and another two-tenement house just over the railroad near the estate of R. Buxton's heirs, caught. It was now a race between whirling cinders and brave men to save what property they could. Pails came from everywhere, coal hods were utilized, ladders fetched, and countless carpets and coverlids were laid dripping wet over the roofs of adjacent buildings while sure-footed men paced to and fro on the roofs of the tenement and hothouses with switches with which they beat out all the flaming cinders as they alighted. Other hands were busy carrying out the furniture of those whose homes were already enveloped in flames. Perhaps the fiercest fight was made to save the Buxton property. The two-story stock house to the mill, with its oily contents, was but thirty feet distant from the Buxton residence, and right royally did the heroes work as they carried water and wet cloths to the roof and sides of the house. It was hot work, and scorched faces and singed hair or whiskers told of the risks taken. The flames were checked, however, and there was but little damage done to the Buxtons.

It had been a hot fire! Less than two hours had told the story and destroyed two two-tenement houses, the large stock house, mill, and their contents. The ruins smoked a greater part of the next day. The unfortunate tenants were looked after and helped to new quarters kindly furnished by the mill owners, while tired neighbors wound their way homeward to the toil of another day, all inwardly vowing that they would vote for waterworks if ever our leading men gave them a chance.

Up in Smoke
January 12, 1900

A double cottage house near the Nasonville Woolen Mill, the property of that company, was almost wholly consumed by fire early Saturday morning. The fire was discovered between 2 and 3 a.m. in the kitchen of a tenement occupied by Alphonse Allaire. It was burning at a good rate when discovered. Efforts were at once made to extinguish the blaze. A line of hose was turned on, and all the night help of the mill participated in the work, but to no avail. At 5 a.m. the fire was still burning, and the building practically in ruins. The cause of the fire is not known. It is believed to have communicated itself from the cellar of Allaire's tenement to the kitchen where it was discovered. The Allaire family managed to save nearly all their furniture, but the family of Cleophas St. Peter, who occupy the other tenement, lost practically all of their household goods. The building, which was probably worth something over $1,500, was partially insured. The fire attracted people from all over the neighborhood.

Tenement Block Destroyed in Gazza
August 22, 1902

At a late hour last Saturday night a large eight tenement block at Gazza was burned to the ground, together with a considerable part of contents. So far as could be learned, only one of the tenants carried any insurance on their household effects. The fire was attended by one fatality—an infant. The babe had been removed safely from the house and, wrapped closely in a blanket, was carried to a place of safety. During the excitement of getting out furniture, the child was overlooked, and when again looked after was found to be dead, having suffocated. The building was owned by Fred W. Whipple, the owner of the village.

New Fire Alarm Installed
November 25, 1904

The installing of the new fire alarm was completed last week and Monday the system was tested and proved to be in good working order. The alarm was pulled in from the several boxes, and the bell in the tower at St. Joseph's Church was found to respond correctly. The only criticism that could be made was the strength of the tone of the alarm. After the apparatus has been in operation for a little time, however, the volume of the tone will increase. There are six boxes, the location and numbers being as follows: #53 - Herald Square. #54 - Fountain Square. #56 - Corner Sayles and Irving Avenues. #48 - Corner Church and Broad Streets. #64 - Fountain Square, Bridgeton. #72 - Near Inman Mill, North Main Street.

The box keys will be located in the following places: A. L. Sayles & Sons office, H. A. Waterhouse residence, P. S. Fagan shop, E. D. Sayles residence, Varnum Steere office, H. W. Rowell store, Griffith House, Telephone Exchange, Fred L. Sayles Co. office, F. E. Paine store, W. A. Inman residence, Anchor Mills office, Inman Mill office, Joseph Denico residence, Laurel Hill Yarn Co. office, Inman & Brooks store, M. O. Bailey residence, Hopkins Machine Works office, W. H. Prendergast residence, W. H. Prendergast office, Philip Dwire residence, J. A. Bailey store, George A. Allison residence, George H. Baker residence, James McLoon residence, Rev. Fr. Mahon residence, Fred L. Sayles residence.

Chief Rounds and Electrician Crosbie will each have a key to the boxes. In case of fire, the person giving the alarm should secure a key and go to the box nearest the fire, unlock the door, and pull the lever down easily. The alarm will then work automatically as follows: The first number of the box will be struck, and after a pause of three seconds, the second number will strike. There will then be a pause of ten seconds ,and the number will be given again. The box number will be automatically sounded four times by the simple pulling down of the hook in the box. When the alarm is sounded from one box, it should not be pulled in from another box at the same time, as it will make a confusion of numbers.

At a meeting of the fire wardens it was voted to purchase 500 feet of hose and four new nozzles. It was also decided to keep one of the hose carts at Bridgeton. These votes were in compliance with a request of the insurance underwriters. The demands of the underwriters will have been complied with when the new hose and nozzles have been purchased, and it is expected that within a couple of weeks the underwriters will come to Pascoag and make a revision of insurance rates.

Big Fire at Mohegan
April 17, 1905

Last Monday forenoon the village of Mohegan was visited by one of the largest fires in its history, when the large and well stocked barn of Ex-Senator Fayette E. Bartlett was totally destroyed by fire, and the adjacent village of Nasonville was for a time in imminent danger of complete destruction. The barn built 28 years ago was one of the largest in this section of the state and had every modern convenience for the economical and expeditious carrying on of farm work. The main portion of the building was 40 x 108 with an ell 40 x 68 and an adjoining shed 24 x 64. On the front of the barn was a tower four stories in height. The barn was very commodious and was so arranged that a load of hay could be driven into the very top of the barn and pitched down into the mows.

The fire was first seen by Joseph Moffit who was employed in painting at about 11:45 o'clock. Mr. Moffit was in the house at the time and immediately started for the barn to warn the men who were caring for the cattle. Almost at the same moment, the fire was seen by the conductor and motorman on a passing electric car and they, too, went to the barn to assist. The fire was on the second floor and the barn attendants were unaware of its presence. All turned their attention to getting the eighty head of cattle and the three horses from the burning building and this was speedily accomplished. The fire had been seen from the Mohegan Mill, and the mill hands left their work and rendered valuable assistance in saving wagons and farming tools.

As the fire gained headway, the sparks were carried by the high wind over the village of Nasonville where only the most incessant work saved further destruction. Several times the school house was on fire, and the roof of the ice house at the Western Hotel was burned off. In a number of places the woods were on fire and large areas of grassland were burned over. Lines of hose were laid from both the Mohegan and Nasonville mills and rendered valuable aid in subduing the fire. Had it not been for the high wind, Mr. Bartlett's residence might have been consumed, and had the direction of the wind been slightly different, it is doubtful if the village of Nasonville could have been saved. Mr. Bartlett was in Woonsocket at the time of the fire caring for a carload of cattle which had just arrived from the West. He returned to find his barn a smoldering mass of ruins. The work of housing the large herd of cattle was no easy task but it was accomplished before nightfall.

Midnight Fire Menaces Pascoag's Center
May 7, 1909

To good fortune and the vigilance of one of our townsmen, the entire business section of Pascoag was saved from complete destruction at an early hour Tuesday morning. What was seemingly a most dastardly crime was perpetrated, and a fire started, which had it not been stopped in its incipiency would have done wide-spread damage.

At 1:15 o'clock that morning, the fire department was called out by a double alarm rung in from Box 54 at Fountain Square. When the department arrived, the portion of Potter & Salisbury's store which was used for the dry goods department was found to be a seething mass of fire. As the water was turned on, the flames burst from the front windows of the store with a violence which drove back the firemen to the center of the square. As soon as possible, a hose was attached to the hydrant in front of the store, and in a short time the fire was sufficiently subdued to give hopes of saving the building.

It was noticed that excelsior was scattered about one of

One Hundred Years Ago in Burrillville by Patricia A. Mehrtens

the store windows, and excelsior was also found on the stairs which lead to the Y.M.C.A. League rooms on the third floor of the building. Tracing the source of the excelsior, it was found that a part of it had been secured in the rear of Malone's Pharmacy and a part from near J. H. Smith's store. The finding of the excelsior pointed toward incendiarism, and that fact was substantiated by James Legg and his brother, Edward, who reside over the post office, and who occupy a sleeping room on the third floor of the post office building with windows facing almost directly toward the building which was visited by fire.

James Legg saw the men making trips to the building with something white, which at first thought seemed to him to be blankets to be used in deadening the sound of safe breaking. The men did not stop at the door of W. W. Logee's insurance office as he supposed they would to get at the safe there. Instead they went inside the building into the hallway leading to the stairs to the floor above. Then two of the men entered the dry goods department of Potter & Salisbury's store. Mr. Legg remarked to his brother that the men were probably about to crack the store safe and they had better take their revolvers and hold up the burglars. Almost as he spoke, a light was seen in the store and the whole interior blazed up. The men rushed from the burning store and down South Main Street. Mr. Legg ordered them to stop and fired his revolver at them. They did not pause, but went on down the street. Mr. Legg sounded the alarm as soon as possible, and in a very brief space of time the firemen had responded and were doing noble work in saving the building from destruction. The stock in the dry goods department was entirely destroyed, and in the grocery department much damage was done by smoke and water. Aside from the fire in the kitchen on the second floor, the entire damage to the other parts of the building was caused by smoke and water, principally smoke.

In the morning, Mr. Legg met in conference with Messrs. Waterhouse and Prendergast of the board of fire wardens and Deputy Sheriff Roscoe S. Wood, and to them he divulged the name of the man whom he positively identified as being present, and of his belief in the identity of the others. Deputy Sheriff Wood visited the parties whom the clue given seemed to indicate, and from investigations made felt pretty positive that those were the men wanted. The Deputy Sheriff swore out warrants charging these men with drunkenness and placed them under arrest. In default of bail, the four men were committed to the Providence County Jail Wednesday afternoon.

One Hundred Years Ago in Burrillville by Patricia A. Mehrtens

AROUND TOWN

Manufacturers Hotel's New Landlord
October 7, 1881

Mr. Albert F. Mowry, who for nearly a year and one-half has been the landlord of the Manufacturers Hotel, on Tuesday last retired from the management and is succeeded by Mr. James Olney who is well known in this community. As soon as possible, probably before our next issue, Mr. Mowry intends establishing a hotel in the Horace Kimball house on the Main Street, Pascoag, where he proposes to cater to the wants of the traveling public. Pascoag will then have two hotels, and the "drummer" who pays his money can take his choice. The old proprietor with a new hotel and the new proprietor with the old hotel both have our best wishes for success.

Brooks' New Store in Harrisville
August 16, 1887

Painters are putting on the finishing touches and the shelves are being loaded with dry goods and first class groceries at the new store in Harrisville, which will be opened to the public for the transaction of business next Monday, August 29th. The store is a beauty: 33 feet in width by 70 feet in depth. Shelves are ranged along each side with dry goods on one side and shelf groceries on the other. No store could be any better lighted as the whole front is glass. The building was built by R. F. Brooks on the site of the large barn that has stood so many years next to Wm. Carpenter's store on Chapel Street. Building new and with the object of a store in view everything was planned so that no grocery store in the country can be more convenient. This store, named Brooks & O'Donnell, is to be occupied by two enterprising young men of sterling qualities, and who thoroughly understand every branch of the grocery business. The parties spoken of are Roswell F. Brooks and Thomas O'Donnell.

Roswell F. Brooks needs no introduction to the people of Burrillville as he has worked ten years and had had for the last seven years, until a year ago, an interest in the old stand now under the management of Remington & Sykes. Thomas O'Donnell is a native of the town. After leaving school, he worked in the mill for some time, but wishing for something different he took a course and graduated at the Bryant & Stratton Business College in Providence. A position as bookkeeper was offered him at the then Remington & Brooks' store. He accepted and filled the position acceptably until last June. Both young men are pleasant and obliging, and there is no doubt but what they will succeed in their new undertaking, for certainly it is the wish of their many friends.

Glimpses in Shop and Store
from *The Burrillville Gazette*
December 9, 1887

Briggs, Photographer - This gentleman on Sayles Avenue, Pascoag, has been among us some time, and judging from the fine quality of work he gives us, he is welcome to stay much longer. Certainly no finer work can be produced in the city than comes from this gallery, and it is a very convenient place to reach. He is making a specialty of Christmas photographs, and now is the time to get one when you are attired in all your Christmas bravery. Go right in, sit down, "look pleasant, please," and the sun and Mr. Briggs' skill will soon enable you to see yourself as others see you. Perhaps Mr. Briggs has the power of making the old look young and the young beautiful, though perhaps the latter would be a useless talent in this locality.

Reuben A. Buxton, Florist - For many years Mr. Buxton has been in the floral and plant business increasing his facilities from year to year until now he has one of the finest and fairest greenhouses in this part of the State. The holiday season demands an extra effort on the part of flower growers, and provisions were being made here to adequately supply that extra demand no matter how large it might be. Mr. Buxton has earned an enviable reputation for artistic skill in the arrangement of baskets, bouquets, and other flower designs. This coming Christmas bids fair to put that skill to a severe test, as the calls for flowers for table and parlor decoration will be very large. While making your dinner table arrangements, do not forget to crown your table and grace the banquet with a dream in flowers, whose richness and color and beauty will please the eye and whose odor, mingling with the aroma of the viands, will soften and sweeten and linger and fade into the memory, like the delicate hues of an autumn sunset.

J. H. Knowles, Dentist - This gentleman, succeeding to the business of Dr. Kendall some three years ago, has achieved a fine reputation for skill and good work in his business, and people no longer think it is necessary to go to the city for dental service. It may be thought a doubtful invitation to ask you to visit the dentist to add to the pleasure of Christmas, but if there are any errors in your ivory department it would be the part of wisdom to have them rectified before attempting to adjust accounts with the noble turkey. Dr. Knowles makes the filling and repairing of teeth a specialty, and does very artistic and durable work in that line.

Michael Lacy, Empire Market - The portly form of the Councilman Lacy is a powerful argument in favor of the superior nutritive qualities of the meats he dispenses. His genial disposition plainly shows that no struggles with "bull-beef" have ever ruffled his placid serenity. To keep a line of meats as good in quality as it is large in quantity has been Mr. Lacy's constant effort, and he has well succeeded in doing this. The Empire Market is fully stocked with the good things of this life. The shelves in this market are completely packed full of tin cylinders, and the legends on the labels assures that the goods are practically in the same condition as when the fruit was plucked.

Huge joints of juicy meat, quarters of lamb, ribs, roasts and steaks greet and satisfy the eye, while at the same time excite the appetite. Mr. Lacy's prices are so fixed that a full stomach does not mean an empty pocketbook. He has made extensive preparations for Christmas, and while you will do well to speak for the bird of your heart a little in advance, you need not fear disappointment if you wait until the last moment, for he will have enough. The turkeys, chicks, and ducks will be carefully selected, while the geese though they may "hang high" will not be so high in price as to be out of reach. If your Christmas dinner table is from the Empire Market, you will have a royal spread, and "May good digestion wait on appetite, and health on both."

Manufacturers Hotel, Mrs. J. W. Olney - That there is a dearth of really good hotels in this town is a regrettable fact, but it is pleasant to chronicle there is at least one place where the

One Hundred Years Ago in Burrillville by Patricia A. Mehrtens

traveling public may be assured of finding the best of accommodations. The Manufacturers Hotel has always maintained a high reputation, and under its present management it always will. A well supplied and served table, nicely furnished rooms, a quiet location, and ample stable and livery accommodations are afforded the guests, and patrons speak in complimentary terms of their treatment while under its hospitable roof.

William Raftery, Boots and Shoes - On Chapel Street in Harrisville, Mr. Raftery has recently opened a store for the selling of boots and shoes, especially a shoe called the "Fitzpatrick," which he claims and with good reason to be as good an article as can be obtained for the money. Mr. Raftery is a practical workman, knows how to fit a shoe to the foot, and furthermore, will say nothing about his goods that the goods do not fully testify to be true. He makes to measure, many preferring this to buying sale work, and also does repairs like a skillful artisan.

J. H. Smith, Tinsmith and Kitchen Furnishings - You have doubtless read of rapid business growths, especially in the Western country, but here is a story of a business in our very midst that points a moral and adorns a tale. Mr. Smith commenced business in Pascoag in 1879 in two small rooms, each containing some 400 square feet of flooring. He did all the work himself at first, but in the autumn of the following year his business had so increased that he hired a workman, and finally another helper. In 1881 he built an addition to his workshop. The partition between the old work and sales rooms was taken down and the whole thrown into one room making 800 square feet of flooring in the sales room. Business kept steadily increasing, and in 1882 a room in an adjacent building was hired and used as a crockery sales room.

In 1883 he added a glassware department, as he does a very large business in this line, importing both glass and crockery and doing a jobbing as well as a retail trade. In 1883 the repair shop of the P & S R. R. Co. was bought and turned into a stock house. In 1885 still another new workshop was built. Now, in 1887, the workshop embraces 950 feet of floor, the front sales room 1000 feet, the rooms upstairs, downstairs and everywhere else are literally packed with goods and trade still increasing. Mr. Smith stands ready to show you a stock of stoves, crockery, hardware, glass, tin and wooden ware, skates, library lamps, and everything else that makes up a mammoth stock, and he quotes prices clear down to hard-pan. A remarkable business success.

Rosamond A. Steere, Millinery and Dress Making - This lady is prominently identified with the millinery business in

One Hundred Years Ago in Burrillville by Patricia A. Mehrtens

Pascoag, and her artistic skill and rare taste is eagerly sought for by the ladies from far and near. She had once decided to retire from the business, but the urgent solicitations of personal friends caused her to rescind that decision to the gratification of the public at large. The evidences of her thorough knowledge of her art are seen daily on our streets, and no words of ours can add to their attractive appearance. In the dress-making department, the same care and skill is displayed, and the garments are models in fit, style, and elegance—but this is telling the ladies what they already well know.

John R. Keilty & Co., Dry and Fancy Goods, Boots and Shoes - This well known store in Harrisville is under the management of Mr. John R. Keilty, a young man who succeeded Landry & Co. about one year ago. Mr. Keilty came from Potter & Salisbury's in Pascoag where he had been employed as clerk for some two years. In his present location, Mr. Keilty is holding out many inducements to the public in the way of large assortments, honest prices, strict attention to business, and treating all with courteous consideration. His line of dry goods is large and seasonable, boots, shoes and rubbers, clothing, millinery, notions, all in infinite variety, style and price. At this time, the most noticeable feature in the store is the display of holiday presents, and this is certainly a large and fine one. Toilet sets, smoking sets, shaving cases, writing desks, whisk broom holders, stationery, novelties in perfumery, and in fact about anything and everything you can think of in the way of a Christmas gift. A line of toys calculated to make the hearts of the kids jump with joy is spread on the counters. When our readers are out selecting Christmas goods, we would suggest a call here and a look at a beautiful French clock that is to be given away. Whoever gets this will have a most valuable and useful household appendage.

John M. Smith, Watches, Clocks and Jewelry - Mr. Smith is one of the oldest established jewelers in town, having commenced his labors here in April, 1856. Without capital, with but an indifferent kit of tools, and with serious physical disadvantages having lost his right hand by an accident when very young, he began the arduous struggle for an honest livelihood. For twenty-eight years he has kept up the good fight, and mark the result. Industry, economy, faithful dealings, and continuous advertising in the home paper have borne their deserved fruits, and today he is serving his old customers and new from a shop well supplied and equipped with all things essential to his trade. A handsome little cottage on one of our main thoroughfares is ready for him when he retires from business.

For many years to come he hopes to still meet his friends who are in need of watches, clocks, jewelry, optical goods, stationery, perfumery and many other articles, which he always keeps in stock. In the way of repairs, he will guarantee that all work entrusted to him will be done in first-class style. His long experience and well known skill renders him adept at his trade and the most difficult jobs are easily accomplished.

Whiteley & Luther, Dry Goods, Groceries, Grain and Provisions - probably there is not a place in town where there is so much business transacted in so limited quarters as by this firm. By honorable exertions and first-class goods they have gained and retained an enormous trade. Without doubt they could still further enlarge it, if the facilities for handling goods were better. The *Gazette* representative looked through the store the other day and asked Mr. Whiteley what special preparations had been made for Christmas. The answer came promptly, "find a place to put them, and we will have Christmas goods in at once." It didn't take a very long look to satisfy the reporter that there wasn't room enough to get in even a Christmas card, unless edgewise, as it were. Never was a store so packed. The reporter was asked to look at the lot opposite the store and if, in his opinion, a two story 100x60 store with furniture wareroom and meat market attachment wouldn't look well there. With the trade Messrs. Whitely & Luther have to supply now, and with the increase that will naturally come when the White Mill starts up, they must have more room. If we were running a Robert B. Thomas almanac under the head of May, 1888, we should predict: Expect a grand new store in Laurel Hill about this time.

Post Office for Tarkiln?
12/13/1889

The people living in the vicinity of Tarkiln Station would deem it a great convenience to have a post office located at the depot. The nearest post office where people in this neighborhood can get their mail is Nasonville, which is over two miles distant. Oakland is three miles away and other offices still further yet. To establish an office at the depot would cost the Government nothing save an extra mail pouch. It would not detract from the revenue of the Nasonville office as dozens of letters are handed to the mail agent of the train when it comes along twice each way each day, and the postmaster at Nasonville derives no benefit from this. Probably there are more letters mailed on this road than any other in Rhode Island for its run. This reduces the salary of postmasters who are dependent upon the number of stamps canceled for their salary. Usually the only motive for mailing letters on the train is for convenience, or to get them started sooner on their way. A post office was established at the Smithfield Station two or three years ago, and was found to be very convenient for those living nearby, who previously were obliged to go to Stillwater for their mail. All the mail facilities possible, especially where the expense will be nothing, should be given the people.

Change name of Post Office?
January 24, 1890

The name of the post office here, which has been Burrillville, has been officially changed to the name of the village. This change is not fancied by some of the citizens here, and the matter was worked so quietly that some of them did not know that an effort was being made to have the name changed, while others had heard some talk about the matter and supposed that it would end in talk and thought but little about it. But, the workers in the matter took the right course and represented the affair in such a light that the sanction of the authorities at Washington was obtained. The name of the post office will now be Harrisville. The sign at the station was changed to Burrillville not many months ago, and in all probability it will soon be replaced by a sign bearing the old name. This change of the name of the station was the cause of the change of the name of this post office. The people are about evenly divided in the regard to the change and sometimes hot discussions over the point have been had. It is hard for some to concur in new things while others are constantly trying them.

The Burrillville Post Office Question
January 24, 1890

Mr. Editor: I was surprised to read the article in the columns of the *Gazette* last week on the proposed change of the name of this office, and especially was I surprised to read that in the opinion of the writer it was already as good as accomplished. Living here in Harrisville and going in and out among the people I had never heard the subject broached. To me it was like a clap of thunder out of a clear sky. I had not seen a cloud as big as a man's hand indicating the coming change. But who has done it? Who proposes to do it? The people of the village and vicinity

One Hundred Years Ago in Burrillville by Patricia A. Mehrtens

who are most concerned have, so far as I know, expressed no opinion on the subject. Who are these magnates who propose, without consulting their fellow citizens, to blot out the name which this post office has borne ever since the town was organized and to substitute the name of Harrisville, which today is inappropriate even as a name of the village. The Harris family has had nothing to do with the business of the place for years. With greater propriety might it today be called Tinkhamville or Woodville, or several other Villes which might be named. But I have never heard that anybody here was particularly anxious for a change of the name either of the village or of the post office. But I suspect this is the work of outside parties. If so, it is an impertinence; an unjustifiable interference with the affairs of their neighbors. All I have to say to such is, "Gentlemen, hands off; when we have need of your counsel we will ask it. At present we think we can manage our own affairs." - Harrisville.

Improvements in Harrisville
August 7, 1891

    Truly Harrisville is showing considerable enterprise. Several new buildings have recently been erected, a new iron bridge made to span the river, the main street graded. A long string of stone curbing is being put in place along Main Street, which will make a line of curbing from the Catholic Church down to the corner of the street, which extends by the mill across the river. The curbing in front of the Universalist Church had been put in place, but was found too low, and Wednesday it was being raised on a line with that of each side. Otis W. Wood, after building his store for his two sons, put in curbing and stone posts, and now he wishes the council to straighten the street near the brook. This would take a piece of Mr. Wood's land but would be a big improvement.

    While these improvements are going on, the Central Hotel is receiving one of the most thorough overhaulings in its history. Since Clarence G. Thayer purchased the furniture and fixtures, the heirs owning the building have laid new floors where needed, repaired broken glass, repainted and papered throughout. Mr. Thayer has taken each room separate, and entirely cleared it of everything; scrubbed it previous to receiving its new coat of paint and paper, put down new carpets and put in new furniture. The kitchen has a new floor, new range, new paper, new sink and one would not know the place judging by its former appearance. New carpets, chamber sets, mattresses, spring beds, have been placed in all the rooms and the old beds burned. Mr. Thayer is putting out hundreds of dollars in refitting the place and intends keeping a first-class hotel. Mrs. Thayer seems adapted to the position of mistress of a hotel, which is so necessary to make guests feel at home.

George Warner still presides over the cuisine department, and Miss Annie Eagan will be table waitress. The barroom with its new floor and paint will make an entirely different appearance with the new bar running across another portion of the room. The outside of the hotel will soon receive a coat of paint, which will be keeping with the inside. The hall connected with the hotel is to be fixed up, and we should not be surprised if lively times were had this next winter by parties given at this hotel.

Fountain in Post Office Square
September 18, 1891

Standing on Post Office Square, Pascoag, looking four ways and seeing the improvements made in a few years, brought to mind this thought: that if our fathers or grandfathers of sixty years ago could arise from their graves and see it now, they would not know where they were. The fountain placed in the center affords three parts, one for horses, one for man, one for dogs—the top basin is expressly for horses, the lower basin for dogs, the door on the east for man. The work was superintended and done by John Thayer and son. Considerable was said by one and another as to the fountain being too high. John said he guessed it was, but continued right on as though nothing had been said. It is now graded and everyone is satisfied it's all right.

Building Our Fountain
January 29, 1892

The remark has been often heard in the past that Pascoag Square would be a good place for a fountain where horses could slake their thirst, and the fountain, at the same time, serve as an ornament. The benefits of such a fountain to the residents of Pascoag and vicinity, the town as a whole, and the convenience it would afford travelers journeying through the town, become more and more apparent to some of the enterprising citizens. The handiness with which the flow of water could be secured, and the water being given so there would be no cost attached, was a great incentive in bringing the matter to an issue.

Saturday, June 17, 1891, the Town Council considered the

question of a fountain and decided by a vote to place a fountain in Pascoag. Thomas H. Fagan attended to his duty as a committee, and the result of his investigation led him to purchase, through Mr. J. H. Smith hardware dealer at Pascoag, a fountain of Henry F. Jenks of Pawtucket. The purchase of the fountain for $135 was consummated August 24, 1891 and it soon arrived ready to be set up.

The services of Dr. Henry J. Bruce, who sometimes handles the surveyors instruments, was brought into requisition, and a grade was established to place the stone foundation for the iron fountain. An underground drain was built along Sayles Avenue to the river for the waste water to escape, which enters the drain directly under the fountain. To get a trench for the supply pipe, workmen first began to dig near the corner of the bank building along the sidewalk towards the bridge on Church street. Only a short distance had been dug when a solid ledge was struck. This is doubtless the continuation of the granite ledge which extends under the bank building, the wing of the mill, and the buildings located on South Main street and extending to the fish market.

The portion of the trench excavated was refilled, and a trench was started on the opposite side of the street from the corner of the building owned by Albert L. Sayles and occupied by Potter & Salisbury as a grocery store, and the lower end of the bridge which spans the stream from the Union Mill. Although no ledge was struck in excavating for the trench on this side of the road, quite a number of boulders were encountered, and the course of the trench was deviated somewhat. The supply pipe was laid and connected with the flume of the Union Mill. Many did not realize its great convenience and need until the fountain was in and bubbling forth clear sparkling water. So numerous were the horses watered during the daytime that the basin of the fountain never filled, although four fair sized streams were continually emptying into it. At night the basin would fill, but in the morning it would be quickly lowered as four horses at a time would be drinking and others be waiting for a chance.

New Post Office in Laurel Hill
May 19, 1893

Charles F. Potter of Laurel Hill has received the appointment dated May 6th of postmaster for that section. The post office name will be Bridgeton and will be located in the building now occupied by A. Hopkins & Co. as a business office.

It will be on the ground floor and entrance will be gained from the door which leads to the hall overhead. This office will be a great convenience to people living in the vicinity. It is estimated that nearly one third of the mail matter which formerly came to Pascoag will eventually go to Bridgeton direct. When the office is opened for business, our many subscribers living at Laurel Hill can have their post office address changed by notifying the publishers by postal card or the postmaster at Bridgeton.

Laurel Hill people are not dozing as anyone can see by a little thought upon various matters arising of late. There is a large amount of business done at this end of Pascoag. This statement is not made at random but can be verified by a little investigation. For a long time the inhabitants much desired better postal facilities. Mail carried by boys who were compensated by the receivers of the letters was an unsatisfactory service because of irregularities. C. F. Potter did what he could to accommodate the people who appreciated his efforts in this line in the past, and there was no dissent in regard to his appointment as Postmaster. Mail was left in bulk in a box at the Laurel Hill store, free for the inspection of all, and instances are not lacking when letters were lost behind sugar barrels for several days or until sweeping time came. A post office was applied for and the petition was granted, and now Laurel Hill has a pretty and well kept office.

Will of Mary E. Smith
March 3, 1894

The last will and testament of the late Mary E. Smith widow of Jesse M. Smith which was entered for probate last Saturday contained the following bequests: Emeline F. Dawley, $5,000; Henry A. Tinkham, $5,000; Sarah E. Tourtellotte, $2,000 and certain articles of furniture and all the wearing apparel and jewelry of the deceased excepting her watch and chain. If the said Sarah E. Tourtellotte should marry or leave the employ of the deceased before her death, the said $2,000 shall be given to the First Universalist Church in Harrisville and the furniture, etc., to Job S. Steere, Jr.

The sum of $9,000 to the R. I. Hospital Trust Co., in trust, the income of which shall be paid semi-annually to the said Sarah E. Tourtellotte during her natural life, and at her death the income shall be paid to the First Universalist Church in Harrisville. Ellison Tinkham, $500; Grace L. Johnson, $500; Ernest Tinkham, $2,000; Fred L. Smith, $2,000 and my portion of the Aaron Smith Farm; to the Baptist Church in Harrisville,

One Hundred Years Ago in Burrillville by Patricia A. Mehrtens

$300; to the R. I. Universalist state convention, $2,000 to hold in trust and devote the income to the maintenance of the First Universalist Church at Harrisville; to the Harmony Cemetery and Chapel Association, $300, to erect a monument on the burial lot of my uncle Peter Tinkham; to the Harmony Cemetery and Chapel Association $3,000 in trust and devote the interest to keeping in proper repair the burial lots of myself and my father, and if the income shall be more than necessary for this purpose, the balance shall go to the general fund of said association; to my nephew Job S. Steere Jr., my home place in Harrisville, together with the sum of $2,000 and all things in the house that are not otherwise herein bequeathed. All the rest, residue and remainder of my estate, real, personal and mixed of which I shall die seized and possessed, or to which I shall be entitled at the time of my decease, wheresoever situated and however described, I give and bequeath unto the Town of Burrillville, in the State of Rhode Island, to have and to hold the same unto said town and unto the successors of said town which shall include said village of Harrisville forever, in trust, nevertheless, and upon the uses and trusts following: namely, that the property thus conveyed in trust to the town shall be denominated "The Jesse M. Smith Fund." That, until the amount of said sum will justify the use of it hereafter specified, it shall be safely invested or deposited at interest to accumulate. That as soon as the amount will justify the undertaking, it shall be devoted to the erection and maintenance of a Public Library in said village of Harrisville, preferably upon my Burlingame lot of land, so called, that conspicuously within shall be erected a marble tablet in memory of my late beloved husband, Jesse M. Smith, on which shall be stated that the property came to me by will from him and that I have erected the Library as a memorial of him and that within the Library shall be preserved for public inspection the following mementos: the large portraits of my husband and myself and all photographs of him and his family and me and my family, our marriage certificate, our large family Bible and two smaller Bibles, one plush covered and one Morocco, with the bookmarks remaining in, the old fashioned clock given my husband by his uncle Martin A. Smith, my husband's watch and chain, my watch and chain, his rifle and its trappings, our two photograph albums with their contents, four pictures of the house in which I live, the little three-legged black stand with gold band and two spindle-backed chairs that came from Father Smith's. The will was entered for probate February 28, 1894 and admitted to probate June 9th of the same year.

One Hundred Years Ago in Burrillville by Patricia A. Mehrtens

Questions about Mrs. Smith's Will
June 14, 1894

There is a vast difference in the opinions of our townspeople relative to the probate of the will of the late Mrs. Smith. Everybody would like to see the town have a good Harrisville library building, provided the will makes ample provision for its care and furnishing. But does it? Then, too, we want to see justice done. If Mrs. Smith was insane and did not know her own mind; if she willed away from her legal heirs property that she would have given them when in her right mind; why we have no right to it. Our sense of justice will enable us to maintain our honor, so that while we protect our rights and demand the proof of insanity, yet we shall, should insanity be proven, be ready to accord to the heirs-at-law that which is their own.

The question presented to the lawyer who wrote the will, "Was Mrs. Smith insane when she made her will?" elicited the carefully guarded answer of, "I am not sure." How foolish then for us who do not know the facts to make careless statements about this question until it has been duly proven by law. The council probated the will last Saturday, the heirs have taken an appeal, and the council will see to it that good attorneys look after the interests of our citizens. More cannot be done, legally or wisely. Let us wait in a spirit of fairness for the result, encouraging our town council by our confidence and support and dealing justly by the heirs who are no more anxious for their own than we might be under the circumstances.

Bridgeton Square Has New Fountain
October 1, 1897

The new fountain at Bridgeton has now been in running order for a week and many an equine might testify, were his linguistic powers more human, to its convenience and worth. The fountain is situated at the junction of Church Street and Laurel Hill Avenue, which has been sufficiently enlarged through the generosity of adjoining property owners to the dignified name of "Square." The macadam road is completed here, and the fountain, besides being a convenience, adds materially to the appearance of this section of the town. Water for the fountain is conveyed from the stream near the mill by a hydraulic ram. The erection of this fountain was authorized by vote of the electors at the last special town meeting, and the committee in charge were

Messrs. W. H. Prendergast and O. T. Inman, and well have they performed their duties.

Father of Forty-One Children
June 15, 1900

Levi Bresson of North Foster, R. I., recently celebrated the birth of his forty-first child—a boy of ten pounds. It was born to his third wife who is the mother of fourteen. His first wife bore him fifteen children and his second wife twelve. Thirty-two of the children are still living, or were up to a few months ago when the father last heard of them. He kept the names of his grandchildren until they numbered over one hundred, and then gave up the record.

Bresson ran away to this country from Canada to marry his first wife, and settled in Connecticut. She presented him with triplets within the first year and with twins the next, and they all lived. In 1862 Bresson went to the war. The family commenced to grow again as soon as peace was restored, and has been growing ever since. After the death of his first wife, Bresson married a neighboring farmer's daughter, who in her lifetime thrice bore him twins in addition to six single babies. All of his children were remarkably healthy, though at one time he had sixteen down with the measles at once. When he moved here from across the Connecticut line a few years ago, the authorities thought an orphan asylum was coming to town.

Burrillville Memorial Library
July 20, 1900

The Burrillville Memorial Library has at last been drawn from the mythland of uncertainty to a state of reality, and the *Herald* is the first among the numerous papers to give the public the inside working of the matter with description of the beautiful new building, which will be constructed of brick, trimmed with stone, 80 feet long, 40 feet wide, and 3 stories or about 48 feet high. The cost will be in the neighborhood of $11,000 or $12,000. The building will be lighted by electricity and heated by steam, and the trustees expect to locate it on the square at Harrisville where the Town Clerk's office and Quinn's newsroom now stand.

The first floor will contain four stores 15x40 feet or two stores 30x40, each having a beautiful glass front. The reading room will be located on the second floor, which will also contain

One Hundred Years Ago in Burrillville by Patricia A. Mehrtens

the librarian's office. These two apartments will occupy one-half the floor, and the other half will be divided into offices for the Town Clerk and other town officials. The third floor will be entirely occupied for hall purposes. It will have a large stage, two spacious dressing rooms, a kitchen and store room. The hall will have a seating capacity of 340 or about 40 more than Music Hall at Pascoag accommodated previous to the fire.

At the last financial town meeting the trustees were given charge of the fund, and these gentlemen have lost no time in bringing the matter to a head. Plans and specifications were obtained, and within a short time the building will grace the village of Harrisville and will be a source of knowledge, pride, and pleasure to the citizens of the town. The deeds for the land where the new building is expected to be located have not been signed as we go to press, but in interview late yesterday afternoon, one of the trustees stated that an understanding and verbal agreement had been made with William Tinkham for the lot on the corner of East Avenue and Main Street. The library will be known as the Jesse M. Smith Memorial Building, and is being erected from a fund left to the town for that purpose by Mary E. Smith, wife of Jesse M. Smith.

Odd Fellows Block
December 21, 1900

The carpenters and painters have finished their labors on Odd Fellows' block, and during the week the electricians and furniture men have been at work. The general appearance of the building inside and out is the same as before the fire. The lower floor has three stores, which have been fitted with large plate glass windows. The second floor is a hall. The walls have been covered with wainscoting up to about four feet above the floor. The rest of the walls are covered with a beautiful pattern of paper and all the woodwork is painted white. The stage is about five inches higher than it formerly was, and has a set of scenery suitable for any drama that may be staged. The scenery, which is newly painted, comprises four sliding scenes and three curtains, excluding the drop at the front of the stage. The sliding scenes are a cottage, prison, parlor and kitchen, and the drops are woods, sea and street. In addition to these, there are also set rocks and other necessary small parts.

Perhaps one of the most noticeable and important improvements is the manner in which the hall is to be lighted. Four beautiful chandeliers with five electric and five kerosene lamps in each have taken the place of the twelve electric lights by which the hall was formerly lighted. The stage has three rows of overhead lights in place of the single row. The wiring of the entire building was done by Electrician Chas. T. W. Crosbie, and his work has been performed in such a manner as to place it beyond criticism. On the upper floor is the lodge room and a spacious dining hall. The latter is large enough to allow two rows of tables side by side and still leave sufficient room for persons to move about comfortably. The lodge room has been papered, and presents a beautiful appearance. Contractor Fred A. Gory received the contract for the rebuilding of the hall. The first event to be held in the new hall will take place New Year's night. A concert and social followed by a grand ball will be held. Active preparations have begun and the initial event promises to be a grand success.

Post Office Burglarized
April 19, 1907

A heavy explosion in the local post office about 2 o'clock Monday morning was the first and only sound made by a gang of daring burglars who entered the post office by means of one of the rear windows and successfully "cracked" the large safe, in which they expected to find a good round sum of Uncle Sam's treasure. Louis Disotell, who resides over the post office, was the first to hear the sound, and rushed to the door to ascertain the cause. He was unable to gain the street by either the front or back doors of his home because the doors were firmly tied with ropes, as were the doors on the house across the way occupied by Mr. Gervais and the door of the store of Edward Legg next door to the post office. This precaution on the part of the burglars gave them a little longer time in which to escape, and rendered their apprehension more difficult.

James Fox, who resides on South Main Street, heard people passing his home soon after 2 o'clock, and being up and about the house looked out of his window. He saw the men take a carriage below his house and drive rapidly away. If the burglars expected to make a haul worth the time and labor, expended to say nothing of the danger, they were sadly disappointed, for beyond a few stamp books and a small amount of change, there was nothing of value to them in the safe. The safe was cracked by the use of nitroglycerine or some similar substance "floated" into the seam around the door by applying soap to the seam to keep the explosive from running out. Two new carpenter's chisels and a coupling pin were the only implements left, which are quite insufficient to trace the perpetrators of the job.

The New "Wet Wash" Laundry
October 4, 1907

The new "wet wash" laundry of the Burrillville Laundry Co. was opened for business on Monday of this week with James F. Dwire as the manager. The patronage accorded the new company on the opening week has been gratifyingly large. It is an innovation in this town to have a laundry where may be sent the entire family wash and have it cleansed and returned within a few hours all ready for the ironing board. Although he has been beset with the difficulties incidental to the opening of any new enterprise and the starting up of new machinery, he has handled it from the very beginning to the entire satisfaction of all patrons.

Fastidious housewives or painstaking washerwomen are no more careful and particular in the handling of the family wash than is practiced at the new laundry. Each basket of clothes, as it is received, is carefully sorted over, and the white and colored clothes separated and placed in different compartments, each of which is labeled with the owner's name. Two and sometimes three and four divisions are made of the clothes so they may all be cleansed to the best advantage. Dainty wearing apparel and laces are placed in a bag of white network so they may not become torn in handling. In this bag they remain until the cleansing and drying processes are complete, and the clothes are all back in the basket in which they came from the home.

There are three washing machines in use at present. One for white goods, another for woolens, and another for colored goods. Each of the machines is divided into compartments, and each family wash has the exclusive use of a compartment until the washing is complete. Afterwards, each wash is put through the extractor separately, so there is absolutely no danger of the washings of different families becoming mixed. All of the clothes are put through five changes of water, and the white goods are given an extra bath containing bluing. At first, cold water is turned on for ten minutes, and then follows a thorough boiling, which is followed by rinsing waters. All the while the clothes are turning in the hard pine cylinders of the machine, and the whole is accomplished without rubbing or pounding or other processes which wear the fabric.

From the washers the clothes go into the "extractor"

where the water is forced out by the centrifugal motion. The wash is put into the baskets and delivered at the home almost dry, having only a sufficient amount of dampness to make them in proper condition for the ironing board, without the need of "sprinkling." The new laundry makes it possible for the housewife to have the basket of soiled clothing taken from the house in the morning, and returned in the afternoon ready for ironing, all without the discomforts and hard work which has long given the title of "blue Monday" to the first secular day in the week. Joseph O'Connell has charge of the gathering and delivering, and has already built up a good list of patrons.

First Mail Service
September 29, 1911

In 1847 the first daily mail service was established in Pascoag, and the first permanent post office was established in the building now occupied by John Acheson's cobbler's shop. At that time, this building stood between the store now occupied by Edward Legg and the Angell Sayles homestead. Previous to 1847, the post office was located here in the residence of James Harris who lived across the street from the present Manufacturer's Hotel. Mr. Harris was appointed postmaster during the term of President Taylor. A weekly mail service was maintained between Pascoag and Chepachet. After dinner every Saturday afternoon, Joseph Clark of Harrisville came for the mail and carried it to Chepachet, returning with the mail the same afternoon. He made the trip on foot, and received the sum of $50 annually. The local post office was contained in a cupboard in the postmaster's house, a space quite sufficient for the needs of the times.

With the election of President James K. Polk came a change in postmaster in this town, and Smith Wood of Harrisville was appointed to have charge of the office then moved to Mr. Wood's residence in Harrisville. The weekly service with Chepachet was still maintained, and the services of Mr. Clark were retained at the same salary to carry the mail. In 1847 Rev. Mr. Lord came to Pascoag as pastor of the Free Baptist church and felt that a service of more frequency than once a week was desirable. He believed he could secure a daily mail service for Pascoag and set about the work with the result that the service was established within a short time, and the appointment of postmaster was given him.

A contract was made with Jonas McKenzie to transport

the mail on his stage between Pascoag and Providence, and the weekly mail and the carrying of it on foot were alike things of the past for our village. Mr. McKenzie had established a stage line between Pascoag and Providence in 1844, and continued the business until 1849, when he sold his line and went to California and operated stage lines for several years. While in California, he had several narrow escapes from death, and it is said he carried several bullet wounds which were mementos of encounters with highwaymen. Mr. McKenzie returned to Burrillville in his later years and died here. After he sold his stage line here, the mail was carried by John Wilkinson.

During the years which have elapsed since 1847, the post office has always been kept in the vicinity of Fountain Square. It is difficult for us of this day and generation to realize, as we see the amount of business which is transacted in the present perfectly appointed quarters, that 75 years ago the business was handled from a cupboard in a dwelling house and that the people of this community were served by one mail each week, where now there are several mails daily.

Free Mail Delivery for Pascoag
February 28, 1913

The Post Office Department by authority of a recent act of Congress is trying the experiment of village delivery of mail, and in each state post offices have been selected for the experiment. Pascoag has been designated as the first office in Rhode Island to test the village delivery and, commencing tomorrow, the residents of the compact part of the village will have an opportunity to have their mail delivered at their homes and places of business twice daily, a convenience until now not enjoyed by the residents of country towns.

The first delivery will be made in the morning when the carrier will leave the post office at 8:30 o'clock; he will start on the second delivery at 5:45 p.m. The following sections will be covered by the carrier: High Street to the residence of M. H. Lacey, Church Street to J. A. Bailey's Store, Sayles Avenue to the residence of Mrs. A. S. Fitz, Main Street to Depot Square, South Main Street to the residence of L. E. Edwards, all of Broad Street, Irving Avenue, Pine Street, Prospect Street and Park Place, comprising altogether a route about two and one-fourth miles in length.

Mail will be delivered to all the residents of this section who so desire, but their wishes must be made known to the

One Hundred Years Ago in Burrillville by Patricia A. Mehrtens

postmaster in order that he may know whether the patron desires to call at the office for his mail or have it delivered at his home. It would be a great convenience if houses were numbered, and it will be a special advantage if patrons have their correspondence addressed to the street upon which they reside. While the postmaster and his assistants know about everybody in the village and where they reside, it is rather too much to expect that the name of each individual member of the household and the occasional visitor is also as well known.

That Pascoag is the first place in Rhode Island to be selected for the experiment is due to Postmaster Logee who is ever on the alert to make the local office the best possible, and to give to the people the highest grade of service. As soon as the appropriation was made by Congress, Mr. Logee made application to have the experiment tried here and "kept right on the job" until Pascoag was officially designated by the authorities. Since Mr. Logee was appointed postmaster, the receipts of the office have doubled, and the cramped and inconvenient quarters have been replaced by a model office—the finest in its class in Rhode Island.

One Hundred Years Ago in Burrillville by Patricia A. Mehrtens

MILLS

Riot at Gazzaville
March 11, 1881

Tuesday evening was an eventful occasion for the inhabitants of Gazza and for the police constables of the town of Burrillville. For some time there have been fights and rumors of fights among the night weavers of Gazza growing out of a too free indulgence in "Jersey lightning." On Tuesday afternoon Constable A. S. Greene went there to arrest Jerry Bowles for an assault on a young man who had ventured to address some not very complimentary language to Bowles and a crowd who were with him. Greene secured his man, and was about to take him to the throne of justice, when a crowd pitched on him, badly bruising him, inflicting several uncomfortable, but happily not serious, wounds, and took his prisoner away. Greene immediately went to Harrisville and Pascoag, and securing a posse of officers, started for the seat of war. At the mill yard, after the arrival of the officers, there was a free fight. Pistols were freely fired and clubs and stones flew through the air in reckless profusion. Michael Murtha, James Smith, and John Riley were finally secured and taken to the lockup at Harrisville. During the melee, Murtha received a bullet in the left ear, which embedded itself in the bone, inflicting what may prove a serious wound. When shot, he was running away from Adin L. Steere who was within two feet of him when the ball struck. Steere and Murtha both fell into the water and were thoroughly drenched.

At 10 o'clock Wednesday morning crowds of the Gazza "bums" as one of them styled himself, together with many of our citizens from all over the town, were assembled in Harrisville awaiting the slow progress of the Court and discussing the riot of the night before. Murtha, who was shot in the ear and whose wound showed signs of inflammation, was removed to more comfortable quarters than the calaboose furnished, as the wound was liable to prove fatal if he did not have careful attention.

The trial of Murtha, after tedious delay in the securing of witnesses, finally commenced at about 12 o'clock. Mr. Driver was the first witness for the State, but beyond stating there was a crowd fighting and reveling at the mill of which crowd Murtha was a member, he could not positively state either as to the individual actions or words of Murtha. During his trial Murtha sat by the table in the Council room by the side of his counsel, Lawrence Prendergast, and did not bear the appearance of a man who was dangerously injured.

Mrs. Elizabeth Gibson was the second witness, and told a straight enough story in regard to Murtha calling her bad names, implying that she was not a woman of good repute, which she said was something he could not prove and which was not true. She swore that he called her these bad names in the "'ouse, outside the 'ouse, and on the 'ighway," a statement which the counsel for the prisoners could not make her alter in the least, although he badgered her almost beyond endurance and required her to repeat the language applied to her something less than a hundred times.

Willard A. Tobey was then sworn and said he knew nothing of Murtha's making a disturbance, and Jerry Mowry, after a long look at the prisoner, was just as ignorant. Mr. Prendergast, Murtha's lawyer, addressed the noble judge and showed that it was not competent to convict a man of being a common railer and brawler unless he was convicted of more than once reveling and fighting upon the highway. He intimated that the judge was a near approach to an idiot and as ignorant of law as a two-year-old baby, which did not have a tendency to make Judge Millard feel kindly disposed towards Larry. He remonstrated with him, whereat the learned counsel indulged in language which would hardly be considered appropriate in any other court but the Justice Court of Burrillville, but which seemed to strike the audience as very much to the point on this occasion. Murtha was sworn, denied railing and brawling on the highway. He was judged guilty by the Judge and sentenced to the State Farm for six months from which an appeal was taken.

J. T. Fiske's New Mill
September 16, 1887

A visit to J. T. Fiske's mill on Tuesday found everyone around the establishment busy. The water privilege at this site in

Pascoag is excellent, there being sixteen feet head of water at the dam. A new addition has been built joining the old mill, which increases the room for manufacturing more than thribble the former capacity. The new part is two stories in height, 120 feet long by 36 feet in width, well lighted by double windows on each side and at the end. The arrangement of the windows is admirable for light, and spaced exactly to allow a loom to set endwise between two of them. By this plan, the weaver gets just as good light at the back of the loom as at the front. There is no choice of looms on account of insufficient light, as each loom has the benefit of two large windows.

A row of new Crompton looms of the very latest design is ranged along each side of the lower floor, fifteen on each side. A row of posts extend along through the center of the lower room to support the floor timbers of the room overhead. These are also placed just the same distance apart as the looms, and in exact range from side to side of the mill, the convenience of which can be seen at once by an observing person and is elucidated by the easiness with which beams can be taken to the exact spot wished on trucks. Plenty of space is seen between the posts on either side, and the inner end of the fine looms. Many things remain to be done before everything is complete and in order, but looms are being started up as fast as possible, and by next week Mr. Fiske is hoping to have all the thirty-two looms in motion. The kind of goods made at this mill are worsted cloths used mostly for men's suitings, particularly for pantaloons and of an infinite variety of pretty patterns. In the near future ,electric lights will supersede the kerosene safety lamps now in use. This enterprise of Mr. Fiske gives renewed courage to many in town who appreciate thrift and enterprise.

Stone Drain and Steps
December 2 & 9, 1887

Through the instrumentality of John A. Bailey and a few others, a stone drain has been put in and planked over across the short cut road leading from Church Street to the regular road to Laurel Hill. This has been a low, wet place where in different seasons of the year, water stood. This piece of road was offered the town last year but was rejected because considerable would have to be laid out on it in repairs. This short cut is quite a convenience to travelers to and from the Hill.

The steps down the bank to the river in the rear of Whiteley & Luther's Store, making a short cut to A. Hopkins and

Co's works and the dwellings on the Ridge, became very much decayed and dangerous to navigate, and the neighbors that were accommodated by steps being there "chipped in" and secured sufficient money to replace the stringers, in some instances stepless, with a "bunkum" new pair.

White Mill & Privilege
December 2, 1887

Sayles & Nichols bargained for the White Mill and privilege, and bought a strip of land a little upstream lying between the highway and pond, last Thursday week. The former was purchased by Edwin Sayles and the land of William and Munroe Wilson. With no loss of time a plan was formulated for a mill 175 feet long and 40 feet wide to be built of wood, two stories high above the foundation and to be placed on the land bought. Ground was broken Monday and Tuesday about twenty-two shovels were busily excavating for the foundation besides two teams with shovels. When this paper gets to our readers, the shovelers will have finished and the wall begun unless snow and severe weather prevent it. The work is to be pushed as rapidly as possible, and under the energetic oversight of Mr. Nichols no stop would be allowed without an extra good reason.

How Turkeyville Got Its Name
April 18, 1890

Dear *Gazette*: by L. D. S. - It has been a long query in the minds of a great many people of this village what first caused or gave the name of Turkeyville now Laurel Ridge. With your kind courtesy and patience I will try to make plain the primitive origin of the White Mill. Arnold Hunt was a man of indomitable will. If his mind was made up on anything, that mind knew no rest until his will was carried out. He being a man of great foresight as well as forethought, he could have his plans all matured ready for action when he said he was all ready. He went to Moses Taft, senior, who owned a saw mill near where the White Mill now stands plus all the land nearby. Hunt told Mr. Taft he wanted to put in a shingle mill adjoining his saw mill as he owned a great amount of woodland on Buck Hill. He would bring the logs to Taft to saw and the small logs he could make into shingles, and wanted to buy a right to draw water from the saw mill pond. Mr. Hunt told Moses Taft and his son, Elisha, to come down to his house, he then living where A. L. Sayles now lives, and they would talk it over and agree upon the price, and he would have a turkey killed and would have a good turkey supper.

The memorial day did arrive, and with it Moses and his son Elisha down to the house of old Major Arnold Hunt. Major Hunt had a liquor cellar about eight feet square made of flat stones on the bottom and top. Mr. Hunt told Mr. Taft he would give him $100 for a right to draw water from the sawmill pond to run his mill, as he called it; "take a little more, this is very good liquor; now you know I want a flume from the pond to my mill about one foot square." "Yes, Mr. Hunt, that is so." (Takes a little more.) After a short time Mr. Hunt says, "Come to think about it, I must once in a while clean out this penstock or flume. I must have it larger - 'take a little more' - suppose we call it four feet square?" "All right, Mr. Hunt." "Suppose we have this all settled today, I must go away tomorrow." "All right, Mr. Hunt." Mr. Hunt goes out and brings in a Justice of the Peace, has the writings all made out signed by Mr. Taft, and they eat their turkey supper and all parties made perfectly satisfied and happy. This statement is the first cause of the title name of Turkeyville.

Great Activity at the White Mill
September 26, 1890

The mill known as the White Mill and the new one close by present scenes of great activity. All the looms are running and over one hundred persons are employed. Since the Perkins Brothers have taken hold, a new dresser has been added to the machinery and they have negotiated for another spooler, so there may be no waits for material. The upper floor of the new building is used for spinning, and the second story for weaving. These looms are of the most approved pattern and most new. The weave room is very pleasant indeed and does not present the cramped appearance, which is seen many times in other mills. Some of the goods made at this mill have been sold already and are a good grade of goods. The dressing and other departments are in the old section. In passing through the dressing room, a new device for regulating the spools from which the thread is run to the dresser was noticed, displacing the paddle and weight. Mr. Slade, the overseer of the dressing room, invented it and has applied for a patent. The help come from different portions of the town, and some of them from adjoining towns. The payroll will amount to about $4000 per month when running full time, which makes the storekeepers and businessmen smile. An era of prosperity, it is hoped, is for the people of this section.

Boiler at Inman Mill Explodes
February 13, 1891

One of the three horizontal boilers at Inman's Mill burst at abut 2:45 Wednesday morning from some unexplainable cause. It was located at the backside of the mill in the stone building which was connected with the main mill. Right over the boiler room was the drying room. The explosion made a loud noise and was heard by those who were not asleep a long distance away. The stone building was almost completely demolished, a portion of the wall on two sides remaining standing, although considerably shattered. The roof was wood and was lifted bodily and stood nearly perpendicular against a portion of wall left standing. The floor timbers above were splintered and torn, and lay with pipes, stone and mortar in a most perplexing mass. The boiler which burst stood next to the dam, end towards the main mill, and it was this portion where the trouble occurred.

The boiler was wrenched from its foundation and projected through the corner of the thick stone building, carrying the wall with it, and dropped high and dry half way to the mill trench two or three rods from its former resting place. The boiler parted where it was riveted. The other boilers were thrown out of place, and the steam gauge was picked up by itself outside the building. Stones were thrown in the air with such force that the coping of the mill many feet above was smashed through. Pressure of the explosion and stones knocked out several of the windows in the main mill. Some of the help knew nothing of the accident until they arrived at the mill to go to work and were rather surprised. A more fortunate time for the explosion could not have been, as no one was near at the time. Had it happened during working hours, doubtless several lives would have been sacrificed.

The cause of the accident was a mystery, as there were only forty pounds of steam on when the watchman last visited the place only a short time before. The three boilers were connected and weighted to blow off steam at eighty pounds. A temporary stopping of the mill is inevitable, but the proprietors will rebuild as soon as possible after the insurance is adjusted. A temporary engine will be placed outside until permanent arrangements are completed, as the water power is not sufficient to run more than half the week. It is unfortunate for the manufacturers, as they have more orders for goods at the present time than for several years before, but they are very much gratified that no one was injured.

One Hundred Years Ago in Burrillville by Patricia A. Mehrtens

Happenings at Random
August 14, 1891

Happenings in and around Mapleville as seen by a casual observer from the summit of Snake Hill, Glendale, which is just beginning to resume her usual industry. Her smokestack tells the tale of the hum of machinery and the clatter of the looms, which is a good omen for the many artisans in that locality. We gazed on Oakland, where is put in shape the product of the silk worm which, in time, adorns our mothers, wives and daughters. At Whipple can be heard the stentorian screams of the locomotive on its visits from Pascoag to Woonsocket and return, but her waters run idly to the Blackstone, there to be carried to the Seekonk, where it is lost track of in one of the mighty rivers of Old Neptune.

Mapleville, where yet stands the ruins of an old factory which looks sad, silent and dark, where once was heard the loud looms of progress, is now like a zealous worshiper of juggernaut. Nevertheless, there is a make-up for this loss in the factory which stands in line with what was once called the little mill. There is not a machine in this factory but that is running to its utmost capacity, which speaks well for the management of the Mapleville corporation, giving in dull times plenty of work, plenty to eat and place to sleep, plus recreation in its turn.

But Gazza, forlorn Gazza, with its shapeless, tottering walls which might be called Sweet Auburn or the deserted village. For like Auburn it was one of the most noted villages in the two Americas. Gazza was spoken of in England, Ireland, Scotland, France and Germany. But she had had her day, her glory is departed, and her future is anything but bright from present indications. Still, let us hope that some enterprising spirit with a little capital will wander that way and renew tottering Gazza to her former greatness so she can again sit among her proud sister villages and be her former self, Queen of Hearts, or the home of the Whipperwill.

Disappearance of Herbert M. Wilson
June 13, 1893

The community received quite a shock last Saturday morning when it was learned that Herbert M. Wilson, the well known yarn and shoddy manufacturer of Laurel Hill, had left the town apparently with no intention of returning. Inquiry revealed that Mr. Wilson has been in financial difficulties for some time past and has been in the habit of borrowing money in any amounts from $5 upwards. The long continuance of this kind of work had encumbered Wilson with a large number of clamorous creditors, and their constant dunning wore upon Wilson's feelings. Mr. Wilson was manufacturing yarn for a Franklin, Massachusetts firm and was expecting to get some money from them Friday. On the strength of this, he made numerous promises to pay creditors Saturday. He was disappointed in getting money, and rather than face the music, he stayed away. His wife received a letter from him saying he should never return, but men sometime change their minds.

As soon as it was known he had gone, quite a number of attachments for small amounts were placed on his property, but we believe Mr. William R. Wilson will satisfy these and will assist Herbert in every way possible. It seems the general impression that Herbert's property will much more than pay his indebtedness and that he was foolish in taking the course he did. We hope Mr. Wilson may soon straighten up his affairs, and again resume his business position among us, for he was an industrious man with no bad habits and would be gladly welcomed back again.

Harrisville's Big Woolen Mill Destroyed
January 20, 1894

The destruction of the Harrisville Woolen Mills last Saturday morning was the most disastrous fire that ever visited this town, destroying nearly half a million dollars worth of property and throwing out of employment over 400 hands in the middle of a winter almost unparalleled in business depression, casting a deep gloom over the community. The mill had several times before caught fire, but was always fortunately extinguished by the sprinklers with but little damage. The origin of the fire is shrouded in mystery. The night watchman made his usual round at 11 o'clock Friday night and found everything all right. The mill closed at 4 p.m. and no one was known to have been in the mill except the watchman. The night was a terrible one for a fire with the wind blowing a gale, but, fortunately, it was from a favorable direction to save the village. The loss would have been almost irreparable, for the main part of the village would doubtless have been reduced to ashes.

The property is owned by William Tinkham of Providence, formerly president of the Providence & Springfield Railroad, and was operated by him and his son, Ernest W., under the firm name of William Tinkham & Co. It was the largest mill in Burrillville and the leading industry of this village. Its destruction at this season of the year is a terrible calamity to the inhabitants of the village.

There is an interesting history connected with this property. Where the company had its office there was once a spindle shop, the proprietors of which were Andrew Fenner Harris and his brother-in-law, Augustus Hopkins. In 1856 Job S. Steere and William Tinkham bought the Harrisville property of Jason Emerson for $30,000, and manufactured satinettes. The following year a dam was built, the factory lengthened 100 feet, and other improvements made at an outlay of $20,000. In 1860 more machinery was added, and cassimeres manufactured. In 1873 Mr. Tinkham purchased Mr. Steere's interest and took in F. S. Farwell as partner. In 1878 the firm was Tinkham, Farwell & Co., Ernest Tinkham, son of William, being admitted into partnership. Farwell withdrew in 1884, and the present name William Tinkham & Co. was adopted. The mill was a well furnished establishment with steam and water power. More than $300,000 had been expended to bring the mill up to the point of excellence it had attained.

Prospects of New Mills
August 11, 1894

The prospect of some new mills in town is one that cheers not only the heart of the laborer but that of the merchant as well. It means more work, more prosperity for the town, more taxable property, more goods sold, etc. There is no way of estimating the actual benefits to be gained. At this time, when there has been a dearth of work for some months, it has an even more significant meaning than usual. Our people need employment. They don't ask for wages they do not earn, but would grasp eagerly at good steady employment. The manufacturers, the laborers, and their families with us, all have suffered on account of the tariff quarrel in the present Congress. Now that it appears as if there would be no tariff bill passed, or at the worst, as if the Senate bill would be substituted for the death-dealing bill passed by the Democratic House of Representatives. There seems to be a ray of light for both the manufacturer and the employees.

The market has been drained of its surplus, foreign goods won't come in and ruin home industry as was promised. We shall have thousands who need clothes, if they are only able to earn the money needed to pay for them. There is more confidence among the buyers, and a prospect of a demand in the near future.

One Hundred Years Ago in Burrillville by Patricia A. Mehrtens

It is because of this outlook that William Tinkham & Son have decided to build a large weave shed and office on the site of their old mill. The buildings will be of wood and will be rushed towards completion and made ready for immediate operations. October first is the day set for their completion. They will be so arranged that the other buildings needed to equip a mill as completely as was their former plant may be added at a very short notice, and in direct harmony with each other.

William Orrell at Glendale has also completed plans for a large brick shoddy mill one story high, which will be located on the opposite side of the river from his present mill, and will be adapted for shoddy and picker work. Perfect arrangements for flooding in case of fire will be added, and the whole plant so arranged as not to affect the insurance on the rest of his property. Two parties are understood to be negotiating with Mr. Keyes R. Brown for the rebuilding of the Mohegan Mill. Messrs. A. L. Sayles & Son are also making a good sized glass addition for the benefit of the finishing department. Mr. J. T. Fiske Jr., has his new mill all completed and ready to run at a moments notice. In fact, there is a general air of activity among the woolen men. Clays are selling well and prospects are the fall market will open strong in a few days, if no new complications set in upon tariff questions.

Magner Bros. Mill Destroyed by Fire
September 20, 1895

Monday night a disastrous fire occurred in this place, destroying the entire plant of Magner Bros. Silver Lake Worsted Mills and endangering nearby property. At 11 o'clock, the watchman made his usual rounds and found everything all right. About twenty minutes later, he discovered the fire, and by 11:30 the whole mill was a mass of seething flames far beyond control. At midnight, the place was a roaring furnace, and at 1:30 nothing but smoking ruins was left of the plant. The fire probably originated in the vicinity of the boilers and then spread to the tower nearby, in which were located the tanks supplying the sprinklers. The flames quickly enveloped the tower, and thus destroyed the usefulness of the sprinklers with which the mill was well equipped. The large fire pump was also located near where the fire started and that, too, was made powerless to assist in subduing the flames.

The heat from the burning structure was intense, and had not the wind been blowing from the southwest, all of the many buildings nearby would have been consumed. As it was, only the most strenuous efforts on the part of the crowd saved them. The house in which one of the proprietors lived was situated but a short distance to the west of the mill and was badly charred. The flames caught from time to time and were extinguished by the bucket brigade, which had quickly been formed. E. O. Battey's Market building and the barn occupied by Walter Smith south of the mill were kept drenched with water and are none the worse for being in proximity to the fire, except that the paint on the market is somewhat scorched.

The burned mill was a combination of old and new parts, built of wood one part two stories and the other one and a half stories high, with the tower, the boiler and engine rooms connecting the two parts. Forty-four looms were operated in the weaving of fancy worsted and cloakings. Two hundred pieces of goods, including those finished and in the process of manufacture, were destroyed. The new two-story addition built about six months ago was equipped with new looms, and at the same time new boilers, engine, finishers, and other machinery were put in. The destruction of the mill throws about 100 people out of employment. The mill was running overtime, and had sufficient number of orders already on hand to operate it in its fullest capacity to the last of December. The plant was valued at between $75,000 and $80,000 and was insured for $65,000. As soon as the insurance is adjusted, steps will probably be taken to rebuild. The Messrs. Magner have the sympathy of the community in their loss. Beginning a few years ago with practically nothing, they had, by indomitable energy and untiring zeal, built up a plant and a business of which they were justly proud. To have it thus taken away is a severe blow to them.

Wm. H. Sheldon's Obituary
February 21, 1896

William H. Sheldon died at his residence on Sayles Avenue Monday afternoon. He was born in Chepachet in 1837 and was in his 59th year. His early life was passed in Chepachet, but when a young man he came here and has ever since been closely identified with the best interests of this town. About 1860, Mr. Sheldon entered into co-partnership with Almon Smith, and together they operated a power wood-working shop at Laurel Hill near A. Hopkins & Co. Machine Shop. This partnership was dissolved after a few years, and Mr. Sheldon carried on business there alone until 1872, when he built a shop on Sayles Avenue near his present location. He remained there until 1881, when he erected the three-story stone building where he has ever since been located. Shortly after the completion of his new shop, he commenced putting in wood-working machinery. His is now one of the best appointed establishments of the kind in the state. Mr. Sheldon was truly a self-made man. By close attention to business and by unremitting energy, he had from a humble beginning built up a business second to none in Northern Rhode Island.

Mr. Sheldon's business as a contractor and builder was very extensive, and for years he constructed the major portion of the buildings here as well as in many in adjoining towns. While he never sought public office, he has held a number of positions of trust in town such as councilman, surveyor, etc. It may be said of him that whatever he did, he did well. He married Mary, daughter of James Preston of Foster, in 1864. She died in 1865. In 1873 he married Nancy E., daughter of Thomas M. Baker of Grafton, Mass., who together with one son, survives him. He has been a member of Friendship Lodge A.F. and A.M. of Chepachet for many years. He was also a member of Pascoag Lodge A. O. U. W., and Pascoag Commandry, U. O. G. C. Funeral services will be held from the F. B. Church today at 1 o'clock. He will be buried with full Masonic honors at Chepachet. His death is a sad blow to the community and particularly to his family, who have ever found him a kind and indulgent husband and father. They have the heartfelt sympathy of all.

Mapleville Mill Sold -1898

Wednesday forenoon shortly after 11 o'clock the Mapleville Mill and the adjoining property, which includes nearly the entire village of Mapleville, was sold at public auction by Oliver A. Inman, auctioneer. The mill property consists of a large woolen mill, about 100 acres of land, the "upper mill" site, at present unoccupied, two large private residences, a store, hall, a large boarding house, seventeen tenement houses and several barns. There were several prospective bidders on the ground at the time of the sale, but when the bidding started, only two entered into it, William Legg and a Mr. Lester of the Centredale Worsted Company. The first bid was for $20,000. Mr. Lester immediately raised it $500 and from that time on until it reached $25,000 the bidding was solely between Mr. Legg and Mr. Lester. It was finally knocked down for $25,000 to William Legg, agent. The mill site cost about $200,000 when it was built something like thirty years ago. It was partially destroyed by fire a few months ago, and the insurance companies adjusted the loss at $25,000. The property was subject to a mortgage of $19,000 at the time of sale, the Woonsocket Institution for Savings being the mortgagee. The price is considered extremely low.

Bridgeton Knife Co.
July 6, 1900

The Bridgeton Knife Co., a new corporation composed of local businessmen, began active operations at Bridgeton on Monday. The plant is located at the Hopkins' Machine Works and is equipped with up-to-date machinery. James Kearney, formerly of Southbridge, is superintendent and manager of the concern, and offices are maintained at Bridgeton and also at Providence. The men employed are all skilled mechanics from out of town. Mr. Kearney has been in the knife business for several years and thoroughly understands every branch. At present the company has orders enough to keep them going for several months, and some orders were refused on account of the rush in business. The new industry is a valuable addition to those already located here, and the new concern has the best wishes of the entire community.

Stone Worsted Mill Destroyed
April 11, 1902

Sunday night, fire practically destroyed the Stone Worsted Mill on Sayles Avenue operated by Samuel S. Mellor, and had it not been for the efficient line of hose from A. L. Sayles & Sons' Mill, the loss would have been much greater. The rain which had been falling in a light shower when the fire began, fell heavily before one o'clock and thus aided in preventing the sparks from setting fire to the roofs of the neighboring houses. Watchman David Stephenson said he first saw the blaze about fifteen or twenty minutes after he made the 11 o'clock round. He said he heard a crackling sound in the boiler room, looked up and saw the flames in the room over his head in which the picker was located. Stephenson immediately gave the alarm and went to start up the pump.

The sprinklers did their work promptly, but the flames conquered the efforts of the automatic system. The hose was quickly coupled to the hydrants in the mill yard, and two lines were laid from the Sayles's Mill located around the corner of

Sayles Avenue and Main Street. Large streams of water were thrown with great force, and in a short time the building was thoroughly drenched. The difficulty seemed to be the inability to get water to the source of the fire. The firemen climbed upon the roof, but the flames were underneath, and it was not an easy task to get at them. The fire burned very slowly, but it did not seem possible to save William R. Sheldon's box shop located nearby the mill and connected with it.

Volumes of sparks were sent high up into the air and fell like snow upon the roofs of the nearby houses. Several times, a large shed, filled with lumber and located in the yard near the mill, caught fire, and the sparks were frantically stamped out by those who fought the flames. The mill, box shop, and the houses near them all seemed to be doomed. Residents of the houses removed a large part of their belongings to a place of safety. While the fire was at its fiercest stage, Mr. Hey, William H. Prendergast, William Mellor, Fred Mellor, and James O'Mara went into the wheel house to look after the wheel. They had scarcely stepped out of the building, when a large part of the fire wall of the mill toppled over and crushed the wheel house as if it had been an eggshell. With the wheel broken, the pumps immediately stopped. The two streams from the Union Mill were kept playing steadily upon the flames, and the fire was gradually brought under control. The contents of the mill, with the single exception of part of the finishing room, are totally destroyed, and the few benches and whatever cloth may be in that room are the only things remaining of the mill.

The Stone Worsted Mill was a three story stone building about 150x60 feet and contained 35 looms, 3 sets of cards, and 3 jacks with the necessary machinery for finishing. The plant occupied the three floors in the main building and also the upper floor of the adjoining building in which the box shop is located. There has been a woolen mill on the site since 1846. The roof was burned off of the mill in 1864 and was partly destroyed by fire in 1887. Mr. Mellor has been located there since 1890, the first four years associated with Wm. H. Prendergast. The mill has been running steadily, and it is a very rare occurrence in its history since 1890 that it has been shut down.

Fly-Wheel Burst
May 24, 1907

A sudden slackening of the speed, a heavy explosion, and the crash of breaking floors and timbers was the accompaniment of a disastrous accident at the Oakland Worsted Mills last evening, when a large fly wheel on the engine burst into many fragments. The accident occurred at 5:40 o'clock just twenty minutes before the closing of the mill for the day. That there was no attendant loss of life seems miraculous, for the heavy pieces of iron were hurled many feet through the floors ,and struck in and about the mill yard. At the time the accident occurred, it was evident the engine must have been running at normal speed, for there was no increase in the speed of the machinery and the electric stop motion would have prevented any increase in speed.

The engine was located on the basement floor of the mill with two floors above it. Through these two floors and the roof, the huge fragments of the fly wheel went crushing thick planks like paper and severing floor and roof timbers like pipe stems. It is a remarkable coincidence that at the time the accident occurred Superintendent William H. White was conversing with a salesman in the office regarding a safety appliance for the mill elevator. Mr. White noticed a slackening of the speed, and as he turned to the window to see the occasion of it, he heard a heavy explosion. At the same instant, he saw a large fragment hurled into the air to a height almost as great as that of the tall chimney. Inside the mill, the rooms adjacent to the path of the flying iron were filled with dust. As the dust settled, careful investigation revealed the fact that aside from two or three who were injured very slightly by flying splinters and silvers of wood, no one was harmed. When it was learned no one had been seriously injured, there was a general feeling of relief and thanksgiving throughout the little village.

The room directly over the engine is the drawing-in room, and near the path of the flying iron was the desk of the overseer of weaving, William C. Hill. He was at his desk at the time and was conversing with Joseph Marsden. Although but a few feet removed, they were uninjured, except slightly by splinters. Only a few seconds before the accident, one of the weavers had crossed this floor, which was torn up. The sewing room was on the floor above this. Three of the employees were in such close proximity to the path that the cuts of cloth upon which they were working were entangled in the wreckage. Joseph Garvin is the overseer in charge of the sewing room, and he promptly prevented any panic among the employees, which might have otherwise arisen. By putting cuts of cloth out the windows, the women were enabled to safely lower themselves to the roof of the dye house a few feet below the windows of their room. When the dust had settled, it was shown that the need of this precaution in leaving the room was unnecessary, as the usual means of egress was not impeded.

Some of the fragments, which went through the roof and high in the air, were estimated to weigh from 300 to 600 pounds. The terrible force with which they struck the earth and went through intervening parts of the building would have brought death to any who might have been in their path. Directly over the flywheel was a large water pipe which got broken and caused a flood of water, until the supply could be shut off. The roof was at once repaired temporarily, and the dangerous places propped up. Arrangements were made so that a part of the mill was started up this morning, water being the motive power used.

The New Harrisville Mill
January 18, 1910

The William Tinkham Co. woolen manufacturers, which recently sold out the old woolen mill to the United States Worsted Company, has awarded a contract to build a $75,000 mill near the old one in the village of Harrisville to the E. K. Watson Company of Warren. The plant will be constructed of reinforced concrete, which is a new departure in mill construction in this state, and will be the largest mill built of this material in Rhode Island. It will consist of two or more buildings two or more stories in height with bays fifteen feet wide, about one-third wider than is usual. This will reduce the number of columns and will economize space. The exterior of the building will be largely of glass, making the interior almost as light as outdoors.

The new Tinkham structure will have concrete cornices and pilasters with moldings, relief ornaments and tower balconies, which will give it a highly ornamental appearance. The designs of the building are by Adolph Suck of Hyde Park, Mass. The dimensions of the largest building will be 170x48 feet and the second in size, which will contain a steam power plant, dye house, storage and drying departments, will be 175x60 feet. It will take almost a half mile of railroad box cars to convey the amount of concrete needed to erect the building.

Stonemason Francis Sprague
March 25, 1910

Francis Sprague, one of the oldest residents of Burrillville and a contractor and builder known nearly all over the State of Rhode Island, died at his home in this village Tuesday night in

One Hundred Years Ago in Burrillville by Patricia A. Mehrtens

his 85th year due to diseases incident to old age. Mr. Sprague had constructed mills and other large plants and buildings in New Haven, Conn., in the state of Illinois, and in Pascoag, Mohegan, Oakland, Harrisville, Graniteville, Burrillville, West Glocester, Riverpoint, and other Rhode Island communities. He was a brick and stone constructor and had completed many large contracts.

    He was born in Glocester, March 6, 1825, the son of George and Sarah (Darling) Sprague. When he was quite young, he cut off wood lots, got out lumber, and carted it to Providence and Pawtucket with ox teams. When he was 22 years of age he learned the mason's trade and worked at it 45 years, becoming a contractor and builder of all kinds of stone and brick construction, plastering, stucco working and hard finishing. In 1860, he came to Mapleville and built a dam for Daniel Whipple, who was a prominent manufacturer at that time. Later he did considerable building for John L. Ross, who formerly owned what is now the village of Oakland. The first contract he made with Mr. Ross was to build the stone office now owned and occupied by the Oakland Worsted Company.

    In the early sixties he did a large amount of work for Lafayette Reynolds when the latter was building up the village of Mohegan. Mr. Sprague built the mill and plastered the houses, including Mr. Reynold's private dwelling, which is now the home of F. E. Bartlett. Mr. Sprague worked on the first woolen mill built in Harrisville, and the first one built in Graniteville. In 1864-65 he built the four-story mill that stood on Main Street in Pascoag, afterward owned and operated by Horace A. Kimball until 1882, when it was destroyed by fire. When Mr. Sprague took the contract to build this mill, he took it with the stone in the ledge and the lumber in the woods, blasting and trimming all the stone, and cutting and sawing all the lumber with the exception of the beams he bought of a lumber dealer in Woonsocket.

    Mr. Sprague built and rebuilt the Old Stone Mill on Sayles Avenue three times. He built the planing mill and box shop on Sayles Avenue, the stock house that stands west of the Union Mill, laid the foundation of the White Mill, and did many other jobs throughout the town. There is not a mill privilege in Burrillville he had not worked on. Mr. Sprague also built many tall chimneys in his day. The one standing at the Anchor Mills in Pascoag was built under his supervision, erected in 1888 for John T. Fiske, Jr. In 1856, Mr. Sprague married Emily Sayles, daughter of Welcome Sayles of Burrillville. Mrs. Sprague died in 1893. He leaves one son, Edward C. Sprague. A funeral will be held Saturday morning at 10:30 and burial will be in Glocester.

One Hundred Years Ago in Burrillville by Patricia A. Mehrtens

RAILROADS & TROLLEYS

Trains Collide
January 5, 1883

Last Saturday at 3:30 p.m. the freight train from Pascoag to Providence was run into between Olneyville and Providence by a special N.Y. & N.E. train. The freight train on our road was on their regular time, and the accident was due to the inexcusable carelessness of the operator in the employ of the New England Road stationed at Olneyville Junction. Both engines were badly disabled. Owing to the fact that the Pascoag train was going very slowly, and also owing to the great presence of mind of those on the engine and cars, none of the employees of the Providence & Springfield road were injured seriously. But those on the N.Y. & N.E. train did not escape so well, nearly all of them being more or less bruised, some seriously.

The train was on its way to Sterling, Connecticut carrying men and material to clear up a wreck there which occurred earlier in the day. The actual money damage to the Providence & Springfield R. R. Co. will probably not exceed $3000, but as it is the possessor of only three locomotives and one of them was in the repair shop, the accident reduced them to only one engine. There has been great inconvenience caused thereby, as it was difficult to procure an engine at short notice. No train left Pascoag Saturday after the 12:35 p.m. and the train which should have left Providence at 4:15 p.m. did not get away until 11:30 p.m. Monday, there was no freight train, and one engine ran down both 5:35 and 7:10 a.m. trains, the latter train being behind time nearly fifty minutes. The 6:20 p.m. from Providence was also delayed, as it was necessary to run the engine back over the road before the next train could start. Tuesday, an engine was procured, which is running the freight trains.

Ever since the new arrangements by which the Providence

& Springfield and the N.Y. & N.E. R. R. Cos. use a common track between Olneyville and Providence, the general public has been prophesying an accident basing their belief on the notorious "accident qualities" of the N.Y. & N.E. The recent catastrophe has shown that the belief was well founded, although it occurred through no fault in the arrangement, but by the carelessness of an employee. It is to be hoped that some other arrangement may be made very soon, if possible.

A Trip Along the Railroad
May 15, 1891

A trip along the Woonsocket and Pascoag branch of the New York and New England Railroad Friday last found work at various localities being accomplished with characteristic vigor. Slatersville presented the most activity. A large gang of men under a boss were laying a side track, which will be on the opposite side of the depot from the main track. This track is about 1,500 feet in length and is designed to be used for a siding for freight trains while the passenger trains pass. It is made necessary because of the additional evening passenger trains put on May 9th. The foreman of the gang said this new siding would be finished for use Saturday noon.

The high bank is being cut away considerably, the loam from the top saved to be used where needed to cover up the sand near the depot. A spur track beside this siding has been put in to give facilities for local freight. The depot building is completed and makes a very neat appearance in its dark colored paint. No station agent had been placed here, but it is talked that James O. Smith, who filled a similar position at Tarkiln Station on the Providence and Springfield branch, is the one selected for this place. If this be so, the citizens and patrons of the road are to be congratulated, for they will find in him a courteous and considerate person. The depot surroundings are exceedingly sandy, it being the natural quality of the soil there. This station is about the same pattern as the others along the line, and consists of a waiting room with ticket office connected and a good sized room for baggage. The Nasonville depot is completed and is to be a telegraph station with the agent at Woonsocket Junction expected to fill the position of depot master and train dispatcher. The deep cut this side of Nasonville does not look as formidable as it did a few weeks ago, as laborers have dug the bank away and dragged the stones which had rolled down the embankment to the open space below the cut and pushed them out of the way.

We notice that caution is taken by engineer O'Brien to bring his trains under perfect control as he approaches the deep ravine with his living freight. This is necessary, because with the sharp curve only a very short distance can be seen ahead of the locomotive as it winds around under the care of its driver. Caution is also taken to have some person in the cut most of the time and especially just before train time, to see that no obstructions have fallen upon the track. As one passes along in the train, water can be seen oozing from the side of the bank. This results in a small stream of water which wends its way beside the track until lost in the sand or until it finds its way into the river close by. The road as a whole has many curves but rides very easy. Quite a straight stretch is seen just below Glendale before the cut is reached. The depot at Glendale was well underway Friday with the frame up and the roof shingled except near the gable. The frame for a depot at Whipple's was partially erected and will be soon completed. At Harrisville, just below the station, a side track of good length has been put in for the accommodation of the midnight freight. The facilities here have been rather cramped and this will supply a great need.

The New Railroad Extension
November 18, 1892

From a descriptive article in the *Providence Sunday Journal*, we make the following extracts: The original plan of the Providence and Springfield Railroad was to provide direct communication to Springfield, and thus with Albany and the West. The Pascoag extension will complete an important link and will reach a similar result by shortening the distance by rail to Worcester. The lessees of the road, the New York and New England Railroad, conceived this plan to enlarge and improve their own system and have taken the work in hand. After a survey of the proposed route by railroad engineers, the construction of the bed and track was turned over to the general contractors, Ward Brothers of Kennebunk, Maine. The general trend of the line is in a northwesterly direction from Pascoag, the present terminus through the sparsely settled and picturesque region of Buck Hill, tapping the main line of the N.Y. and N.E. at a point about two miles above East Thompson Junction.

No serious obstacles exist on the proposed route, although in the village of Pascoag two bridges will be required. In the intermediate sections, several substantial ledges have been encountered, and the last few miles are being constructed through a densely wooded territory. From the Pascoag station, about 100 yards of track have been laid up to the first abutment of the bridge, which is to cross the Reservoir outlet near the woolen mill of John T. Fiske. This bridge, about 300 feet long, is to be of iron of the ordinary viaduct type and built to accommodate a single track. Besides the two granite abutments at either end of the bridge, there will be nine sets of double granite piers, making in all 18 intermediate supports. Beyond the first bridge, the grade has been practically finished for a distance of about an eighth of a mile up to the shoddy mill, or what is known as the "Hopkins privilege." Another deep cut is here, which will necessitate a second bridge over the road and thestream from the Reservoir.

At the present time there are nearly 500 men employed on the entire road, and the great majority of them are Italian contract laborers. The colony at the Pascoag end affiliate in a single old-fashioned deserted farm house on the outskirts of the village. The building is two stories high, low studded, and is divided up to accommodate the 100 Italians who are purported to live there. On the Stanfield farm in this section, another obstacle is met in the shape of a large compact ledge, which crops out in several places on the high land, and extends deep into the ground. Two steam drills and a steam derrick are constantly at work at this point and, although the stone covers a considerable distance, no great delay is anticipated from this cause. Further on beyond the ledge the course lies through a rough territory, very stony and covered with a growth of scrub pines.

About four miles from Pascoag the road enters the Buck Hill woods and passes for a distance of about two miles along the shores of Wallum Pond. It is here that a view of exceptional attractiveness is afforded. The shores of the pond are lined with a dense growth of pines which, with the clear, sparkling waters of the lake, combine to give an effect of rare beauty. The entire region of Buck Hill constitutes one of the most picturesque localities in Rhode Island, and the proposed railroad will traverse the most interesting portion winding round the base of the hill following the line of shore. In the woods, the pioneer gangs engaged in felling the trees and cutting away the underbrush have nearly finished their labors, and the route is now clearly defined through the tall trees. Much of the tall lumber from the clearing in this section will be converted into ties for the new road, which has proved one of the advantages of the route.

A short distance from the main line the road divides, and the two branches will join the main track in opposite direction to form the "Y." One arm of the "Y" is already finished and ready for the rails, while the other is rapidly approaching completion. For a distance of a quarter of a mile in from the main line, a double track is to be laid. The remainder of the line will consist of a single track with convenient sidings at various points. An excellent opportunity is given here to see the workings of Italian contract labor. The contractor who furnishes the laborers is colloquially termed the Italian "King" and the title is singularly appropriate.

There is such little doubt as to the ultimate advantage of the business interests of Providence as well as the development of the surrounding territory that the near completion of the line is looked forward to with interest here in the city and in the towns along the line. The inhabitants of that portion have been greatly benefited by the original Providence and Springfield road, but the existence of a through line communicating with the other New England states and the West, without having first to depend on the connection with Providence, will doubly increase the advantage to the small manufacturing establishments in the various towns, beside adding to the facilities for the transportation of freight to and from Providence.

Oakland Station Accident
December 16, 1892

A rather curious and fatal accident occurred Wednesday, just after dark, near the Oakland station, which resulted in the death of Fred Himes, a brakeman in the employ of the N.Y. and N.E. Railroad Company. Because of the heavy freight business on the road, an extra freight was made up at the Providence yard and followed the local freight train west. The extra was in charge of Conductor Smith and Engineer Love. As Oakland was neared, the extra slowed up, as the local was at the station. Himes, who was head brakeman, was on the engine as the locomotive slowly moved towards the station, and just as the bridge spanning the neck of the Oakland Pond was reached, he stepped off in the darkness supposing the bridge had been crossed, and went down about eight feet into the water on the side next Mapleville. He was heard to cry out, but he could not swim, and sank to the bottom. The train men rallied with lanters and hooks secured from the engine, and endeavored to find the body, but without avail. Other help arrived, and a boat was procured to assist in the search. The water at this point was not frozen over for quite a distance around. Several worked with a will but gave up the search for the night as fruitless and returned home. But as one party became tired, there were others to take their places, and the search continued for hours. At 11 o'clock the body was found about 20 feet from where the unfortunate man had stepped in and below the bridge. Calvin Aldrich immediately started for Coroner Wilcox of Pascoag and notified him of the discovery of Himes' body. Wilcox, being satisfied it was simply an accident, gave Aldrich permission to remove the body to Waterman Bros., Pascoag, arriving there about 3 o'clock Thursday morning.

The accident is a very sad one indeed. Fred was congenial and well liked by his brother employees. It was like a thunderbolt from a clear sky to his wife who is grief stricken. Mr. Himes was about 25 years of age and had two children, the oldest not over 3 years of age. They lived in the house which is located near the tracks at Smithfield station. Many times as Fred passed this station, his wife held the little one up at the window to see its papa. The parents of the unfortunate man live at Pascoag, the father having charge of the round house near the station, and the blow is a very severe one to them. While it may look to some as a very curious accident, railroad men say that it was nothing strange, as doubtless when Himes stood at the side of the cab to step off the headlight showed solid ground a little back from the head of the locomotive. The deceased was a member of Granite Lodge No. 33 I.O.O.F. and had been in the employ of the road for several years.

Laurel Hill to the Front
July 28, 1893

Laurel Hill people are not dozing as anyone can see by a little thought upon various matters arising of late. There is a large amount of business done at this end of Pascoag. This statement is not made at random, but can be verified by a little investigation. For a long time the inhabitants much desired better postal facilities. Mail carried by boys who were compensated by the receivers of the letters was an unsatisfactory service because of irregularities. When boys would be minus for the above purpose, C. F. Potter did what he could to accommodate the people who appreciated his efforts in this line in the past. There was no dissent in regard to his appointment as Postmaster. Mail was left in bulk in a box at the Laurel Hill Store, free for the inspection of all. Instances are not lacking when letters were lost behind sugar barrels for several days or until sweeping time came. A post office was applied for and the petition was granted and now Laurel Hill has a pretty and well-kept office. Over 70 letter boxes have been let. So much for that.

A committee has been appointed regarding a school house, and Laurel Hill people will be pleased with a school building located sufficiently near to accommodate those having children to send to school. The old building is in bad shape, and in a short time a new building would be necessary. It looks as though those engineering the project are on the right track. But we did not begin this article to talk about the new school house, but to bring forward the idea of a change of the location of the passenger station from its present location to a point near what is known as Sayles Grove, Sayles Avenue.

Since the laying out of the railroad extension, the idea of having a depot at the Ridge has never for an instant been absent from the minds of the people living in this vicinity. A petition has been circulated and numerously signed asking for a station in the rear of Col. Hopkins' residence. A meeting was recently held in Hopkins Hall when the matter was discussed. The project of having a union depot and have it located there was broached and seemed to gain in favor. Olney T. Inman, A. S. Hopkins, and Andrew Luther were appointed a committee to consult with the businessmen of Pascoag and get their opinion. If Laurel Hill people cannot secure a union depot suitably located, they will persistently press their claim for a station at the Ridge.

At first thought, it might strike some that the changing of location was rather a radical measure, but the more it is investigated, the more feasible it appears. It surely would be more central and much better accommodate the people. The station at present is away to one side. It is not known how the officials of the New England road will look upon such a change, but it is thought that if the people of Laurel Hill are all in favor and nearly all of those in Pascoag, it will carry considerable weight. The distance from Fountain Square to the proposed new site is but a trifle more than to the present location, and would be a great accommodation to Laurel Hill. With a union school house, why not have a union depot, and eventually one central post office? Laurel Hill and Pascoag are gradually growing together, and the time is not far distant when the open space will be all built over.

Andrew Hubbard Killed by Train
December 31, 1893

The passengers on the first train from Woonsocket on Wednesday morning were somewhat startled when the train suddenly stopped on the bridge between Whipples and Harrisville. Looking out they saw the mangled form of Andrew Hubbard, a respected citizen of Harrisville, who had been walking up the track from his work at Whipples where he had been night watchman for a number of years.

Mr. Hubbard was caught on the bridge, and when the whistle blew the danger alarm, he became confused, and did not hurry ahead, but gazed vacantly about as if undecided which way to go. The engineer reversed his engine, but the train could not be stopped until the cow catcher had caught the unfortunate man, breaking one leg in two places, tearing off the foot, and stripping the flesh from the bone of the other in a terrible manner, after which, mangled and bleeding, he was thrown upon the bank in full view of the passengers as they sat in the cars. The opportunity for immediate assistance was quickly seized upon, and trainmen and passengers soon placed him upon the stretcher and laid him in the baggage car. Undertaker Wightman, who happened to be aboard, and Mr. G. W. Esten quickly bound up the wounded members with stout cord.

As soon as the train arrived at Harrisville, doctors were at once telegraphed for, but as they were not immediately available, he was carried to Pascoag. Here doctors were also sent for, but as one had arrived at Harrisville, he was at once carried there. Dr. Wilcox, medical examiner, and Dr. H. J. Bruce both rendered all the assistance possible until the 12:40 train for Providence arrived. Mr. Hubbard was conveyed to the Rhode Island Hospital Dr. Wilcox accompanied him and ministered to his wants during the journey. At Providence, the hospital ambulance met the train and took Mr. Hubbard immediately in hand. He had received a severe shock, and it was seen that his age, 59 years, and condition were all against him, and a little after 6 p.m. Wednesday night, he died. Before death, however, he acquitted the railroad and employees of all blame in the affair, saying it was all his fault.

Fast Train through Burrillville
May 15, 1896

Away back in the sixties the residents of Burrillville cherished fond hopes of seeing express trains whirl through their town enroute from Boston to New York over the projected "Air Line" Railroad. In their dreams they could see clouds of dust and cinders roll from under the rapidly revolving wheels and even the bushes along the line came to have a perpetual swaying motion caused by the rapid rush of the trains. Awaking from their dreams, they would go out and watch the laborers busily engaged in preparing the roadway at intervals along the route. But alas for the hopes of man! The "Air Line" Road ended abruptly at Woonsocket, and the unfinished roadbed this side was left to crumble away and serve only as a monument of an unfinished project.

Never since then has the dreamer even in his most visionary fantasies ever thought of Boston and New York limited express trains speeding across the confines of Burrillville. The improbable sometimes happens, and the visions of a former day become realities of the present. To this generation came the pleasure of witnessing the unusual and unthought of sight of the Boston and New York "Five-Hour Flyer" rushing through town at an almost incredible speed. There have been other trains galore ordinarily run on the main line, but none have attracted so much attention as this. Even a majestic bandwagon with its two score of horses and its following of gaudy circus wagons, would have been passed by the small boy as of little consequence compared to the sight of a "limited" in Burrillville. Thus the loss of the two great railroad bridges near Blackstone, deplorable as it was, and entailing great monetary loss and much inconvenience, caused the visions of a former generation to be realized, and made Pascoag for a brief time the principal town on a "Trunk Line" railroad.

Columbian Street Railway
July 30, 1906

Town Council Meeting - The Columbian Street Railway was directed to change the location of its tracks in Rich Hollow between Nasonville and Mohegan to conform to a plat on file at the Town Clerk's office. The highway, at this point over which the state road will be constructed, is to be raised and straightened, and the change of the tracks is made to conform to the plan. The approval of the location of the grade crossings of the Worcester & Providence Street Railway tracks, and the granting of a franchise were taken up. Plans of the entire route of the proposed road were shown and examined by the board. It enters the town near Oak Valley, crosses the highway at several points, then enters the highway several hundred feet south of the Western Hotel. Leaving the highway north of the hotel, it crosses the Glendale road, intersects the Columbian Street Railway tracks near the Mohegan Mills and crosses the highway several times between Mohegan and the state line.

The principal point at issue regarding the grade crossings was whether it would be better to locate the tracks in front of the Western Hotel or run behind it and cross the Glendale road higher up the hill. All things considered, the former plan seemed most feasible and best. The franchise presented for adoption had been changed somewhat from the outline originally before the board, and various features were considered at length. The representatives of the company seemed perfectly willing to embody anything that was reasonable, and so expressed themselves. The company will make three regular stopping places in town, viz: At Oak Valley, Western Hotel, and at the intersection with the Columbian tracks. Accommodation cars will also stop at all highway crossings in town to take or leave passengers.

The rate of fare within the limits of the town will be 5c, with a 20c fare from any point in town to Providence. A half rate was agreed upon for school children. It was decided that all cars, both passenger and freight, should come to a full stop before crossing the Glendale road on the Western hill. Waiting rooms or stations will be erected at the three stopping places in town. Other features were considered, and it was decided to continue the whole matter to Wednesday afternoon of this week for further action. The railway company was represented by President Hinds, Chief Engineer Fisher, and Attorneys Tillinghast and Bartlett. Walter Tabor addressed the council in behalf of the owners of the Oak Valley Mill, urging the granting of the franchise. The representatives of the road expressed themselves as being anxious the franchise be granted as soon as possible so the work of construction might not be delayed. Adjourned.

Pleasant Trolley Trip
June 21, 1907

If one cannot afford the luxury and uncertainty of an automobile, the next best thing is the trolley car on which one may now visit many sections which heretofore were not reached by public conveyance. The trolley car does have its limitations. For that matter so has the automobile, as everyone will testify who has experienced some of the strange freaks which the automobile has of unexplainably "bucking up" and refusing to be coaxed, cajoled or frightened into budging. At last some little nut or trivial screw is tightened up or loosened and, presto, the machinery starts with a whirl that makes one forget it had been causing discomfort and danger of breaking the commandment which forbids the use of certain expressive language. But all this is digressing from the subject of the story. Whether automobiles are an entire or limited blessing does not concern this narrative. Trolley cars are all right, and with the company of a congenial friend or the more rollicking trolley party, one can find trips which are delightful and at the same time inexpensive.

When you have the combination of spare time, an inclination for sightseeing, and pleasant weather, you can start on a pleasant day's outing by taking the morning train from Pascoag at 9:40 to Webster. The scenes from the car window are picturesque as the train steams over the high railroad bridges of Pascoag and Bridgeton, and passing through intervening field and woodland, skirts along the shores of Wilson's Reservoir and Wallum Lake. Glimpses of the State Sanatorium may be had over the treetops. At Wallum Lake Station passengers will alight to visit this great and beneficent institution located on the most healthful spot in all Rhode Island. Nearby the station is O'Neil's Camp where before the days of the Sanatorium many an invalid found a renewal of health by camping under the pines and breathing the pure balsam laden air. At the north end of Wallum Lake are the large ice houses and a cluster of summer cottages.

A few hundred feet beyond Wallum Lake, the Pascoag branch joins the "main line" of the Midland division. At East Thompson the train leaves the "main line" and goes on to the Southbridge branch. Soon the train is passing along the shores of one of the most beautiful lakes in New England, popularly known as Webster Lake, which has another name whose aggregation of syllables makes its pronunciation and spelling a feat well nigh unaccomplishable. At Webster there will be a wait of twenty minutes, and at 10:45 the Consolidated trolley may be taken for a ride down the picturesque Quinnebaug to Danielson. A short distance beyond Webster is a branch line to Perryville, and farther on is the little village of Wilkinsonville. Then comes North Grosvenordale with its handsome brick mill, and farther on is Grosvenordale where a smaller factory is located. There are several smaller villages before one reaches Putnam, and the scenery is ever-changing and beautiful.

In Putnam, the route is through the principal streets, under the railroad tracks near the commodious new station, and then by somewhat of a tortuous course through the residential sections. Passing by the fair grounds, the car comes again to the shores of the Quinnebaug, and soon Dayville is reached. At exactly noon, the traveler comes to the little station at Wildwood Park, a trolley park located on the shores of a clear sparkling lake whose natural beauties have brought for it more than local fame.

At Elmville, the Providence & Danielson road connects with the Consolidated. From Elmville the car climbs up, up, up, through a beautiful valley where there was once a chain of small mills with their attendant tenements and thriving industry. Although this section is officially designated as East Killingly, it is more familiarly known as Chestnut Hill. To describe the ride from Chestnut Hill through Foster does not require many paragraphs for it is in the main uninteresting. There are spots, however, that are attractive. At Foster Center is the old town house, the little church, and school house, and the large building where is located the town clerk's office, and from there on the view again becomes attractive.

Clayville, with its massive elms, has an inviting look, and the villages of Rockland, Richmond and South Scituate, with the busy little factory village of Ashland nearby, draw the attention of the traveler. A glimpse of the once thriving factory village of Saundersville is seen just before the car reaches the "new Mill" at North Scituate. The last named village is the largest passed through since leaving Danielson. A short distance beyond is Lake Moswansicut, another beautiful sheet of water. Farther on is Waterman Reservoir, beyond which the railroad passes over a private right of way. In a few moments the city of Providence is presented to view and the journey over the Providence & Danielson road is soon at an end.

By the time one reaches Providence, his appetite has been fanned by the breezes of Northern Rhode Island, Massachusetts, and Connecticut to a pitch where a good dinner has an irresistible appeal, unless there has been a lunch basket accompaniment on the trip. For the hungry there is nothing more satisfactory at this time of the year than a dinner at Field's Point. The arrival in Providence at 3:40 gives ample time to take the 4 o'clock boat to Col. Atwell's establishment and get the best shore dinner on earth. The trip home from Providence can then be made over the fast trolley to Woonsocket, and by the Columbian to Burrillville, or over the steam road directly to town as suits the fancy of the individual. The cost of the trip is nominal and is as follows: Pascoag to Webster, 30c; Webster to Danielson, 35c; Danielson to Providence, 65c; Providence to Pascoag by trolley, 35c.

Providence & Springfield RR History
August 14, 1908

The Providence and Springfield Line opened for traffic August 11, 1873. Thirty-five years ago last Tuesday morning

One Hundred Years Ago in Burrillville by Patricia A. Mehrtens

the first regular passenger train pulled out of the local station, and the arduous and difficult task of constructing a railroad during almost unprecedented hard times bore fruition in the opening of regular passenger traffic and the uniting of this section of the state with the outer world by indissoluble bonds of railroad iron.

This date may well be termed the opening of a new epoch for Burrillville and the intermediate towns on the line to Providence, marking as it does the ending of the stage coach days and bringing this section into easy and quick communication with the outside world. The new railroad not only cheapened the cost of freight transportation, but also made the handling of large quantities of merchandise and supplies possible at prices which permitted competition with other localities. To the coming of the railroad much of the prosperity of our town is due, for without it the material prosperity of Burrillville could not have increased with such splendid strides as the past 35 years have witnessed. Those men who labored under the most discouraging conditions and battled against adverse circumstances for the building of the Providence & Springfield Railroad are deserving of the utmost praise from the citizens of this generation for the persistency with which they prosecuted their endeavor and completed the undertaking.

On August 11, 1873, the railroad was far from final completion. The road bed was new and imperfectly ballasted, stations had not been constructed, and platforms were conspicuous in most instances by their absence. The locomotive "Hercules" which had been used in the construction work on the new railroad, was taken from that prosaic duty and given the honor of hauling the first regular passenger train from Pascoag to Providence. After a short time the "Hercules" was assigned to freight work, where it fully sustained the expectations which its name would imply and the "Stentor" was purchased and put into the passenger service. The "Stentor" was later refurbished and emerged as the "William Tinkham" in honor of the president of the road, and under that name did long and effective service. The "Achilles" was a later purchase and was used in the freight service.

During the first few years there were only two trains each way a day, leaving Pascoag shortly after 7 o'clock in the morning and between 12 and 1 p.m. On the return trips, Providence was left about 9:30 a.m. and a little after 4 o'clock in the afternoon. Besides these, there was a theater train Saturday nights. In those old days the crew on the Saturday night train were allowed fifty

One Hundred Years Ago in Burrillville by Patricia A. Mehrtens

cents each for supper. It was the custom to have an officer on the late train to assist the conductor in seeing that passengers conducted themselves with due order and decorum. The presence of the officer was made advisable not because of the actions of those who patronized the new road, but by those who might be termed transient inhabitants of some of the villages.

When the freight service was commenced, it was remarked that "one freight train a month will bring all the freight that is required" but the road was yet new when special trains were operated to bring coal to the manufacturing establishments. For some time there were no freight houses, and merchandise was either unloaded on the ground or kept in the box cars until removed by the consignees.

The road was opened before the passenger stations were built. George W. Esten, who was the first station agent at Harrisville and to whom we are indebted for the major facts concerning the early history of the road, says that he kept the railroad tickets in the town clerk's office, and before each train went out he would put into his pocket as many tickets as he expected to sell, go down to the railroad, and supply the required needs. William Blackmar, who was the first agent at Oakland, pursued a similar course, having his office in the lobby of the stable now occupied by C. O. Remington. William H. Vaughn was the first agent at Pascoag coming here from the station at Douglas. James O. Smith and Mr. Hubbard were the first agents at Tarkiln and Georgiaville, respectively. The station at Pascoag was constructed first and the Harrisville station was completed in January following the opening of the road.

W. I. Fox was the first passenger conductor, and was followed by W. C. Patterson, who had charge of the first freight train. He was succeeded by George W. Esten who was promoted from station agent at Harrisville. Samuel Stebbins was engineer and Charles Vars fireman on the first passenger train. The latter was for several years an efficient engineer on the road. Ephram Taylor as engineer and Michael H. Lacey of Pascoag as fireman had charge of the locomotive which drew the first freight train over the new road. James Drury of this place came on the road as fireman two or three months after the opening and was soon set up as engineer in which capacity he has served continuously ever since and is rated as one of the best engineers on the New Haven system. Conductor Albert F. Ballou came on the road during the early days as freight brakeman under William Hutchinson. From that position he rose rapidly and has been a conductor for many, many years.

One Hundred Years Ago in Burrillville by Patricia A. Mehrtens

SUMMER RESORTS & PARTIES

Shore Resorts in Burrillville
July 17, 1885

Although Burrillville is an inland town, it contains two natural "shore resorts" namely, Wallum Lake and Herring Pond—or correctly speaking, Lake. Wallum Lake is a natural sheet of water three miles long and one mile wide at the broadest place and is said to lie in three states, Rhode Island, Massachusetts, and Connecticut. In some portions of the lake the water is very deep, some claiming that no one has ever been able to touch bottom in those places no matter what they used. As it contains many kinds of the finny tribe, it attracts many of the disciples of Isaac Walton, who scarcely ever go away without a good string of fish.

Upon a hill near the lake a fair view of Dudley, Mass. is obtained in fair weather. About a mile further towards Douglas away to the north, north-east, three mountain peaks may be seen: Wachusett (which can be seen the plainest) and Mt. Tom in Massachusetts and Mt. Monadnock in New Hampshire. So it will be seen that this is very high land. The lake is situated in a valley and its fine beaches, clear water, and beautiful scenery makes it very attractive to all. The "North end" of the lake was formerly opened to the public and visited a great deal more than the "South end" for it has the best beaches, groves, etc. But picnic parties and others will have to content themselves with visiting the latter place now as the former place is fenced in.

Picnics on July Fourth
July 6, 1888

The weather was all that could be wished for, and July fourth was well celebrated by picnickers in various parts of the town. The Methodist Society held a bake in Ara Paine's Grove and it was well attended. although not as many as last year. The clams were excellently baked under the supervision of the veteran caterer Elisha Daggett and were pronounced sweet and of good flavor. Five bushels were baked and disposed of. Two strangers with accordions furnished music for the entertainment of the picnickers. The table where ice cream, confectionery, fruit and cake were on sale was well patronized, also the booth where lemonade was dispensed.

Carson's Grove presented an animated appearance. The clams served here under the care of Mr. Duty Place were never better. Teams were hitched among the trees quite thickly. while the owners were in different sections of the grove imbibing lemonade, sarsaparillas and sodas of various flavors. A canvas was stretched from the trees shading the stand for dancing. which was well patronized. Mr. Riley prompted, with his usual good voice, the music, consisting of four pieces which gave rhythm enough to satisfy the most obtuse timest with the pedal extremities. There were at the least calculation seven hundred persons on the grounds. The many light and airy white dresses worn by the ladies made the scene a pretty one. Many of our citizens visited the grove in teams, stopping for a short time. During the day the trains stopped at the grove giving every facility for those not being the possessor of an equine steed to get to and from the picnic. The ice cream disappeared like dew before the sun. Swings, games and other amusements made the day pass pleasantly away. The picnic at this place will be known in history as a great and grand success.

A party of fifteen couples of young people took everything palatable with them and picnicked on the shore of beautiful Wallum Pond. Baseball was indulged in here and a game of Old Maid. Boating also was enjoyed. Private clambakes and picnics were numerous, one being reported on Page's Island, one on the mainland on the shore of the Reservoir, at Herring Pond, and many other places. Altogether the day was enjoyably and pleasantly passed, the reporter only hearing of one accident from the use of articles used for celebrating. Many families had fireworks of their own, which were much enjoyed by themselves and neighbors.

Sunday at Herring Pond
August 9, 1889

The shores of this beautiful sheet of water and also the crest of the pond were alive with humanity last Sunday. The day was perfect not being excessively hot, neither too cool for comfort. Many of our townspeople availed themselves of the opportunity to visit the many enchanting nooks placed by nature along its rock-bound borders.

Not only were many Burrillville people present, but parties came in large teams and private teams from Slatersville, Woonsocket and Uxbridge. Over one hundred souls were present to enjoy a day's outing. The boats were in great demand and had there been fifty more the owners would have had no trouble in letting them at renumerative prices. In fact, boats were at a premium, and many who wished to enjoy a boat ride upon the surface of the pond which glistened in the sunlight were unable to fulfill their desire.

The shores of Herring Pond—five-sixths of its circumference—are bounded by large boulders with here and there a clear place suitable for landing from a boat. A wharf has been built at the south end at the island, and one at the beach near Comstock's Grove for the better accommodation of boating. The pond was dotted with boats of all colors, many of them flitting hither and yon as the occupants desired and at the will of the oarsmen. Others were anchored in various localities with lines out trying to entice the wary "kinies" and big mouthed pouts to give their lives for the delusive bait. Some had but little luck at this sport, while others caught very respectable strings. Comstock's Beach is truly a splendid one. The fine white sand extending with a gradual slope into the deeper water.

The "Little Rhody" a large boat which was fitted up with side wheels last season and arranged to be propelled by steam, which was a failure for the projectors, lay with its bow well up upon the beach, a silent reminder of shorn glory. Children were seen playing between its capacious sides enjoying themselves fully as much as though it were afloat and they were its occupants. There was no clambake on this side last Sunday, and the most of the visitors brought well-filled baskets and enjoyed the day as a regular picnic. Two booths or small buildings dispensing liquid refreshments were well patronized. On the west shore there is a secluded, smaller, sandy beach which the young male portion utilized for bathing. A little further south is the quarry which is now being worked and from which a good quality of granite is obtained. The shanty which marks the spot is plainly seen.

The principal attraction for Burrillville people was at the south end of the pond where Philander Putnam holds his Sunday clambakes. This part of the shore is well adapted for pleasure, and those not otherwise busy sat on the many seats in the grove enjoying the fine, cool, refreshing breeze, which frequenters say is invariably present. The dinner hour was set for two o'clock, and exactly on the dot the bake was opened and the steaming clams were placed before the hungry party. The dinner consisted of clams, clam chowder, green corn, brown and white bread, onions, cucumbers, watermelons and other fixings. The clams were delicious and the corn extra. The chowder was hardly up to that of Boyden's or Atwell's. Over one hundred partook of dinner, which was a success beyond question. Liquid refreshments of a light character could be obtained at a building located on what is called the island some distance away from the place of the dinner, and it was well patronized. The day was quiet, and no one was seen under the influence of liquor, and not the least sign of any jar or trouble came to the notice of the writer. There are many who believe these Sunday bakes entirely wrong, while the more liberal ones believe them to be beneficial providing they are conducted properly and quietly.

The Last & Best Excursion
October 3, 1890

The last and best excursion of the season transpired Wednesday, September 24th. It was made by the Laurel Hill Band called the second edition, the first edition going up the Monday previous. This band assembled at the Pleasant View House on Inman Street; the day was fine but cool. The excursion was to be from the Pleasant View House to Mrs. Caroline H. Brown's two miles west of Laurel Ridge. Mrs. Brown came after the band about 8 o'clock a.m. The band was carried in the golden chariot (so-called). When the chariot was about to start there were seven of Eve's fair daughters, all seated and numbered and started from the front gate of the Pleasant View House. The line of travel was up Inman Street to Salisbury Street, up Salisbury Street to Highland Street to Brown Avenue to the mansion of Mrs. Caroline Brown. The time of march was two hours and forty minutes. All the scenery and sights along the road was enjoyed. Upon arriving at the mansion, Mr. Mills took the horse to the stable to give him rest from his fatiguing labors preparatory for the return trip.

The forenoon was spent in singing of hymns and reading of the Scripture and solemn prayer for the good of all Christians and the conversion of the worldly to Christianity. All the eatables were prepared and carried by the band. Dinner was called at noon. A blessing was invoked by Mr. Mills (it being his daily habit). All the delicacies of the season were on the table, and the band did the dinner ample justice. The afternoon was spent same as the forenoon (only more so). Supper was served at 5 p.m. A teapot Brittania two feet long with a wooden handle graced the table, the teapot being over 80 years old. A child present was rocked to sleep in a cradle over 100 years old.

The chariot was brought up to the door about one hour after tea all ready for the return trip, Mrs. Brown carrying the band home. Mrs. Brown has been in feeble health a number of years but being of a hardy enduring race she retains her strength and vitality to a remarkable degree. The band came back the same way they went arriving home about 9 o'clock p.m. They all pronounced the excursion a perfect success socially, religiously, morally with a prospect of being repeated in the near future. We hope Mrs. Brown will live to enjoy many more of the same kind of social entertainments as that is her nature and her nature helps to make these meetings pleasant and agreeable.

Drum and Fife Band of Pascoag
April 8, 1892

The Pascoag Drum and Fife Band made its appearance on the street Monday evening for the first time marching from their band room on Sayles Avenue to the Primitive Church. On the return it was noticed that each man was decorated with a buttonhole bouquet. A short serenade was given in front of the post office, and three selections were played in front of their hall before breaking ranks. The band was organized January 20, 1892. William H. Gould was elected president; Fred Deverall, vice-president; Frederick C. Guy, secretary; Herbert Whatley, treasurer.

The full roster is: Drum Major, Ed. W. Carpenter; Leader, Ben. Spedding; Asst. Leader, William Spedding; First Flutes, Fred Morris, Fred Deverall, Herbert Whatley; Second Flutes, George Gould, William Doel, George S. Doughtery; Bass Flutes, William Guy, Henry Guy, William Smith, Jabez H. Gingell; Bass Drum, William H. Gould; Snare Drums, Thomas M. Maloney, Frederick C. Guy; Triangle, Master Herbert Stephenson.

Since organization, very rapid progress has been made in the mastering of the instruments. When the organization took place quite a number of the members could not tell one note from another. It is truly surprising to note the excellency of the rendering of the selections they did while marching to the church and back. It has been only a trifle over three weeks they have played all together. Ben Spedding has taken great interest in the matter and has given instructions individually and collectively, which with the application to study of the members has brought them on the plane they now are.

Although called the Drum and Fife Band, in one sense it is a misnomer, for the instruments are flutes such as are used in the old country and can be played any key where the fife cannot. This enables them to take up a higher grade and better class of music than they otherwise could, and we shall expect much in the way of music from this organization if it holds together any length of time and interest does not flag. The drums are of the best and so far as instruments they are well equipped. Bands of this kind are rare in this country, and it is difficult to get music properly arranged for the different parts. Most has to be sent from England. Music hath charms to soothe the savage breast.

One for Dixie
July 14, 1894

The times there are to be in Dixie no one can tell. It's such a lovely little nook with just the right proportion of green grass and luxuriant shade, all intermingled. The view is so perfect as you look to the east over the waters of the Reservoir toward Pascoag and its environs. Any tired body could find rest reclining in a hammock on the hillsides underneath the aromatic pine trees where, enjoying the cool breezes, life loses much of its cares. That sounds a trifle flat, do you think? It's boasting over much for a spot in this section? You wouldn't think so if you had visited Camp Dixie and taken a prospective view of its inhabitants and habitations. There are no swell surroundings, no grand majestic scenery, but it is quiet, cozy and perfectly enchanting all the same.

You may come by water if you will, and as you pass from the boat in the glare of a midsummers day up the banks across the greensward to the dwellings of the campers, it comes almost natural to throw yourself upon the ground and enjoy the shade and ease, so easily obtained in this sylvan abode. There are only five or six families here each with their white spread tent or bed chamber, and close adjoining are as many well arranged cookhouses, dining rooms, etc. Some are painted and some finished in the rough but all are tidy and look as if they would wait on appetite to make the savory stores of the campers prove delectable. The boats are all nearby and occasional fishing

One Hundred Years Ago in Burrillville by Patricia A. Mehrtens

expeditions help to beguile the fleeting hours.

The grocer Mr. R. F. Brooks who's camp is handy by makes the cares of the housewife light as each daily trip to and from his store brings help to depleted larders. Dentist J. H. Knowles looks in vain for teeth that might need a bite of steel, and not finding those willing to ache in nature's fairyland contents himself with the sports of an old time camper. Young Albert Sayles, all life and animation, is ready to show the guests some pleasant spot, or study up a new plan to add to Dixie's fame. There stands the veteran camper nor looks he like a patriarch as Whitford of Gypsy tent comes into view. The pioneer of these haunts still thinks there is no place like Dixie, and with him the camp ladies and guests are always ready to agree. Pascoag cannot brag of the number of her resorts, she has no public park, no famous falls, or noted caves but so long as Dixie retains the pristine beauty that now surrounds her, there will always be a place where campers tired of town and city life or rusty with indoor exercise, may come and renew their youth, make health and happiness.

Wallum Lake House
May 3, 1895

A brand new summer resort seems about to spring to life at the southern end of Wallum Lake. Its plan embodies not only a railroad station at the junction of the highway and railroad near the south end of the lake with a platform on the south side of the railroad at least 100 feet long and ample to accommodate a large sized excursion party, but it also contemplates a large summer hotel with 23 rooms to be known by the title of "Wallum Lake House." Sylvester Angell of this village and C. H. Smith are the proprietors. They promise weekly clam bakes, excursion parties, one of the finest groves in the state, plenty of boating, bathing and fishing and abundant accommodations for all.

Quite a number of guests have already engaged board for the summer, and the hotel will be open and ready for business by June 1st, 1895. The location is familiar to most of our readers, being very near the site of the old Lapham Cotton Mill ruins and just beyond the Clear River, which at this point is most picturesque as it leaves Wallum Lake and dashing down over the foam-strewn rocks forms many a delightful cascade. The hotel just beyond and within a few seconds walk through a beautiful white pine grove of the extreme southern end of the lake is well situated on land that must approximate 700 feet above the sea level at Providence from which it is scarce 27 miles distant. This makes it possible for the businessmen to leave that city via the N.Y. & N.E. Railroad at 4 p.m., and in one hour's time be in one of the coolest and most comfortable summer resorts imaginable. With trains so near at hand, 15 hours of the 24 of each day may thus be spent in recreation or with the cool breezes of the lake blowing about you. At 8:05 a.m., or thereabouts, you can leave for Providence and way stations which can be reached at 9:06, thus giving one nearly seven hours in the city for business. One of the main plans of this scheme will be the erection of a number of summer cottages to be leased or sold as desired. Taken as a whole, it appears to be a promising plan and if generously carried out will bring thousands of dollars to its promoters as well as an increase to the taxable property of the town.

What "Quiet" Girls Did
May 18, 1900

Monday, May 7th two demure visions of loveliness alighted from the 5:15 p.m. train at Pascoag and proceeded arm in arm to Manufacturers' Hotel on South Main Street. To the casual observer it was a case of "innocence abroad" and when they told a pathetic tale of being thrown upon the cruel world, they struck a sympathetic cord in Proprietor Francis' heart. They registered as Emily Watcher and Loretta Reilly. Miss Watcher volunteered the information that her folks were all dead and that Miss Reilly was her cousin with whom she lived. Miss Reilly's story was a pathetic one. She lived in Providence off Pawtucket Avenue. Dame fortune had turned a frowning face upon herself and immediate relatives, and she had come to Pascoag as a pioneer seeking labor for those at home. Soon after leaving the bosom of her family, she was notified by telegram that her little brother was ill with scarlet fever. On this account, she could neither go nor send for her wearing apparel. She stated this accounted for their scanty wardrobe which they carried in a single tiny Boston hand satchel.

During their stay at the hotel, the maids were models of propriety and were regarded by all who met them as nice "quiet" girls. They kept early hours and attended to their work. Sunday they remained about the hotel all day and strolled out early in the evening. They did not return until between nine and ten o'clock. When they came to breakfast Monday morning, they did not manifest any dissatisfaction with their surroundings, although they had previously told a boarder their stay in the metropolis of northwestern Rhode Island depended upon the good graces of an aunt. When the models of simplicity went to work, they took with them their "baggage" namely the Boston handbag. At the mill, the overseer was informed that papa said they must come home immediately, and a settlement of wages was asked for. From the mill the pair went to Joseph Legacy's bicycle room on Sayles Avenue, and by representing they were related to George Francis, proprietor of the hotel, and depositing 50 cents, they obtained two wheels "just to ride about the town." The young ladies very rudely shook the dust of Pascoag from their dainty feet and wandered hence into the hither.

Miss Watcher was known at the mill as Emily Watson. She was about 16 years of age over five feet tall, light complexion, very light hair, wore a plaid waist with skirt to match and a white straw sailor hat with black band and trimmings. Miss Reilly was known at the mill as Loretta Kelly. She was about 16 years of age somewhat smaller than her companion, dark complexioned, dark brown hair, wore tailor made suit, slate color shepherdess hat and a waist of mixed novelty goods which she had borrowed from the proprietor's daughter.

The Pascoag people, who were intimately acquainted with the girls, felt hurt when they learned their hospitality was abused in this manner. The bicycle man desired to see the clever dames long enough to obtain the number on one of the wheels, and the proprietor of the hotel wondered who was going to settle the board bill. After a consultation, it was decided to send the girls a special invitation through Town Sergeant Haniver to return to Pascoag. The wheels taken were a Keating, number unknown, and a Standish number 11109. The unlawful career of the youthful misdemeants was brought to an early end by the authorities in Providence Monday evening. Town Sergeant Haniver sent a description of the girls to the police there, and when the young girls arrived they were immediately recognized. They will be brought to Harrisville for trial tomorrow.

Arrested for Taking a Bath
March 28, 1902

Sunday forenoon Special Officer Roscoe S. Wood was called to Sweet's Hill and arrested a man named John Hannon. Hannon had been acting queerly, and the residents of the vicinity were alarmed lest he should do injury either to himself or others. Early Sunday forenoon the man called at a house on Sweet's Hill and asked for a piece of soap. He said he wished to clean up and was going over to Herring Pond to take a bath. The resident told him it was rather early for a bath in the open air and did not grant Hannon's request. Later in the day he was seen dancing about in a muddy pool of water below Sweet's Hill. He was partly stripped, and it is said he thought he was a frog. All of the large boulders in the field he thought were gravestones.

He was locked up, and during his confinement in durance vile, he manifested his ability to adapt himself to the circumstances in which he was placed, and sang songs, preached sermons, and stood on his head. He was brought to the courtroom at Harrisville Monday forenoon and examined by Drs. E. V. Granger and Paul Demarais. The physicians found that he was very eccentric, but did not pronounce him insane. Hannon said he had been arrested because he was washing up, and as soon as given his liberty he shook the dust of the town from his heels and went where he hoped to find a place where he might wash up to his heart's content even in midwinter without being restrained.

New Year's Party at Overlook
January 3, 1902

Tuesday evening at Overlook Hall was a memorable one for the upwards of fifty couples that watched the hand of time swing from the declining 1901 to the bright and sturdy year of 1902. Right royally were the guests entertained by the genial host and hostess, and it is safe to say that nowhere at any time did a New Year dawn upon a more happy throng than that which gathered in Overlook and exchanged greetings for a bright and happy new year while the old year lay a dying.

The guests began to assemble at 8:30, and shortly afterwards, the tables in the hall were taken for whist. Until 10:30 the game went on merrily. This was the time at which the playing was to be discontinued, and prizes were awarded to Mrs. E. W. Tinkham, Mrs. Nancy Sheldon, Warren W. Logee and E. W. Tinkham. A dainty lunch was served by Victor Gelb of Providence in the carriage room which was prettily arranged for the occasion. About 11:30 o'clock, Terpsichore took possession and reigned supreme. Just before midnight, the "Soldier's Joy" was played by the orchestra, and the guests joined in the dance. The dance was carefully planned, and just as the distant bells in the village tolled the death knell of 1901, the merrymakers wended their way through the grand right and left, each wishing the other a Happy New Year as they grasped each others hand.

One Hundred Years Ago in Burrillville by Patricia A. Mehrtens

The decorations in the hall and throughout the stable were especially dainty and beautiful. An abundance of evergreen and laurel was used, and the display of electric lights has probably never been equaled in this vicinity. The evergreen was twined in graceful festoons within the hall proper and formed a solid bank in the rear of the alcove where the orchestra was seated. In large red figures upon the green background was "1901-1902." In a gable at the end of the hall, another solid bank of green bore the word "Welcome." Another dainty bit of decorating very pleasing to the eye was that in Mr. Sayles' den or smoking room. The wall over the fireplace was completely hidden by a bank of green upon which in prominent letters was the inscription "A Happy New Year."

Camp Notes on Wallum's Shore
July 29, 1903

On a sunny western slope of the big hills that embrace Wallum Lake at its extreme northern end, where the coolest of spring water flows free for all with old Wallum itself spreading out a broad expanse of water, now ruffled with a western breeze. Anon placid and peaceful in quiet sunshine, its very borders touched off by green verdure that adds refreshment to the scene, —here, where in the depths of nature's own lake the agile black bass lies in wait for some alluring bait—where clear water and sandy beaches make bathing one of life's greatest pleasures—with berries that wild about us grow, trees overspread and where breezes blow—camped upon this all attractive ground, Camp Bellows first is found. The house of H. F. Bellows and family who let you boats and give a meal, or entertain a picnic party and furnish shelter for many a sportsman. Here entertained the past week were Mrs. Hattie Place of Providence, angler Wilcox of Pineside floral fame who's well skilled in tempting wondrous large fish to leave their dark retreats. Fisherman and manufacturer Mr. W. A. Inman and family, and our village druggist and wife here dine while their commodious tents hard by give abundant shelter.

Editor Fitz and family (two tents) with the editor's oldest sister, Miss Nellie, are close by. Next comes Camp Taft, presided over by him whose dinners at Chepachet have given him a wondrous hotel fame. Just below is "Camp Mystic Four," two tents, it's Chepachet also from whence they came. Far up the hill close by the spring were camped three sturdy Worcester men and below, upon the highlands sheltered in the grove camped Dr.

One Hundred Years Ago in Burrillville by Patricia A. Mehrtens

Granger, Mr. R. S. Wood and family and others, who enjoy the shade. Over on the western shore are two Woonsocket tents. Here wave o'er head the stars and stripes. This week visitors have come to camp a full score, and now Division Superintendent Offutt has given us a flag, where will be as many more. We thank the obliging superintendent who made it possible to come and go by train, and should he ever come this way we'll meet him and most royally entertain. We will make this stop a merry station that will bring his road a lot of coppers more, for there is no more beautiful historic spot than the camping grounds about old Wallum's shore. We bid you welcome—there's room for many a one.

Man Found in a Cabin
September 25, 1903

Early last week two young men from Pascoag were walking along the Reservoir Road and came near the small house owned by George I. Eddy just beyond the ledges. They heard a feeble cry for "water" coming from a small building nearby, which was built several years ago for a cabin. They investigated, and found a man inside the building. He seemed very weak and was only able to speak in a tone that was hardly audible. He had evidently been there for considerable time and was in an extremely emaciated condition.

Special Officer Collins was notified and took the man to Harrisville where he was placed in the lockup, that being the only available place where he could be cared for. Dr. Eugene N. Granger was called and found the man's condition to be extremely grave. On his clothing was the name "William Cory" and little by little his story was gotten from him. He said he had worked in South Kingston during the spring, but after the first of June he did not seem to remember where he had been until he came to the cabin where he was found. He said he had been in the cabin for about twenty days, and that the first part of the time he had subsisted on green grapes and other edibles which he found in the woods. For the last week he had nothing to eat, which statement seemed to be borne out by his condition.

A telephone inquiry at the state institutions revealed that he had been an inmate of the insane asylum, having been discharged from there several weeks ago. At that time, a sister from Connecticut had agreed to care for him, and he seemed to be nearly recovered from his insanity. It is probable he had strayed from his sister's home, and his demented condition had come on again, and for some reason he had hidden himself in the cabin. Who his relatives were could not be learned. In fact, he stated he had no relatives in the world that he knew of. Under the doctor's care he seemed to gain a little strength, although when he was removed to Cranston he was unable to stand and had to be carried on a bed in the baggage car. He was brought before Assistant Justice Lace Tuesday night and was ordered committed to the State Insane Asylum. He was taken down Wednesday morning by Officer Collins. That he could have been in the cabin for twenty days without being seen or heard seems almost incredible, for the cabin is but a few feet away from a highway which is much traveled. Owing to the fact that he had been discharged from the insane asylum, he could not be returned there except by being recommitted by order of the court. If he had escaped, he could have been taken back without the formality of court proceedings.

Ballou Reunion
June 7, 1907

In June, 1860 the Ballou family held a reunion at the old homestead near the Glocester line, and for the 47 years which have elapsed since that time, similar gatherings have been held each year. For a long time the second Thursday in June has been set aside as the date for the gathering. No matter what may have been the demands upon the individuals of the family, that date has always been devoted to attending the reunion. There are many who have attended most of the gatherings but there is only one, Mrs. George W. Esten of this place who has been present at every one.

At 10 o'clock yesterday morning the descendants of the original family commenced to gather at the old farm, which until its recent purchase by General Hunter C. White, has been in the family for generations. From the hour of arrival until the shades of night approached there was a delightful reunion of the ties of kindred. At 1 o'clock a clam dinner was served in the orchard, the bake being prepared under the supervision of Thomas Gross. Never before were clams so toothsome and sweet, and the abundance of other good things made up a meal which was ample and delicious enough for all. There was the usual ball game, and then rambles through the old familiar fields and an inspection of the house, which was built by one of the family many long years ago.

There were 45 persons present, all but two of whom were

descendants or relatives. It was universally agreed that so long as there was a descendent left, these gatherings would be maintained. Cousins were present from Milford, Woonsocket and Providence, among them Mrs. Harriet Ballou, widow of Job O. Ballou, who was the last of the family to reside on the old homestead. Although the farm belongs to Gen. White, the family is free to use it for their gatherings, and he is ever ready to assist in any way possible in adding to the comfort and enjoyment of the day set aside for the reunion. A group photograph was made during the day. There are few families who for 57 years have had an unbroken line of family gatherings, and the Ballous may well feel proud of the ties which have bound them together for so nearly half a century.

Oakland Whist
June 21, 1907

The L.E.W. Club held a highly enjoyable whist and social in Recreation Hall in Oakland last Saturday evening, the event marking the close of a successful series of whists held during the winter and spring. The hall was attractively decorated for the occasion. In the center of the room was suspended a huge Japanese umbrella, and about the sides of the building were Japanese lanterns and flags. On the stage was draped an immense American flag. The first part of the evening was devoted to whist, after which a programme of dances was carried out, music being furnished by Clough's Orchestra of Woonsocket. Refreshments were served during the evening. There were a large number in attendance, and the members of the club saw that each guest had a good time.

One Hundred Years Ago in Burrillville by Patricia A. Mehrtens

CHURCHES

Baptist Church Dedicated at Harrisville
April 29, 1881

On Wednesday evening, the meeting house of the Berean Baptist Society at Harrisville was solemnly dedicated to the service of God by appropriate exercises participated in by the pastor, Rev. Dr. Granger, and several clergymen from Providence and other towns. The edifice is an addition to the village of Harrisville and the town of Burrillville, not only by its architectural beauty but as a moral landmark which will ever exercise a salutary influence on the people. The pastor and people are to be congratulated on the progress of this church, which started five years ago with a membership of thirteen and has so increased in power and numbers and in its influence with the people, to be able to erect this elegant and commodious house for worship.

The dedicatory exercises were opened by reading of the scriptures and prayer by Rev. Mr. Dennison, followed by an address by Rev. Dr. Granger who showed the progress of the church, the trials which it had undergone, notably in the death of Deacon Remington who had been very active in the building of the house. He expressed his gratitude to those friends in and out of the church who had contributed so liberally towards the building and furnishings, and to the audience for the large attendance at the exercises. Dr. Granger's address was of a very interesting character and held the undivided attention of the audience. Several other speakers reflected on the importance of the church, hymns were sung, and Rev. Mr. True of the Central Baptist Church of Providence made the closing address speaking of the sacred character of a church, and showing how from the most ancient to the present time the costliest buildings have been built for the worship of God, showing the hold which religion has upon the world and the world's need of it. The exercises were closed by the singing of a hymn and the benediction of the pastor. A large number of those present from Providence and other towns on the road returned by a special train, which left Harrisville at about 10 o'clock.

Life by Mrs. Edwin S. Bates
January 19, 1883

"Let me go! My soul is weary of the changes that bind it here." Yes, weary of life. How many there are who are weary of life, weary of its joys, its sorrows, its cares, its pains, toils, hopes, and its laurel crowns. Weary of life. How hopeless, how despairing these words sound. We utter them when we have been deceived, when we have trusted and been betrayed, when we have given friendship and received injury and insult in return, when one has shown kindness and bestowed sympathy and have been repaid with ingratitude and slander. The sky that bends above us seems filled with dark clouds, the path before us with thorns. But the earth is still very beautiful, my friend. The clouds have linings of silver, the pathway before us contains roses as well as thorns, yet under the first heavy stroke of sorrow we are apt to deem life valueless or containing naught but sorrow and gloom.

Dear one, there is much to live for, much to be accomplished, and we must not grow weary until our labor is done that our Heavenly Father may consider us worthy, a blessed reward. There are fainting hearts to be cheered, erring ones to be led back to the faith of virtue and honor, those encouraged whom kind words and acts may serve and cheer by casting ashes over the unpleasant memories of a bitter past. What if we are repaid within gratitude and injury? There is One who sees every act and deed of love and charity; One who will not forget unselfish work this side the vale.

What if called upon to bear heavy trials while we journey here below? We know that hereafter will come peace and happiness. Let this thought cheer our hearts in hours of affliction so we may not grow weary of life. When called upon to endure crosses and sorrows, let us gather in new strength, gird faith's armor on, and take our places in the ranks with renewed energy to fight the great battle of life. We will find some good in everything and every person on earth, if we only go to work the right way to find it. So let us never grow weary of life or in well doing.

One Hundred Years Ago in Burrillville by Patricia A. Mehrtens

Catholic Excursion to Oakland Beach
August 28, 1885

The annual union excursion of the members of St. Patrick's and St. Joseph's Churches occurred last Saturday, the objective point being Oakland Beach. Arrangements were made with the Providence & Springfield Railroad Co. for transportation and they laid plans for a special train to leave Pascoag five minutes after the departure of the regular 7:10 train. By the burning of the railroad round house and destruction of two of their locomotives August 20th, this arrangement of necessity was changed, and the excursionists went to Providence on the regular 7:10 train, which consisted of thirteen cars arriving at the city twenty-five minutes late.

The regular passengers disembarked, and the train was drawn on to the track of the N.Y. P. & B. Railroad Co., when the C. M. Miller, a large and powerful engine, relieved the Achilles, which is doing double duty since the fire. Three cars were then detached and the other ten sped on with its throng to Oakland Beach, which was reached without mishap.

The cars were soon empty, and the people scattered in all directions. Some amused themselves in shooting and riding on the wire railway, while others sought rustic and grassy seats in the shade under the majestic and gnarled oaks, whose towering branches, covered with a thick foliage of leaves, furnished ample protection from *Old Soleil* whose majesty did not deign in the morning to show his brilliant and shining countenance.

Dinner time soon came, and a large number of the party secured tickets, which was the key to the large dining room where the smoking bivalves, clam chowder, fish chowder, baked fish, green corn, clam cakes, watermelon and other fixings are served. The clams were very nice, and judging by the piles of shells heaped around the plates of the feasters, were heartily appreciated. We never ate better clams in our life, and the corn was sweet and excellently cooked. To expatiate more on the excellency of the dinner would be useless, as it is conceded by good judges that Maxfield's shore dinners cannot be excelled. The waiters were very attentive and anxious that each one should have their fill. Others not wishing for a clam dinner patronized *la salle a manger* where a different variety of food could be obtained, while a few paid a visit to the hotel and enjoyed whatever called for.

The afternoon was spent in roller skating, boating, fishing, dancing, singing, playing nine pins, social conversation, riding the flying ponies and swinging. Many were interested in bathing, while more enjoyed themselves in looking on. Nearly all the afternoon there were no less than twenty in bathing. Some of the bathers courted deep water, but most of them clung close to the shore. One young man became so interested in bathing and trying to cover another bather up in seaweed that his girl, left on the bank, became tired of waiting, picked up another lad, and went away.

The English Coach Cafe was well patronized, and so were all the establishments on the ground. Three musicians made music in the *Soda Garden* with banjo and songs for the amusement of the patrons. They seemed to be jealous of that right, for when a Harrisville fellow tried to help, they became incensed. Several of the party present stated the fellow was a fine singer and asked to allow him to sing, but this request was refused point blank. The party left the garden in disgust, wondering if they did not come down for a good time, what they did come for.

Thirty or forty of the party left the grounds on the three o'clock train in order to take in Providence, and just before the 4:45 left the Beach, the clouds looked so threatening many skedaddled for this train filling it to overflowing. Some of the young ladies were glad to accept the knees of the sterner sex for a seat rather than stand up as many were obliged to do. The regular excursion train left Oakland Beach about an hour later, and after a little delay in Providence, the train glided slowly away on its homeward journey. Many stopped in Providence until the 11:15 p.m. left, and the six cars composing the train were packed solid, standing room and all. Everything connected with the excursion passed pleasantly, and the day which looked pretty lowery in the morning was all that could be asked for. The number of excursionists was six hundred.

Friends Meeting House Celebration
September 18, 1891

Last Friday the Friends resident in this part of Rhode Island and portions of Massachusetts met together at Mapleville at the old meeting house, the gathering being in honor of the edifice having arrived at the dignity of a century. The gathering did not disperse until the Sabbath day had closed, and a large number of Friends and friends were present a greater or less portion of the time. Isaac Steere, a member and leader of the demonstration, read numerous extracts from the minutes of early meetings from 1791 to 1800. Later, addresses were made by Salome C. Wheeler of Uxbridge, Revs. Lovejoy, Dennett, Byron and Granger of this town, and some others, prayer and praise being offered at intervals. On Sunday, David Douglas, the well known preacher, spoke and was greeted by a large audience.

This old meeting house, the centennial of which has been thus fittingly celebrated, has a history dating back to Nov. 11, 1790, when a committee was appointed by the Smithfield Quarterly Meeting to see about its erection. The report of the Committee was as follows: "Your committee having all attended to the matter and conferred with the Friends in that neighborhood think that a meeting house should be built at a place near Cooper's Mills if a suitable lot can be obtained and that the bigness of the house be 24 by 28 feet upon the ground, with a chimney at one end and a fireplace above and below. N. B. The committee were Paul Green, Sylvester Weeks, Jonathan Chase, 2d, Joseph Farnum and David Anthony."

The building was completed on the 12th day of the 9th month 1791, the expense being 109 pounds, 12 shillings, 6 pence, not being lathed or plastered. The Committee in charge of the building and the raising of the money necessary was Jesse Battey, James Smith, William Buffum, Walter Allen and Charles Smith. The Glocester Friends also erected a horse shed on the lot. The meeting house was remodeled in 1848, lathed, plastered, clapboarded and painted, since which time there has been no material change made in its general appearance. Moses Cooper donated the lot on which the house was built, but owing to difference between him and the society they afterwards paid him between $7 and $8 for the same. Meetings were held in the dwelling of Joseph Battey before the house was erected.

Soliloquizing
May 20, 1892

This is surely getting to be a town of churches, and it can boast of some very good ones. This thought comes to the mind more particularly of late because of the demands upon the people to help in building so many new ones. The questions arises with some, how can so many be supported? We hope that all may be, and doubtless they will be, in a certain way so long as earnest workers are to be found in each of the societies. Although dissension is usually to be deprecated in churches and has caused the downfall of some, there are many instances where much good has followed a division and starting up of new societies. Perhaps the motives might in some cases be selfish ones or a desire to have one's own way, but when this point is reached more energy is apt to be expended in gaining the coveted points and consequently, good comes out of it.

Within a few years, two very pretty churches have been built in Harrisville, the old one at Laurel Hill torn down, and a new one nearly finished and ready for dedication, a chapel built at the "Four Corners," a new church on South Main Street, Pascoag, a new one at Glendale is underway on the site of the one recently burned, and Mapleville feels as though they would like a place of worship. There is a stirring around, and a part of the money has been raised for a new one on Church Street, a lot already having been secured. Another faith has begun in a humble way to worship in Pascoag which may in time develop to such an extent as to wish for a building of their own. One denomination or creed has the same right as another and should be recognized by all, and unless it is a community, must be narrow in its views. Small beginnings many times make in after years something substantial and lasting, and a great power for good in the community.

Laurel Hill Methodist Episcopal Church
June 10, 1892

The first recorded Methodist preaching in Burrillville was in 1810 by "Elder" Britt, who about that time erected the Old Douglas Meeting House. In 1813 meetings were held in the Huntsville Emporium at the place now known as the White Mill. There was preaching occasionally also at the house of Mr. Moab Paine. When the present Free Baptist Church was erected in 1839, the Methodists for a while went there. Some ten years after this, Mr. Geo. W. Marsh, a fervent Methodist, began business at the old Mill recently occupied by Mr. Joshua Perkins at Laurel Hill. Mr. Marsh inaugurated regular religious services at that place, which were held in the upper part of the stock house destroyed by fire last April. In 1846 or 1847, John Cowen, the overseer of the weave shop, preached every Sabbath. Mr. Cowen was from the Isle of Man, an enthusiastic exhorter of the old fashioned kind, sincere and gifted, who often made the ungodly laugh by his rough and ready ways. At this time and for many years afterwards, the Methodists often held religious and social gatherings in Masonic Hall, now the residence of Mr. Edward Salisbury on Laurel Hill Avenue.

In 1847, the first Methodist Church was built in Pascoag.

While Brother Cowen was minding the weavers' cloth in the old Mill on weekdays and caring for the souls across the road on Sundays, his employer with help of a few others was building a more suitable sanctuary on the site of the present edifice. The "Old Church" as we now call it, cost abut $3000. Mr. Geo. W. Marsh was the mainstay of the new society then formed, one of its first treasurers, trustees, stewards and class leaders, a man of great integrity, public spirited and generous—the father of Pascoag Methodism. The Laurel Hill Methodist Church was formally organized in 1847, a little while before the dedication of the Church. Its original Board of Trustees was composed of Simeon B. March, James K. True, Livings Shumway, and Samuel White Lintern. Upon the evening of their organization on September 18, 1852, Bro. Marsh deeded the lot and church building at Laurel Hill to be held in trust for the Methodist Episcopal Church. Thus the little vessel was launched upon the uncertainties of a long voyage.

The Advent Church
October 7, 1893

The Advent Church has been erected after years of patient waiting on a well located lot on Church Street. Artistically designed by Mr. P. D. West of Woonsocket and built in the latest approved manner by Wm. H. Sheldon, a well known contractor of this place. The lot was purchased of Mr. Eli Bailey about a year ago, and presented to the society by Mr. Irving Morse of Woonsocket about the time of the organization of the church last fall. The present pastor, who is the first elder of the church, is Rev. H. B. Woodmansee of this place.

Some years ago a few leading spirits gathered together in the upper part of this village and formed an Advent Society. It was with hard work they braved the storms of winter and the heat of summer, gathering together week after week and adding their mites to the fund needed to maintain the expense of the Society. As is usual in such cases, they found at first but few who looked with favor on their new society, but with warm hearts and willing hands they toiled on, knowing that with God, even though their numbers be few, they possessed a majority, and in due time they would be blessed. At one time they met in the old Stock House at the White Mill, but the fire some year and a half ago destroyed their abiding place and caused them to remove to the house of a warm-hearted brother and subsequently to a tent on the lot where they are building. Last September the tent was blown over, and they at present meet with Brother C. A. Hollingworth. The foundations for the new church were laid last fall. The well planned and architecturally beautiful church shows how well Architect West did his work.

The building is not large, but is amply adequate to the needs of the society for some time, and will be a valuable addition to our village. The outside measurement is 32 1/2 by 48 feet with a projection on each side. The tower posts are to be of hard pine, the outside finish of good clear pine with eave brackets on front and rear gables. A porch extends in front, supported on turned columns. A finial will grace the top of this tower. The inside of the church is to be sealed up as high as the windows with cypress and plastered above. The painting and shellac work, for both outside and in, are to be of the best with double or triple coats as needed. It is expected that the church will cost about $3,000 when done, and it will be a very well arranged building for the amount of money expended.

Mysterious Ringing of Bells in Glendale
May 21, 1897

Great excitement prevailed in this village Monday night when the people were awakened from their peaceful slumbers by the vigorous pealing forth of the tones of the church bell. Fire was the first trouble thought of, and everybody expected to find either the mill or church in flames. Fred Esten was the first to arrive at the church, and seeing it all in darkness decided to enter and "interview" the man at the bell rope. He broke the front door of the church in, rushed for the man at the bell rope, jumped onto the intruder, and gave him quite a shaking up. Mr. Esten recognized the voice of the "church seeker" as that of Martin Paine, a fruit peddler who lives just outside the village. Esten asked him what he meant to do and Martin replied, "I paid $5 towards this church and I've a right to stay here and ring this bell."

By this time everybody in the community had arrived on the scene, and as Paine stepped onto the porch he said, "Well, I got quite a crowd out, didn't I?" It was quickly realized that Martin was insane, and the fright became lessened somewhat. Paine was then ushered into the auditorium where guards were placed over him till the good old "Squire" could get there. Paine entertained his "company" by talking in a disconnected manner. He was under the delusion that the judgment day had come, and upon being asked why he entered the church, he replied, "I expected to find Jesus here, and I thought Bacon was here, but I got left." Sheriff Bacon of Uxbridge was the man he referred to, he having arrested Martin a short time ago for peddling without a license and obliged Paine to pay a fine of $50. Martin has been out of his right mind for some time, his trouble with Bacon probably being the cause."Squire" came and in a jovial manner asked if there was a "watch meeting" going on. He entered, and as Martin glanced at him he remarked, "Here is the Harrisville minister." Martin is a large, powerful man, and it was expected it would be hard work to get him off but the "Squire" coaxed him along without his making any resistance.

As Inman prepared to handcuff Paine he remarked, "You've big wrists, Martin. If I had known this was going to happen, I would have bought a new pair." Paine replied, "They'll fit me all right." Squire" got into the carriage with his intruder and said to him, "Well, Martin, tell the people when you are going to hold your next praise service." Martin in a frightened tone replied, "Well I guess I'll never get around here again to hold another." They disappeared in the darkness for the Harrisville lockup, and the "meeting folks" dispersed to their homes, being grateful that nothing more serious happened. Martin had attended church two Sundays in succession recently and testified in one of them. He gained entrance by breaking a catch on the rear window of the vestry and raising it. He was taken to the Insane Asylum at Cranston Tuesday.

Mapleville News
May 24, 1907

A pleasing and successful entertainment was held at the Casino Monday evening under the auspices of the Ladies' Aid Society of the M. E. Church. There was a good attendance, and all felt amply repaid for being present. The programme which consisted of vocal and instrumental music, readings, etc. was well rendered. A prominent feature was the trial of "Peter Sloper for Sleeping in Church." This was presented by talent from the Zion P. M. Church of Pascoag and was received with hearty favor by the audience. Several of the numbers were also rendered by visitors from Pascoag.

Last Sunday was the closing one for Methodist services at the Casino. Next Sabbath and thereafter until the new church is ready, the society will worship in the fine newly renovated hall over the post office. Sunday school at 12:30 and preaching at 2 and 7 by the pastor, Rev. W. D. Woodward. Norman H. Williams, instructor on the clarionet and soloist of Brown University Glee Club, was a guest at the parsonage Monday afternoon. The first quarterly conference is to be held this evening at the parsonage at 8 o'clock.

Mapleville Catholic Church Dedicated
May 31, 1907

The Church of Our Lady of Good Help between the villages of Oakland and Mapleville was dedicated yesterday morning by Rt. Rev. Matthew Harkins, Bishop of the Diocese of Providence assisted by a large number of priests. The impressive exercises commenced at 10 o'clock and were followed by a solemn high mass, after which a large class was confirmed by the Bishop.

Long before the appointed hour, the members and friends of the parish began to assemble in the sacred edifice and it was estimated there were more than 500 persons in attendance. The dedicatory service was impressive and was eagerly followed by the audience. Immediately afterward, a solemn high mass was celebrated, Rt. Rev. Bishop Harkins assisting. A choir of twenty voices rendered the Sixth Harmonized Mass arranged by Prof. Philie, director of the Precious Blood Choir of Woonsocket. The sermon was delivered by Rev. Rodier of Notre Dame Church of Southbridge, Mass. and was an eloquent discourse. At the close of the mass, Bishop Harkins spoke eloquently and impressively, congratulating the pastor and the parish upon the great work accomplished during the two years since the parish was formed, thanking all those who assisted in the work. A class of about sixty boys and girls was then confirmed. The ceremony was preceded by an address in English and French, impressing upon the candidates the importance of the step which they were taking. The exercises were concluded shortly after 1 o' clock.

A banquet was served in the basement of the church during the early afternoon, covers being laid for 350 people. At the head table were seated the visiting clergymen and the members of the town council, who were especially invited guests. An elaborate menu was served. During the banquet the pastor took occasion to thank all, both the members of the parish and others, for the generous contributions which had been made toward the building fund and for the hearty cooperation which everyone in the community had shown in the work. Many clergymen were present from all over the area.

One Hundred Years Ago in Burrillville by Patricia A. Mehrtens

Many Listen to "Shang" Bailey
June 7, 1907

If the announcement had been made two years ago that "Shang" Bailey would speak in church on a certain day, the announcement would have been considered so utterly improbable that no one would have taken the trouble to attend that church with the idea he would be present. In those days, "Shang" was not engaged in pursuits of exactly this nature. "Shang" was the drawing feature at a social service held in the Zion P. M. Church Sunday afternoon and at the Laurel Hill M. E. Church in the evening, both of the meetings being union services participated in by the several Protestant churches in the village. It was a damp, disagreeable day such as usually exerts a powerful influence in keeping people at home. However, each of the churches was comfortably filled by people who were anxious to see this man who formerly lived in the town and of whom so much has been said during the past two years.

From the moment he commenced to speak, it was not difficult to see that the "Shang" of today is diametrically different from the "Shang" of other days. Any doubts of the genuineness of his reformation were dispelled. He said that since his conversion he had been anxious to come to this, his native town, and speak. He was born in the village of Gazza on June 12, 1842, and during his boyhood lived in almost every village in town. He informed his hearers that he was a bad wicked boy. He attended Sunday school in the morning and in the afternoon played poker, at first for marbles, and afterwards, as he came into possession of limited amounts of money, for pennies. "That was life in Burrillville 60 years ago," he said, "Is it any different today?" After his father died, he went to sea and was in Cuba at the time the Civil War broke out and Fort Sumter was fired upon. He came back to Rhode Island, and enlisted in the Second Rhode Island regiment of volunteers and was in the war for three years. At the expiration of his term of enlistment, he re-enlisted in the Navy, where he remained until the close of the war. He came back to Burrillville, and remained until 1870, when he joined a circus. He was rapidly promoted, and in less than a year was boss canvasman. It was while in the circus business that the name of "Shang" was attached to him on account of his great stature, and not because he impersonated the famous Chinese giant who bore the same name. He wished to refute any statements to the contrary and to brand them as falsehoods.

In 1876 he opened a rum shop in Philadelphia and in

1888 came to Burrillville again and engaged in a similar business at Round Top where he remained 11 years. He went to the town of Johnston, where he paid license fees of $410 a year "for the privilege of sending men to hell." During all the years, he only closed his place of business one Sunday. He gave a graphic description of the time of his conversion, saying that one minute before Christ came to him he did not know he was never again to sell rum. At the close of business one night, his wife asked him if he was not going to set down the day's receipts in a book as was his custom. He replied that he had sold his last drink of rum. It was his plan to lease his place to someone, but he found his new way of living would not sanction this, and could not sell the place for such purposes. Mr. Bailey poured his liquors into the highway and ordered an axe taken to a slot machine which had been a great money getter for him. He spoke for more than an hour in each of the churches and was closely followed by his hearers.

Glendale Clambake
June 21, 1907

The clambake given on the grounds of the M. E. Church in Glendale last Saturday afternoon was a highly successful affair in every way. There was a large attendance, and a comfortable sum was realized as the net profits of the affair. The large crowd was handled nicely, and the patrons felt everything possible was done for their comfort and enjoyment. About $130 were the net proceeds, an increase of 75 per cent over last year. People were present from Woonsocket, Providence, and East Greenwich, besides all the neighboring villages in Burrillville and Smithfield.

Confirmation at St. Joseph's
June 28, 1907

The sacrament of confirmation was administered to a class of about 75 boys and girls by Rt. Rev. Bishop Harkins at St. Joseph's church last Sunday morning at 10 o'clock, the service preceding the high mass. A congregation, which completely filled the sacred edifice, was present to witness the impressive service and to greet the bishop. The girls wore white dresses and veils and the boys were attired in dark clothes. The scene as they approached the altar to receive the sacrament for which they had been preparing for several weeks was a beautiful one. The sanctuary was beautifully decorated with cut flowers. In administering the sacrament, Bishop Harkins was assisted by Rev. Fr. Redihan and Rev. Fr. O'Brien. Miss Mary Black acted as sponsor for the boys and Miss Alice Hayden for the girls.

Following the confirmation, high mass was celebrated by Rev. Fr. O'Brien, and the sermon was delivered by Bishop Harkins. The Bishop congratulated the pastor and parishioners upon the beautiful appearance of the church, which has undergone extensive repairs. He commended Father Redihan for his efforts in behalf of the parish and the parishioners for their cooperation with their pastor in promoting the interests of the church. To the members of the class confirmed, the Bishop spoke words which tended to impress upon their minds the importance of the sacrament received and their duties as Catholics. He especially asked the boys to abstain from liquor until they have reached the age of 21, stating that habits firmly fixed at that age would probably continue through life. He asked the girls to be obedient to their parents, to shun evil associates and places of amusement which might lead to temptation. The objects of the Holy Name Society were spoken upon, and the Bishop urged the men of the parish to become members. The work of renovating St. Joseph's Church was recently completed and the extensive work done has made it one of the most beautiful country churches in the diocese.

Dedication at Mapleville of M.E. Church
October 22, 1909

The handsome new Methodist Episcopal Church, which has been in process of erection for some time at Mapleville, has been finished, and will be dedicated next Sunday with appropriate exercises. The dedicatory exercises are to be in charge of District Superintendent Rev. J. H. Newland of Norwich, Conn., and Bishop John W. Hamilton will officiate at the dedication. Stafford C. Clough of Woonsocket, organist of the Globe Congregational Church, will play the new pipe organ, and the choir from the Globe Church will render the musical selections morning and evening. Joseph T. Hunter, a former resident of Mapleville, will be the soloist of the day. Special singing in the afternoon will be rendered by F. E. Kettlety and Robert L. Donaldson of Woonsocket.

It is expected there will be a large attendance at the morning, afternoon, and evening services. For the convenience of visitors, carriages will connect with the electric cars at Oakland Center and refreshments will be on sale in Mapleville Hall between the services which will be held be 10:30, 2:30, and 7:30.

The new church edifice is one of the finest buildings of its kind in Northwestern Rhode Island, and is the first structure of any note to be made of concrete. The entire superstructure is built of molded concrete blocks which rest on a foundation of solid concrete. On the front is an imposing tower, entrance to which is gained by substantial steps. Adjoining the commodious auditorium are double parlors in the rear, which can be thrown into the main room by the opening of doors. The auditorium has paneled wood ceiling and a paneled wainscotting, the latter being cypress, stained dark. In the auditorium is the handsome new $1400 pipe organ with its case of dark oak, surmounted by gilt pipes, built by the Moller Company of Hagerstown, N. J. Andrew Carnegie contributed $500 and Joseph E. Fletcher $200 toward the pipe organ, and the balance of the cost was made up by other contributions. In the basement is a Sunday schoolroom 32 feet square; also a kitchen with abundant cupboard room, sink, stove, etc. Nearby is the furnace room which is made fireproof by being built of the concrete blocks and having a metal ceiling. A souvenir programme of the dedicatory services, as well as the programme of jubilee week, has been issued from the *Herald* job department and will be distributed next Sunday.

Free Baptist Church of Pascoag
December 27, 1912

A short sketch taken from the Free Will Baptist pulpit on the life of John Colby, reads thus: Thursday, Sept. 10, 1813, I went to Burrillville and preached in the evening. This was the beginning of a series of meetings in this and adjacent towns which continued with but little interruption during the entire autumn and winter. A revival almost immediately commenced and progressed with astonishing rapidity and effect. Card players abandoned their practices, and came and burned their cards in the presence of the preacher, lovers of the ballroom became lovers of the church assembly, and gray-haired captains and justices for the first time acknowledged their allegiance to God and tearfully sought the great Captain of Salvation.

The Church was organized in Burrillville on the 15th of December 1812 by Elder John Colby with nine members. At a church meeting held Feb. 11th, 1813, Brother Andrew Ballad and Duty Salisbury were chosen as deacons, and also to arrange for communion. On Sunday, Feb. 14th, 1813, meeting was held at John Woods Hall, Harrisville. After the meeting, the brethren and

One Hundred Years Ago in Burrillville by Patricia A. Mehrtens

sisters all came forward and commemorated the love of Christ for the first time, and it truly was a precious time to our souls.

A quarterly meeting was held in the Burrillville Meeting House, March, 1814 at 10 a.m. and was quite crowded, being the first ever held in Burrillville. Elder John Colby and his brother Jonathan were present, and gave very powerful and solemn exhortations. In a few years, its numbers increased to about two hundred. It maintained a visible existence without a settled pastor for about 29 years. Monthly conferences and meetings of social worship were held regularly in school houses and private dwellings with preaching by different ministers on occasion.

The greater number of monthly conference meetings were held in the Lafayette School House and the old Burrillville Meeting House. These meetings were well attended, many times 50 or 60 being present. In those years, the discipline of the Church must have been very strict, for in one place it is recorded that a council was called to see what action should be taken about one of their members playing ball. We cannot find any report where a vote was taken to change the name of the church, but thought it might have been when the present edifice was built, which was in 1839 and dedicated in October of that year.

At a meeting of the church society in March, 1839, the following were appointed building committee: D.W. Hunt, Jesse Harris, and Augustus Hopkins. The land was purchased of Angell Sayles. The first reference to this building reads, "The Western Rhode Island Quarterly meeting held its first session at the Pascoag Meeting House, Dec. 4, 1840, Elders' conference, Friday, Dec. 4. Public meetings, Saturday and Sunday following. On account of the inclemency of the weather, our preaching brethren did not arrive as we expected, however, we had a good time throughout the series of meetings. —John Walling, Clerk."

Previous to the building of this church, Sunday school was held in the building now occupied by the post office. The present church has been remodeled and enlarged two or three times. When first built, the pews faced the entrance, later, 1857, they were changed facing the north as they do at present. The pews were owned by individuals and the church was supported by subscriptions. Later the pews were given to the church society and were rented each year. Ten or twelve years ago, the weekly offering system was adopted which encourages systematic giving. In 1865 the building was enlarged and the vestry fitted for Sunday school, evening meetings, etc. The church at the present time numbers 72 resident members. (Partial History by Mrs. E. A. Manchester.)

One Hundred Years Ago in Burrillville by Patricia A. Mehrtens

SCHOOLS

Unprovoked Attack on a School
June 4, 1880

On last Thursday, a scene took place at the schoolhouse of Jackson District No. 13 probably never before witnessed in this town's history. In the forenoon of that day, a large band of invaders entered the premises and reconnoitered for a time, then somewhat hid themselves in the grove adjoining the school grounds probably consulting. When suddenly and apparently with one accord, they rushed toward the object of their vengeance. But the worthy teacher Mrs. E. F. Blackmar was equal to the occasion, closing the doors and windows in time to prevent the entering of the riotous mob, who on seeing they were repulsed made another charge, this time showing a piece of strategy never before equaled. Angered by their first failure, they came on with redoubled vigor armed with deadly weapons and with power that would baffle the bravest of men. The chimney seemed to suit their convenience, and with universal agreement they made this the point of attack. This time the battle proved favorable to their side, for they were bound to go to school any way. Entering the chimney and finding the schoolroom by way of the stovepipe, they made their attack upon the scholars. Eddie Taft, a bright little fellow, was wounded severely, but he bore the intense pain with the courage of an "old soldier." Others were "more frightened than hurt." Had the School Superintendent been present he would have had a chance to test his surgical skill. The battle raged so fiercely that teacher and pupils were compelled by the overwhelming force to retreat and seek shelter in the adjoining forest.

Aid being sent for, numbers soon arrived at the scene of action, including Mr. Fred Phillips who decided at once on the means of capture. Mr. Phillips brought with him a rope to hang the culprits, a "winding sheet" and other articles of considerable importance. Ladders were soon procured, and preparations made to scale the heights and carry into execution the plans for the capture of the invaders, the greater part of whom had taken up their quarters in the chimney. "A little smoke on the subject" drove them near the top of that structure. After all means of force failed, a little moral 'suasion was thought best by Mr. Phillips whose courage never was daunted and who was calm at this period of the action.

The forces he was dealing with, though natural enemies to mankind, generally making attacks without provocation, speedily succumbed to the influence Mr. Phillips exercised over them. Some sticks of wood were placed across the chimney, and a kind of "freedom trap" placed thereon. The home forces then retired to await the results. In the meantime, seeing their foes were somewhat quieted, the occupants of the building came from their retreat and resumed their duties. To cut a long story short, by the charming influence brought to bear upon them which caused them all to "stick to the trap" they were removed from the chimney and "hung" with the rope brought for that purpose from the gable end of the building and lowered to the ground, when "the winding sheet" was brought into requisition. Thus secured, with the exception of a few sentinels on the outposts, they were conveyed to the nearest house about one-fourth of a mile north of the schoolhouse, where in their hive on a bench under an apple tree in a suitable situation they are living happy and contented. Thus on the 27th day of May, 1880, a valuable swarm of bees was hived on the chimney of Jackson Schoolhouse without the loss of life or limb.

Troubles at the Schools
October 7, 1881

Two boys by the name of Ritchie were before the Justice Court Tuesday for defacing the Alam Pond school house and the furniture therein. They were bound over for trial. The boys are but eight and twelve years old but their outrageous actions at the school house and subsequent brazen attempts to lie out of it and fasten the act on someone else indicate a degree of depravity rarely attained by bad boys of more mature age.

The School Committee was in session last Saturday to hear complaints against and petitions for the removal of Miss Harris teacher of the higher grade at the Laurel Hill School. Their decision in the matter was reserved till Monday next. We have no desire to comment on the case before the Committee renders their decision but would say that while the charge of excessive whipping was sustained in a measure, the provocation thereof was great. It came out in the course of the hearing that the trustee of the District had executed his power by forbidding one of the offending pupils to attend school.

School District #11
April 10, 1885

The annual meeting of School District No. 11 was held in the school house at Laurel Ridge last Saturday evening at 6:30. The following officers were then elected for the ensuing year: Moderator, H. J. Bruce, M. D.; Trustee, David Warner: Clerk, E. A. Farwell; Treasurer, James A. Potter; Collector, Chas. F. Potter. It was then voted to continue the school while the money for the same should last, which will probably add another month to the usual school year. Quite a discussion ensued regarding purchasing an organ for the grammar school, but no definite action was taken. Considerable amusement was caused by some of the suggestions and remarks that were made relative to the purchase of the musical instrument referred to, one voter proposing they purchase a pipe organ, while another thought a jews' harp would answer all purposes. School began Monday with the teachers of last term in charge, Misses Esten and Taft.

Rumpus in the Nasonville School District
November 18, 1887

According to reports, the finances and management of the Nasonville school district is at a low ebb. For several years past, the school has been under the able management of Mrs. Ellen Walling, a teacher of experience and ability, and one who has taught school in this town for more than thirty years. With her ability and her record, the Nasonville school attained a position second to none in the town. Her scholars, from her deportment and manner, patterned after her, and many of her pupils have become teachers themselves.

Among the number who aspired to teach is the young daughter of the trustee, and to suit the girl he appointed her as assistant at a salary of five dollars and a half per week. Mrs. Walling thereupon resigned, took herself away, and her place was supplied by a Miss Hannah Stephens from near Boston. The new teacher boarded with the trustee, and things went happy as a marriage bell through the spring term. Undoubtedly, the young teacher felt her importance in emerging from her home each

One Hundred Years Ago in Burrillville by Patricia A. Mehrtens

morning in company with one of riper years. Upon entering on the fall term, the size of the school had evidently diminished, and with the diminished school arose the importance of the young teacher. The scholars felt dissatisfied, and the elder teacher had to assume control, in many cases to the dissatisfaction of the younger one and her parents. Matters by this time became serious, and Miss Stephens applied for advice to the superintendent, who told her to resign and also paid her off.

The citizens of the district began to enquire what the trouble was, and found to their dismay that the teacher had gone and the funds were low. Mrs. Walling taught on a salary of eleven dollars a week, and Miss Stephens was hired at the same rate. This, added to the sum paid to the assistant, had so depleted the exchequer that it was found the school could not be maintained longer than the first of January, and so it was closed last week. The average attendance had not any time exceeded thirty scholars, which number for two teachers seemed absurd.

The outlook for a school at Nasonville the coming winter is not bright. Many of the citizens are watching with anxious eyes for the return of Mrs. Walling. Others are seriously considering the calling of a school meeting to raise funds and possibly place them in safe hands for better management. Under any circumstances, it is a misfortune for a teacher to board with a trustee or in any way be holden to him, and also for a trustee to appoint his own child a teacher. Whether the child as teacher did right or wrong, the public would naturally look with distrust upon it. In serving the public in any capacity, self and family must be kept in the background at all times.

School Committee Meeting
June 22, 1888

An adjourned meeting of the School Board took place last Saturday afternoon in the banking rooms of the Pascoag National Bank. James S. Cook was elected Chairman and Philip O. Hawkins Clerk. A vote was taken to meet the first Saturday afternoon at two o'clock p.m. of each month. The school money was apportioned among the fifteen school districts as follows: District #1 - $306.84. #2 - $298.64. #3 - $413.40. #4 - $398.64. #5 - $733.51. #6 - $305.80. #7 - $1069.09. #8 - $307.90. #9 - $301.50. #10 - $833.90. #11 - $1669.93. #12 - $379.30. #13 - $285.70. #14 - $263.21. #15 - $303.74. Total Amount - $7871.10.

The amount of money for schools came from the

following sources: Unexpended balance, $115.60; from dog license, $468.20; Registry tax, $367.12; Town, $4100; State appropriation, $2820.18. The appropriations were nearly on the same basis as last year. District #3 received about $80 less than last year.

Changes Needed in the Schools
November 15, 1889

The change of the present school system in the town is almost a necessity, as much better results would be obtained in many ways. When a competent teacher is found, his or her services should be retained. By frequent changes of trustees, new teachers are hired. This works detrimentally to the school and to the advancement of the scholars. No two teachers have the same ways of conducting a school. Much valuable time is wasted before the new teacher becomes accustomed to the scholars and surroundings, and the scholars become accustomed to the teachers.

Algebra should not be taught in the grammar schools, especially where teachers have sixty scholars under their care. Crowding so many studies into the school sessions gives altogether too little time for the recitations and thorough drilling required for scholars to make rapid advancement. Parents, in many instances, are at fault for the slow progress made by their children in obtaining an education, by allowing them to stay out frequently. This breaks in upon their studies and injures very materially.

Some of the schools are poorly supplied with the many helps to teachers and scholars that good schools should possess. We are compelled to believe our schools do not come near the standard they should. The sooner the town system takes the place of the district system the better. When this is done, a superintendent should be appointed with a salary sufficient to enable him to devote all his time in raising the school standard and gaining uniformity in the methods of conducting the schools, and also in teaching. Each school would commence on the same day, and the terms would be of uniform length. We do not wish to infer that all the trustees are incompetent, by any means, for in many instances this is not the case. Much greater progress and less petty jealousies would crop out providing the power of hiring teachers and managing the schools was placed under one management. We believe anyone who will look at the matter squarely will not gainsay this.

One Hundred Years Ago in Burrillville by Patricia A. Mehrtens

Tarkiln School
December 13, 1889

The school here in Tarkiln has now been in session two weeks on this term. The register shows twenty-six names, sixteen boys and ten girls. Some of them come from quite a distance and bring their dinners with them. The boys play hop scotch as was evidenced by the markings on the playground. Several charts on anatomy and geographical maps hung upon the walls, something that every district cannot boast of as possessing. An organ stands upon the platform which is used in meetings held in the school building, and which comes handily into play when the school has singing exercises. The ages of the scholars attending this school are nearly all under ten, but a few over that age. The scholars behaved well and seemed to be interested in their studies and eager to learn. Miss Alice M. Smith is the teacher, and has the greatest respect of all her scholars, and we should judge has little cause for the use of the birch.

Meeting in District #7
April 8, 1890

A school meeting was held in District # 7 last Monday evening. The hour set was seven o'clock, but it was nearly a half hour later when Everett B. Sherman, the trustee, called those present to order. Great interest in this meeting seemed to be manifested notwithstanding it had been reported that a quorum could not be gathered. There have been rumblings of an uncertain nature for some time about the short term of the school year in this district and the loose way in which the books have been kept. Over sixty were present, and when order was called, hats came off. Those having weak eyes suffered considerably by the smoke which poured forth from the stove and tear drops fell down their cheeks. One not posted might have supposed that these tears were caused by the smoky situation which was liable to break forth into a raging fire of hot and hasty words, but this was not the fact.

On call for a moderator, Oliver A. Inman was chosen. Edward L. Gannon was elected clerk and Thomas Hanaway treasurer. The minutes of the last meeting were not read. The treasurer's report was called for and was not very satisfactory. It seems that about four years ago a tax of $400 was ordered by vote and the report showed only $313 collected. A portion of the balance it was claimed had never been collected. Inman asked if no time was set for collections to be made and the negative was the reply. Squire Inman thought it a wonder that they collected any of it. Inman said it had been so long since he had attended a school meeting, that he was hardly posted in the business as he should be.

It was voted to make forty weeks the school year. It was voted to raise a tax not exceeding $1000 nor less than $800 to repair the buildings and fences, place a furnace in the new school house, and two new stoves in the old building. Thomas Cunningham made considerable talk, and at times it was thought he was opposed to everything, then he would take a tack and those present would think him in for improvement. In fact, he opposed, and then he didn't oppose. Some were not much wiser as to his position on the matter when he finished than they were when he began talking. E. W. Tinkham made some remarks regarding the betterment of the school. Mr. Sherman explained some matters to make them clear in the minds of those present.

Rev. A. H. Granger made himself to the meeting what the rudder is to the ship and helped steer around shoal places. He said the statement in the *Gazette* that they had only had 22 weeks of schooling the past year was erroneous, that in the first term there were 12 weeks, the next 11, and the last 9, making 32. He was questioned about the money appropriated for evening schools the past year and what became of it. The collector of the town taxes was made the collector of the school tax, to be returnable by July 1st next. A warm and smoky time was had but no friendships were lost, it is hoped.

Valuation of School Property
October 14, 1891

Mr. Editor: If I were to judge from the article in the Providence *Bulletin* of Monday night, an article which evidently had its inspiration in Pascoag, I should conclude that the whole community was in ferment about this matter and that there was danger that the collector would be mobbed when he came around for the taxes. Yet, we see no signs of anything of the kind as we walk the streets, but every man is quietly attending to his own business. Pascoag people are evidently "a law and order" people satisfied, however, that there is a misapprehension in regard to this matter which can easily be set right.

In common with the great body of the citizens of the town, I regret that the commissioners appraised our school property so high. A lower estimate would doubtless have given better satisfaction. The greatest objection I have heard comes from Pascoag. The statement is made that their school property is valued "ridiculously low" and that one building alone cost all that both were appraised for. Is $7,000 or $3,500 each "ridiculously low"? Is it any lower than $2,500 each for the two buildings at Harrisville? Doubtful.

But says the objector, "one of these buildings cost $7,000." What of that? We do not estimate buildings by what they cost but by what they will bring in the open market. How often are dwellings sold for one-half their actual cost. This is frequently the case everywhere. But this is not going down to the root of the real difficulty. Suppose the valuation of the outlying school house, to which objection has been specially made, had been put 25 or even 50% lower. It would hardly have lowered the taxes of the taxpayers in Harrisville, Pascoag, or Laurel Hill one per cent on their large valuation, while it would sensibly affect the little taxable property in these purely farming districts.

Compare the Logee district with a valuation of $18,550, or the Wallum Pond district with a valuation of $15,300 with Pascoag, which is assessed at $908,950 or Harrisville which pays taxes on $677,250. Our villages furnish and must furnish the larger share of the funds to pay the expenses of the rest of the town because the bulk of the taxable property is here. They receive but a comparatively small rebate ie:, a small percentage on their taxes, because their valuation is so large.

Here we have the whole thing in a nutshell. It is not the commissioners who have done the mischief, but it is an evil which grows out of the unequal distribution of property in the different districts. The truth is, there is little wealth in the purely farming districts of the town. To tax them so as to maintain a school on our present scale without outside help would be to ruin them and increase the number of "deserted farms." They must lean on the village and the village must lend them a helping hand. If the farmers of our town know "on which side their bread is buttered" they will never vote to give up the town system of schools and go back to the district system. Yours Respectfully, A. H. Granger. October 14, 1891.

Flag Raising
June 17, 1892

There has been of late a growing interest in the community in flags for our school houses. This interest is not confined to this town or state, but extends all over the country, and hardly a school house can be passed in some sections without seeing the pole attached to the building or planted in the ground in the school yard. The teachers in Harrisville were the first to fall in with this sentiment, and to take steps towards securing a flag and raising it. June 17th was selected as an appropriate day for the ceremonies of the occasion, as upon that day the Battle of Bunker Hill was fought for American Independence.

It was intended to hold the exercises in the school building but when the day opened so sultry, warm, and close, it was decided to have the exercises out-of-doors. A platform was built beneath the grateful shade of the branches of a noble oak in the school yard, upon which was placed a cabinet organ, chairs for the speakers, and rows of board seats and settees at each side for the children, who numbered nearly 200, from the small Primary scholar to those of maturer years in the Grammar school. Seats in front of the stand were reserved for members of Guild Post, No. 27 G.A.R., who at a little past two o'clock marched in a body from their hall on Chapel Street to the scene of animation and bustle headed by the Harrisville Brass Band.

Carriages filled the street, and the yard adjoining which were loaded with occupants. Many brought chairs from residences in the village, and thus were more comfortable. An awning protected the children from the hot rays of the sun and the G.A.R.'s were in the shade of the schoolhouse. The arrangements were very comfortable and showed forethought on the part of the teachers and Superintendent. The stand was trimmed with bunting and flags in an appropriate manner. George Legg presented the Flag to the school children, which was accepted by the Superintendent A. H. Granger. Bands played and speeches about patriotism and the flag were made. The members of the G.A.R. entered the school house after the exercises and were treated to lemonade, after which they repaired to Thayer's Hall where a collation of sandwiches, cake, bananas, and lemonade was discussed. Cigars ended up this part, when all departed for home, having been delayed somewhat by the heavy shower which had come on.

The Schoolhouse Gone
July 8, 1893

The old story has been repeated. The tall flagstaff capped with vane and rod on top of our Grammar school building on Sayles Avenue proved too attractive for the electric fluid that flashed back and forth over our village on Wednesday night. It was about 10 o'clock, when most of our people had gone to bed, a blue sheet of flame, a dull crash and a terrific thud, followed by a zip! ziz! ziz! as the lightning tore down the flagpole of the schoolhouse, through the belfry and out at the front and side of the building. One great sheet of flame, and the whole top of the building was on fire. People hurried to their windows, saw the fire, and rushed out into the storm, some one way and some another, as the vivid lightning flashes made it almost impossible to locate the fire at first. Soon lines of hose were laid toward the schoolhouse, and the crowd all congregated there, each aiding as best he might in the efforts to save this and the adjoining property.

The pumps at the mills of A. L. Sayles & Sons and Miller & Pendergast were quickly started, but as the hydrants near the fire proved out of order, long lines of hose had to be laid. The force of the water was greatly retarded, and it did but little good. Down crashed the chimney, and sparks flew like fireworks in every direction. Men hitched ropes about the timbers and pulled them down to the ground where the fire could be put out. Others brought water in pails and smothered live sparks wherever found, and still others pulled till strong ropes parted and they rolled over each other in the mud.

The neighbors adjoining were all busy keeping their own property wet and free from sparks that were driven everywhere by the strong wind. It was an exciting time for three full hours, and then, with the fire under control, the tired multitude sought their beds again. The building will have to be rebuilt at once or there will be no place for Grammar and Intermediate schools this fall. The fire again broke out from the smoldering ruins Thursday evening, and for a few minutes created a small commotion among people of the vicinity.

Dedication of New Pascoag School House
October 13, 1894

Last Saturday was a gala day in the history of Burrillville, schools for the new school building at Pascoag was dedicated with appropriate ceremonies. Directly in front of the building were settees for the pupils, and on the opposite side of the lawn near the fence were seats for the visitors. These were comfortably filled before the hour appointed for the exercises to begin. At two o'clock the pupils, marshaled by their teachers, marched out of the schoolhouse in excellent form and took the seats assigned them.

One Hundred Years Ago in Burrillville by Patricia A. Mehrtens

The program was well conceived and excellently carried out. The children evinced special interest in their several parts, seeming to take much pride in their handsome new building. The addresses were exceptionally good and were listened to with an unusual degree of interest. The building committee consisted of three members, viz: Dr. J. J. Lace, chairman, John T. Fiske, Jr., and Andrew Luther. This handsome building, which graces Sayles Avenue midway between Fountain Square and Laurel Hill Avenue, will stand for many years as a monument to the efficient manner in which they fulfilled the trust imposed upon them.

(A portion of Dr. Lace's address follows.) The burning of the Pascoag grammar school by lightning on the evening of July 5th, 1893, called forth the need of a new school building. There was doubt in the minds of some as to the advisability of erecting so large a building. It was claimed that Pascoag was not so densely populated as to need so many schools in one building, and some of the rooms would not be used for years. On the other hand, it was claimed a large building could be run more economically, and better work and better grading of the schools could be secured. That the latter plan found favor, both with the school and building committees, is evidenced by this structure.

The want of proper school accommodations is a question that confronts all great centers of population today. We need to build for the future. Burrillville, in erecting this building, has not built much in advance, however, as a review of the school registration will show. We have twenty-four schools in the town, eight of which are located in Pascoag including the primary at Laurel Hill. Total pupils in Pascoag school district - 450. The number registered in the other sixteen schools of the town - 488. It will be seen by these figures that in the Pascoag district is registered nearly one-half the school children of the town. Can anyone believe the building is too large with this number of school children within the radius of one mile? Five out of the six rooms are already occupied, and in all probability before the present year is past, every available space, from cellar to garret will be in use.

History of Burrillville Schools
at Pascoag Dedication
October 13, 1894

(Synopsis of an address given by Rev. W. E. Dennett entitled Growth of Schools in Burrillville.) Facts concerning our

One Hundred Years Ago in Burrillville by Patricia A. Mehrtens

schools of a hundred years ago are not very numerous nor accessible. It is an occasion for just pride that our town so early manifested an interest in the cause of education. The part played by our ancestors in this important work was an honorable one. The first bill presented to the Legislature providing for free schools was drafted by a Burrillvillian and is of deepest interest to us on this occasion. My present purpose is to indicate briefly the growth of our schools by a comparison of statistics. For these facts I am indebted to Rev. Wm. Fitz and the *Pascoag Herald*.

Our first recorded history was in 1790, earliest record of a schoolhouse 1806. The town records contain nothing previous to 1828, when the school committee consisted of twenty-one members. The next year, the number was reduced to sixteen, and in 1846 to six and the next year to three. At present it consists of five members. The first superintendent was Rev. Mowry Phillips, July 11, 1871. His salary was $200. From 1880 to 1885 the salary was $100 then $200 until 1891, when it was raised to $1,000.

In 1808 the Round Top school house was built at an expense of $300; 1832 the Buck Hill house for $200; 1848 the Harris school house at an expense of $134; 1863 the school house in District 7 for $760; 1873 Plainville and Oakland $2,000. 1870 Harrisville house for $4,500, and in 1893 the magnificent structure which we today dedicate at an expense of $18,000.

In 1814, Lydia Brown taught in the Glendale district for eight shillings. In 1840, her daughter, Betsey, received one shilling more. In 1832, the wages in the Buck Hill district were $8 per month. Wm. A. Mowry taught in 1848 for $12 a month and the next year he received $15. James O. Inman taught in 1853 for $18 and board. The wages in the Jackson district in 1849 were $10 and board. Mrs. J. L. Phillips, now a missionary, in India taught in the Logee district in 1857 for $1.50 per week and would have taught for less. Salaries now range from $7.50 per week to $60 per month.

The town appropriations for schools ranges from $300 in 1828 to more than twenty times that amount at present. Our state money in 1828 was $199.88 and in 1871 was $2592.99. It is a time for just pride and congratulations, but not for complacency. What does it mean if so many of our boys and girls are obliged to seek their education either away from home or by private tuition? Others still in our own and surrounding villages would gladly avail themselves of a high school if it were located in our midst. This portion of our state should now be enjoying the benefits of a high school, and this new building is just the place.

One Hundred Years Ago in Burrillville by Patricia A. Mehrtens

School Census Figures
January 26, 1900

The school census has been completed, and returns made by Superintendent of Schools Allen P. Keith. They show a favorable condition and an increase in all the villages except Mapleville. The statistics are as follows: Total number of boys attending public schools, 521; number of girls attending public schools, 523; total, 1044; number of girls attending Catholic schools, 2; number of boys attending select school, 2; number of boys not attending any school, 57; number of girls not attending any school, 76; whole number of boys, 580; whole number of girls, 601; total number of school children, 1181. The total number of children in 1899 was 1186. The stopping of the Mapleville mill made a loss of 50 to 60 children to the town. Although the total number this year is less than that of a year ago, the census shows a marked increase in the several villages.

Of the number of children not attending any school, 85 are under seven years of age and 21 over fifteen years, leaving but 27 who come within the law limit. There are also 4 who attend school less than 16 weeks, thus making the number of children of school age not attending any school, 31. Last year the number was 52. The superintendent states that the overseers and proprietors of the mills in town are becoming accustomed to demand certificates of the children before they are employed, and in many of the mills it is impossible for a child to obtain employment without it.

Round Top School Celebration
July 25, 1902

Tuesday afternoon the celebration at the Round Top school, which is the first step towards reclaiming the old schools of the town, was well attended. Several numbers on a very interesting program were given the closest attention. The older townspeople of Burrillville were perhaps familiar with the erection and service of the little one story building, which nestles beside the road leading from Round Top to Douglas, almost hidden by a growth of underbrush. They may have heard their fathers tell of how the little building was erected at the cost of $800 in 1806, soon after the town was incorporated. It originally stood on one of the corners in the hamlet of Round Top, but when the little village began to expand, the site of the school was needed for stores, and it was removed to its present location.

Beneath its tattered and weatherstained roof, students who in later life have delved in the mysteries of law, medicine and theology acquired their rudimentary knowledge, and a number of those whose names are not unknown in the intellectual and scientific world returned to the scenes of their youth, and gratefully sounded the praises of their first alma mater. Men and women who have passed a number of the milestones of life's pathway, again wended their way to the little building as they had so often done in the days of huskings and parings. Out of the hazy vista of the past came a vivid picture of the olden long ago, the harsh lines mellowed and toned down by the years that are no more. At the sound of the school bell, memories were stirred up, thoughts awakened and scenes recalled to gray-haired men and women that have lain dormant for a period of more than half a century.

The exercises were not held in the school building because of lack of accommodations. The committee in charge of the program cleared away a large space on the hill overlooking the little edifice, and seats were laid along the hillside in tiers. The arrangement was somewhat after the style of an amphitheater with the platform for those who participated in the exercises in front covered with a tent. The gathering was called to order by Mowry Arnold about 2 o'clock. After the program was rendered, the party went to the old house at Stony Bottom and played games and danced. The ball which was to have been held in the evening was postponed on account of the rain.

Recollections by Manning Wood
April 6, 1907

In trying to recall those who taught school in the old Harrisville school house, one I remember more distinctly was named Michael Hayden. Perhaps it would have been better if I did not remember him at all, but he impressed himself on my memory so that to forget him is impossible. For him to lick a scholar was more enjoyable than a good breakfast. A chance to drive a book across the room at one's head was more substantial pleasure than a good dinner. To make a boy stand stooped over and hold his finger on a nail in the floor while he played a tattoo on his buttock with a ruler, was more solid comfort than the best of suppers. To have them all happen in one day would be such a symphony of good things that the memory of their wailings would lull him to deep sleep and pleasant dreams.

But Michael's reign was short. One day when the birch

switch had been more busy than usual and books and ruler had been flying at unlucky heads, he called another culprit up for a good dressing down. Martin Smith, who was the biggest boy in school, arose from his seat and told the teacher he must not punish that scholar. Filled with astonishment, Hayden demanded a reason why. "Because I say you mustn't"and then Moses Smith the next largest boy also arose. The teacher looked at the sturdy youths and cast his eyes along the bench where other boys had laid their books aside. He did the only sensible thing of his whole administration and said school was dismissed. There would be no more sessions until a new teacher was obtained. Exit Michael.

Whether this incident gave the school a bad name or not, I do not know, but there was some talk that it would be necessary to get a teacher for the next term who could manage the scholars instead of being managed by them. If this object was in view when procuring the next teacher, it resulted in the most pronounced success. There was no rebellion during the next administration. I have a unique subject to describe, and I wish it thoroughly understood in the beginning that I am not attempting to draw a caricature because if I did so I would draw down on my head anything but blessings from all the boys and girls who used to unite in singing those good old songs to the accompaniment of his violin.

He was tall, six feet three inches when he stood erect, which he seldom did having an habitual stoop. He was very slim. Nature was not prodigal in finding material to surround the figure she so ambitiously commenced. His head was rather small, but the mouth was rather large ,with a full under lip that had a habit of rolling out further on occasions of displeasure. From the mouth, the face sloped away to his long neck without any intervening chin, which nature had evidently mislaid in the makeup. Arms, body and legs, long and loosely put together so that the limbs seemed to dangle around , and very large feet.

He wore a tall black silk hat and claw-hammer coat, and his long neck was enclosed by an old fashioned stiff black stock. The garment that most impressed itself on my memory was his over garment, which instead of being an overcoat, was a cloak. It was made of an old-fashioned linsey woolsey plaid fastened at the neck with a large heavy hook and chain, the garment reaching to the feet with slashes at the sides to thrust the arms through instead of sleeves. Over this was a cape of the same material about two-thirds as long as the cloak. When his long, loose form was enveloped in this garment with his big feet peeping out at the bottom and the whole surmounted by the stovepipe hat, and he walked off smartly with his wabbly knees striking the long cloak knocking it this way and that, he made a figure to attract attention. To see him when he had been ambushed by fifteen or twenty boys with full magazines of ammunition in the form of water-soaked snowballs, would provoke the risibles. Snatching up the cape to protect the head and bending the long body into the shape of a jackknife, he would speed away with the long cloak fluttering behind like a banner. He placed himself beyond the reach of the fusillade which had been lawfully conceived and executed under the rules and regulations which he had himself adopted. The rules were that no snowballs must be thrown within certain bounds around the school house, and no complaints would be considered for the same thing occurring outside of these bounds, for everyone was supposed to take care of their own heads whether they were pupils or teacher.

If I had drawn a fairly good photograph there would be no necessity for writing the name for every old scholar of his who has read these recollections has probably exclaimed, Old Keep." Yes, "Old Keep" and yet he couldn't have been old either, not very far from thirty-five. For the information of the younger generation or anyone who did not have the opportunity of sitting under his instruction and have knowledge driven into their heads whether they wanted it or not, I will write the whole name, Calvin S. Keep.

TOWN BUSINESS

Burrillville Census of 1880
July 30, 1880

We have been at considerable pains to gather from the recent census of Burrillville such computations of facts and statistics as we thought would be interesting to our readers. The population of the town is 5,719. The increase has been 170 since 1875 and 1,045 since 1870. The number of dwelling houses is 863—78 more than in 1875. The families number 1,171, an increase of 114 since 1875.

As to the nationality of our population, 2,279 are of native parentage and 3,440 of foreign parentage. The native born number 3,848 and the foreign-born 1,872. Of the former, 2,777 had their birthplace in Rhode Island and 993 in other parts of the Union, mainly coming from the two neighboring States of Massachusetts and Connecticut. Of the foreign-born 727 came from Canada and the British Provinces, 704 from Ireland, 358 from England, 17 from Germany, 16 from Scotland, 4 from Portugal, 3 from Wales, and 1 each from Spain, Peru, the Isle of Man, and the Isle of St. Helena.

In regard to occupations, 1,649 of our people are employed by the woolen industry alone, and about 150 in other manufacturing. Next in number to the mill operatives, though a long way behind, come the men who till the soil for a living. They number only 361. Of the various mechanical trades, the carpenters take the lead numbering 52. There are 31 masons, 24 machinists, 16 blacksmiths, 15 painters, 8 shoemakers, 8 wheelwrights, 5 tailors, 4 harness-makers, 4 tinsmiths, 5 barbers, 4 jewelers and watchmakers, 3 cabinet makers, and one soap manufacturer. A few of our people follow a mixed occupation sometimes working on a farm and sometimes at a trade.

The Providence & Springfield Railroad gives employment

in one way or another to 22 persons resident here. The outdoor employments are represented by 28 laborers, 20 teamsters, 11 peddlers, 3 woodchoppers, 1 lightning rod man, and 1 wood sawyer. Of miscellaneous occupations, there are 8 butchers, 5 printers, 3 stable keepers, 11 hostlers, 13 saloon keepers, 2 bartenders, 8 watchmen, 4 hotel keepers, 10 bookkeepers, 1 photographer, 1 sawmill proprietor, 1 boardinghouse keeper, 2 designers, 1 dentist, 1 surveyor of lumber, 1 keeper of house of ill repute, 1 beer manufacturer, 1 undertaker, 1 sexton, 2 quarrymen, 1 stage driver, 1 detective, 1 keeper, 2 deputy sheriffs, 1 trial justice, and 1 town clerk.

Quite a number of our citizens are engaged in trade. The several variety stores in town require the services of 41 persons. There is also 1 clothing dealer, 2 druggists, 1 dry goods dealer, 1 fish dealer, 1 lumber dealer, 1 furniture dealer, 1 coal dealer, 1 wood dealer, 1 cattle trader, and 1 horse dealer. The ladies of Burrillville are also active in many pursuits. Besides the considerable number of females employed in the mills, there are 63 domestic servants, 31 dressmakers, 23 school teachers (two or three males), 6 milliners, 1 seamstress, 2 nurses, 2 tailoresses, and 1 insurance agent. The learned professions are represented by 9 physicians and medical students, 7 clergymen, and only 1 lawyer and 1 law student. There are 2 bank cashiers, 1 retired manufacturer and 1 retired merchant.

Of the social condition of our people, 2,151 are married and 3,565 single (including all ages). There are 181 widows, 99 widowers, and 26 divorced persons. The sexes are very nearly balanced, there being 2,841 males and 2,868 females—a slight preponderance of the latter. There are comparatively few aged people in town only 35 being recorded between 80 and 90, 1 (Dorcas Jenney) 95, and 1 (Bassille LaFarge) 104. As to illiteracy, 899 of our inhabitants cannot read or write and 122 can read but not write.

Political Communications
May 29, 1885

There is considerable talk about this time by the opposition party in regard to the administration and management of the affairs of the Town for the year, and the way the present Town Council has expended some of the Town's money. From the time the Democratic party came into power in the Town some eight years ago, up to the time it came into the hands of the Republicans, they had such a system of patching up things,

One Hundred Years Ago in Burrillville by Patricia A. Mehrtens

bridges and highways, etc., all for the sake of reducing taxation to keep themselves in power by their small expenditures of money and, as they thought, great economy. The time had got to come when there would be a big outlay for repairs. As the Republican party happened to be in power when the blow came, they have got to take the blame of the expenditures. Their aim was, lots of money in the treasury, and let the town go to ruin. If anyone doubts this, let them take a look at our Town House and Poor Farm buildings and see if they can guess when they were painted last.

The first outlay of any account was to build a bridge at Gazza, the old one was so rotten that it fell down with a loaded team upon it. The town was very fortunate that the man and team escaped accident. The present bridge is two feet wider than the old one and very substantially built. The next outlay was to build a bridge near Harrisville, Shippee Bridge so called. This bridge was also so rotten that some of the timbers were broken in two.

The next was the widening a portion of the street and building a wall on Sayles Ave. at Pascoag near the schoolhouse. Anyone acquainted with the locality will not dispute but that it was badly needed, and that the job was well done. The last but not least which has caused the most noise and bluster is the building of a bridge over Graniteville trench, and the building of a wall on Sayles Avenue at Pascoag. The leaders of the opposition party have for the past month been traveling all over the town using these two last jobs as a handle for their arguments to show why the present administration should be turned out and they put in.

In regard to the Granite bridge, they tell the parties living outside of the villages and the farmers, that the Republican party is putting up at great expense to the town a job that does not belong to the town to do at all, that the bridge and abutments should be built and kept in repair by the party who owns the Graniteville property.

If you will just stop and think for a moment, you will remember that Graniteville trench was in existence some twenty years before the present road was built, therefore the bridge belongs to the town to keep in repair. The bridge is three feet wider than the old one, and the cry is "three feet more bridge for the town to take care of." This is a good job, both wood and stone work, and an honor to the town and the party having the matter in charge.

In regard to the wall that has just been built at Pascoag on Sayles Avenue near the bridge which has caused the loudest wail, we will say that some three years ago when the present bridge was erected, there was a wall built as was supposed upon the line of road, but three to five feet upon land owned by the Hon. H. A. Kimball. After the wall was built and the road widened by filling in, the work was so poorly done that the filling all washed into the pond owned by him to the great detriment of the parties operating the mill. Mr. Kimball tried to get the last Council to rebuild the wall in a good substantial manner, saying that he had no objection to their taking his land and would give them a deed of what they had taken, but they must put it in shape so as not to damage him any more; that if something was not done there would be trouble. The old Council appointed a man to do the work over again but it was not done under that administration.

Now this same man is telling all through the town that the present Council is doing a job with the town's money for private individuals, that Mr. Kimball had the town in his power and the Council thought it would be cheaper for the town to rebuild the wall as it should be than to fight a lawsuit, get beat, and then build the wall. The improvements that have been made through the town the past year are all substantial and will last for years without further outlay. They were all very much needed and the work has been honestly and faithfully done and a credit to the parties who had them in charge. Work that the present Council is not ashamed of, and any man who is not prejudiced in his opinions will agree with us.

Notwithstanding the cry of extravagance by the opposition of the present administration, the Town Treasurer's report for the fiscal year ending March 31st shows more money in the treasury than the one a year ago under their administration, and great economy, with over a thousand dollars less received for licenses at that. How are they going to explain that?

Letter from Horace Kimball
May 29, 1885

To the Town Council of the Town of Burrillville: Gentlemen. Sept. 30th, 1882 a vote passed your board instructing Mr. A. S. Green to widen the bridge on Sayles Avenue in Pascoag. This was done, but in so unworkmanlike a manner as to cause me serious damage by reason of the wash from the street emptying into my mill pond. At the time of building the wall, the town took possession of my land and erected thereon a very ungainly and unsightly wall. Now to the occupation of the land I make no objection, but to the construction of the wall I enter my protest. Since this wall was built I understand through Messrs. Sayles & Nichols that the town intends to rebuild this wall and make the necessary filling, doing it in workmanlike manner and to the satisfaction of the interested parties. I wish to call your attention to the same and respectfully ask that the repairs be made as soon as convenient. Respectfully, Horace A. Kimball.

Communication from a Taxpayer
February 26, 1886

There has been much said and much written since the *Burrillville Gazette* issued its first number in Pascoag. It is also the case with our town's highways relative to convincing the public mind of the great importance of having good and safe highways. Good roads are a moral obligation to God, man and beast. Persistent agitation brings about great reforms, in no matter what line. What is the cause of our bad roads? What is the cause of our bad sidewalks? Changing and interchanging of town officials caused by politics which make many changes in our town district highway surveyors.

If we get in a good surveyor, one who is willing to faithfully work out the taxes on the roads, one who will use the shovel or the hoe more for tools of labor than for staves to lean upon and rest fifteen minutes in every hour, not much is gained for the surveyor goes to the taxpayer and says: "Do you want your taxes worked out?" The taxpayer says: "Yes," and he hires Tom, Dick and Harry who do not care if they but get hold of the money. The surveyor tells the citizen that there is not money enough or that there is not tax enough or there is not gravel, chipstone, or dirt enough to make a good road.

Sayles Avenue from the blacksmith shop until you get to the school house is mid, mad, mud, and slish, slash, slush, three-fifths of the year. Another bad place is from the Catholic Church to the small bridge and beyond until you reach Grove Street. It is almost impossible to travel the length of Sayles Ave. in a dark muddy night and find both rubbers on at the end of the trip. It is not an uncommon thing in passing along the Avenue in the morning after a rainy and muddy evening to see two or three rubbers stuck fast in the earth, and frozen in so another thaw must be awaited to get them out. But, says one:"What can be done?" We can do what all towns do that have good roads. "Let the town pay the road tax in money and then put in one or two good men, live men, to take charge of the roads and be responsible for their condition, or bid out the right to make good

One Hundred Years Ago in Burrillville by Patricia A. Mehrtens

roads, and allow toll gates to be erected and require toll of those using them," but have better roads under any circumstances. The boys and girls six years of age and the old man and woman eighty-six years or more, in fact of all ages, travel these roads and it is no more than right that they should have good easy and safe roads to travel on no matter whether they go for necessity or pleasure. -Taxpayer

Burrillville Voting List
March 2, 1888

The voting list as just printed contains 840 names which is considerable of an increase over last year. Every voter should examine the list and see that his name is on correctly, both in initials and spelling, and if it is not, have the mistake rectified before election day. There are some peculiarities about all voting lists in the various towns of our state. Some names are common in some sections while in others they are rare. Puns are frequently heard or seen in papers about Smiths and Jones being so common. This holds good among the names of the voters here in regard to the Smiths, but we fail to find even one by the name of Jones. Burrillville air did not seem to agree with the Joneses.

The letter S takes the lead as an initial letter on the list, that letter containing 120 names. Of these names, 47 or more than one-third of them are Smiths. Only two Smiths appear where the names are just alike, and those are Thomas Smith. In this case we hardly see how law can prevent one from voting on the other's name. There is an Owen Smith and an Owen Smith, Jr.; also a James O. Smith and a James O. Smith, Jr. There are several John Smiths but the lack of a middle name in the one instance and different initial letters of the middle names in the other cases preclude all possibilities of mistake and marks the individual as distinctly as though his name was entirely different.

Among the S's the name of Sayles is quite prevalent with 16 voters. Next to the S's, names commencing with M predominate, there being 94. Mowry and Mathewson are most frequently seen in the M's. There are 27 Mowrys—17 under real estate, 6 personal property and 4 registry. The next letter used the most in the list is, C-88, the next is B-78, then W-63, H-43, P-42, T-41, and F-37. D and R are equally represented, there being 30 names under each letter. Then comes G-28, A-27, L-25, E-22, I-19, K-15, N-12, O-11, Y-7, J-4, V-3 and Q-1. It will be noticed that U, X and Z do not appear, the town not as yet being able to produce a voter whose name begins with any of those letters. The letters, although rare, here appear on some lists in the state, and we now have a representative in the Assembly named Utter. Q comes pretty near getting left as you see—only one under that letter.

We have one King but others will soon be in the field and then there will be war. The town has Knights but no "Days" although the latter is a very common name in some localities. It has Hills and Knowles near the Rivers and Brooks. Fair-fields are seen and Woods are plenty where Hunts occur. Bacon and Fowles are not extra plenty. Coffee is scarce but Cooks are plenty. The place should be attractive to outsiders, as we have a good number of Darlings and Angells. We have Mills and Millers, and of course, Noyes must be here.

Paines are quite prevalent. Sweets are scattered through the town, and the Roses blossom while the Starrs look upon them in the Spring. We have Trainors but they keep within the Laws. We have Carpenters, Coopers, Bakers and Barbers. We have Barnes here also, but we need one more at the Town Farm. We have but one Sly voter and that is George W. Plumbs are not extra plenty but still there are some. We have Taylors so no need exists of going away from home to get clothes made. It may seem a big story but the town holds France. There are 19 men here also that never grow old because they are always Young. The whole number of names under the real estate head is 369; personal property 103; registry 368; total 840.

Feeding of Tramps
April 8, 1890

The regular council meeting was held last Saturday in the accustomed place. Inman, Thayer, Lacey, Honan, Fitz and Copeland were present. R. S. & F. W. Wood was allowed a bill of 71 cents for material for lockup. Joseph N. Smith was allowed $21.25 for care of lockup and feeding prisoners and tramps from February 22 to March 28. The size of this bill brought forth some remarks from Town Sergeant Fairfield who thought the town was too easy with the floating population, and that it was poor policy to allow the same persons to put up night after night at the town's expense. Some of them stay around in the daytime and live on the charity of people and sleep in the lockup nights. He had known of their making brags that when they could not find any other place, they could always get put up at Burrillville. It is customary for those in search of work to make it their headquarters, and if they went to Chepachet to find work and did not get it, they would return.

Mr. Inman didn't know but what it was a credit to the town. One of the councilmen suggested they be made to saw wood enough to pay for their meals and lodging, but others said this could not be done unless someone was hired to see that they did it. President Inman remarked that he had carefully considered the matter, and if anyone had a feasible plan to make it known. Mr. Fairfield said there were instances where those deserving of help were thrown upon the town for a short time and must be taken care of, but something should be done to prevent a certain class from beating the town and taking advantage of its hospitality. Mr. Inman said that when the tramps were in the lockup they were safe and were not in barns where they were liable to set property on fire, and if not in the lockup they would seek other places where damage might be done. Mr. Fairfield thought the town too easy with them, and considered it poor policy to allow men to be put up nights and planning robbery daytimes. No line of action in the matter was taken, as a person could not be arrested for being a tramp unless he was caught begging from house to house. No plans were formulated to help the matter. Adjourned.

Liquor Licenses Granted
May 6, 1892

At the Town Council Meeting, granting 2nd class liquor licenses came up, and the following were granted a liquor license without opposition: John H. Ryan, William T. Fagan, Alvin R. Bowdish, E. C. Griffith, George O. Fairfield, Frank Fagan, James Hoey, Joseph Forcier all located on Main Street, Pascoag. Wm. Hanniver, Jr. near Garvey's ledge south of Pascoag, Patrick Black at the flats in Pascoag, John A. Breault, Charles D. Beauregard, Terrence J. Smith, Chapel Street, Clarence G. Thayer, Daniel W. Mowry, Main Street, and Thomas Cunningham near the depot all in Harrisville. Patrick Lynch at the Western Hotel, Nasonville, Patrick F. McCabe, Glendale, Patrick Smith, Mapleville, Joseph Whittaker between Oakland and Mapleville, Joseph F. Hines, Oakland. This made 21. When the application of Louis Bousquet was read, Wm. S. Malone said he had no objections to Mr. Bousquet getting a license, but did not see how they could grant him a license where he was already located and had applied. The board considered this matter was something they had nothing to do with, and granted Bousquet a license to apply to the Harrisville

One Hundred Years Ago in Burrillville by Patricia A. Mehrtens

Hotel. When the application of Wm. S. Malone was read, James Sykes objected to the board granting one to him to apply to his building, saying he had let the premises to another party. This was rather a puzzler and was discussed at some length, but the board concluded that the parties might settle the matter among themselves as to tenancy, and granted Malone a license to apply to the same place as Bousquet.

When the application of Peter Germain was read, Councilman Griffin objected to granting it on the ground of its general bad reputation. He said he understood it was a house of ill fame, and a party stood ready to come before the board and swear to that. Officer Timmins was called upon to tell what he knew concerning the place, and said it was talked a great deal and by consent considered a hard place. He had been there one or two Sundays and found business under full headway, but of late he had not heard so much, and the place had been quiet. Officer McDermott was called upon to say what he knew about the place run by Mr. Germain and said he had been there a number of times but had never seen any girls there; saw a maid who did the work. Deputy Sheriff Inman was asked concerning the place and said he knew nothing about it, had had no occasion to go there. The petitioner was given leave to withdraw. The license fee was placed at $250. Some of the petitions had coupled with them a hotel license, which was objected to by Councilman Steere, who said he preferred to act upon them separately, and the hotel part was marked out. The bondsmen of persons granted a license were accepted without exception.

Burrillville Senators since 1843
August 26, 1892

Not so very ancient but sufficiently modern, below is a list of the Senators from Burrillville since 1843.
Otis Wood 1843-1845. Solomon Smith 1845-1846. Israel Tucker 1846-1848. Dutee Lapham 1848-1851. Daniel M. Salisbury 1849-1850. Lyman Hawkins 1851-1852. Elisha Mathewson 1852-1853 and 1882-1884. Burrill Logee 1853-1854. Esten Angell 1854-1855. Stephen Eddy 1855-1857. Jeremiah Olney 1857-1858. Jason Olney 1858-1859. James S. Cook 1859-1860 and 1869-1876. Martin A. Smith 1860-1862. John L. Boss 1862-1863. Joseph O. Clarke 1863-1864. Job S. Steere 1864-1866. Stephen Emerson 1866-1867. Horatio L. Hopkins 1867-1868. Jesse M. Smith 1868-1869. William H. Clarke 1876-1877. Horace A. Kimball 1877-1879. Fayette E.

Bartlett 1879-1882 and 1890 - —. George B. Richardson 1884-1885. Erwin J. France 1885-1887. Addison S. Hopkins 1887-1890.

Board of Canvasser's Meeting
March 3, 1893

There may have been a more thoroughly disgusted canvassing board somewhere in the State than was the Burrillville board at midnight last Monday—there may have been voting lists elsewhere made up under chronological, alphabetical and zoological difficulties—there may have been five hours of more genuine fun in some variety theater—but we doubt it. The canvass of a Burrillville voting list is always unique. The members of the board have an easy, conversational way of settling disputed questions, while every spectator feels at liberty to inject breezy remarks and free advice to his heart's content, if not specially to the content of the board.

Last Monday evening at seven sharp, five of the seven members gathered around the table, one of them making the confident remark, "We'll finish this job in an hour." They didn't. Right away after the call to order, someone said that the naturalized voters ought to be notified what to do about showing their papers, and this innocent little remark cost an hour's time—with no result. Then the members squared away for business when the door opened and an individual with an elegantly large "jug" aboard, a supernatural impediment in his speech, and a snow bill in his hand, blew in. The necessary explanations made before the bill was passed threw the board into convulsions but finally everything quieted down.

Just as the president opened fire on the letter "A" a couple of Frenchmen, innocent of English but both enormously drunk, rolled in. One of them explained as well as he could that they had come to testify in favor of their friend Councilman Lacy whom they heard was on trial for something. They were accommodated with seats on the floor and "Arnold" was called again. Once more the door flew open, and a wild-looking individual burst in with the breathless announcement "I'm all right—me horse has run away and me sleigh is broke—but I'm all right." He supplemented this information by saying there was a man "just below" outside who was disrobing himself preparatory to going to bed in the snow. Deputy Sheriff Inman started out but didn't find this particular man—probably he'll show up when the snows melt—but he did find another one peeping from under his bedclothes of snow and gathered him in. The little side shows had brought the time to nearly nine o'clock and the president read the riot act and said "now for strict business."

The board was endeavoring to canvass the general and the three district lists at one time, the president calling from the main list while the other members watched the district lists, the personal taxpayers, the registry book, and each other. The board went at the letter "A" again like a pack of hunters at a five rail fence, and had reached near the bottom of the list, when a name was struck that appeared in two or three places on every list. This man was chased up and down, erased and replaced, given a real estate status, and then reduced to the registry ranks assigned to district number three, and then transferred to number one and finally lost track of altogether. In losing the name, the members lost their serenity of temper and tackled the letter "B" somewhat savagely. With about the first "B" called, the misbegotten "A" man bobbed up again, and he was chased like a flea up and down the lists once more. He was finally planted for keeps somewhere, but the board got into a dazed "where are we at" condition in doing it. "Samuel Bolivar" sang out the president. There was a rustle of paper as the lists were turned over and intent looks following forefingers down the columns of names. "Can't find him" finally came up in chorus. "Who are you looking for?" roared the president. "Lemuel Gulliver," "Ramuel Tolliver," "Manuel Dollivar," "Daniel Ollivar" roared back the badgered canvassers. That settled it. Refreshments were sent for and under their soothing influence the normally placid tempers of the members were fast coming back, when someone suggested it was growing late and that labor and refreshment must literally go hand in hand.

The optical feat of keeping one eye on the zenith of the ceiling, the other on the nadir of the table, was more or less successfully accomplished, and the work went merrily on. Frequently a name would be encountered and the sepulchral cry of "dead," "dead," "dead," would arise in different tones around the table, and by vote the name would be stricken from the list. It happened pretty frequently, too, that after the name had been disposed of and four or five succeeding names had been passed, a belated idea would strike one of the board with a resultant, "Say there, that dead man ain't dead, that's his son." This would open up a genealogical survey, the dead man would be brought to life, his son legally killed, and the waltz would go on again. The question of when a man lost his residence was also a prolific source of argument. Some wanted to strike a man off soon as his coat tails crossed the border, while some appeared to think a man should send in an affidavit that he was never coming back to town before his name should be obliterated. About eleven o'clock the board was galloping through the "K" column at a winning gait when the word "Knowles" was struck. No one seemed to know much of the family history of this particular son of Adam, so reference to the registry list was ordered. Three of the board tackled the list and looked; then they partook of refreshment and looked again; then they had in internecine quarrel—and looked again; then the other two members looked; then the town clerk looked; then an outsider looked and discovered that the search was being prosecuted in the 1890 list of the letter "N." Mr. Knowles was finally found under his proper caption but fifteen minutes had gone forever.

The "M" column was a source of great tribulation and objurgation but when the perennial "Smith's" were reached, the misery of the board reached its lowest depths. The famous "John" was finally placed in his several proper places—but it is well to draw the mantle of silence over the cursory remarks made by the board while doing it. This was the last hard struggle, as the letter "W" was finished with only one wrong man killed. Just before 12 o'clock the president signed the completed lists amid the heartiest kinds of "amen." The two Frenchmen were invited to go home, which they did with lingering reluctance, evidently fearing that "mon cher amie Monsieur Lacy" might be hanged without their knowledge. Thus passes into history the makeup of the general and district voting lists of Burrillville for the year 1893.

Saturday Night's Rally
November 6, 1896

Never was a man welcomed to Burrillville in a more enthusiastic manner than was Congressman-elect Adin B. Capron last Saturday evening. It was truly a princely reception, and in it the citizens may well take pride. The cause for the outburst was the Republican rally, and while notice was somewhat brief, each citizen seemed to vie with his neighbor in making the affair a success.

Shortly after 7 o'clock the Pascoag Brass Band marched down Main Street to the station where the people had begun to gather to await the arrival of the 7:35 train upon which Mr. Capron and Mr. Stokes, the speakers of the evening, were expected to arrive. Just before the train came in, the gathering was seen to be far too large to be accommodated in Music Hall, and it was decided to have the rally in Fountain Square that all might be enabled to hear. Just then, the train whistled, and the crowd turned toward the track expecting to see the glimmer of the headlight. But they saw it not, for when the whistle sounded, the train was still at Carson's Grove. Engineer Drury was aware there was to be a celebration and he was anxious to assist a little. He slackened the speed of his train and whistled not little short toots but one long blast that awoke the echoes for miles around. As the train came in, the band commenced playing patriotic airs, and the crowd gave vent to their feeling by prolonged cheers. Every part of Depot Square was illumined by red fire, and as the procession marched up toward Herald Square such a fusillade of rockets and Roman candles was sent up from J. T. Fiske's place as to make the heavens seem filled with shooting stars.

The procession halted in Herald Square and cheered long and loud and then marched to Fountain Square, the entire length of Main Street being brilliantly illumined with colored fire. Arriving at the Square the speakers, town officials, and several others were escorted to the upper plaza of Sayles Hall from which addresses were delivered. Both speakers were heartily applauded by the audience at frequent intervals. The audience numbered more than 2000 and each person listened to the speakers with an attentiveness that was pleasing to see. The band rendered a number of selections during the evening. The demonstration was by far the largest and most enthusiastic ever held in town.

Alvah Mowry, Ex-Town Clerk
March 6, 1896

Burrillville has lost one of her oldest and most beloved citizens in the death of Alvah Mowry who died Sunday night aged 79 years and 3 days. He was the son of Benjamin and Alcy (Smith) Mowry, was born in Burrillville, and had always made his home here. His early life was spent on a farm, and at the age of 18 he left the farm and worked a number of years at his trade of shoemaking. In 1854, he was elected town clerk, which office he held for thirty-six years. In 1843, he married Abby, daughter of John Whipple of Burrillville, who died February 19, 1891. They had no children.

Mr. Mowry's father was the first town treasurer of Burrillville, having been elected to that office immediately after that town was set off from Glocester. He had seven brothers and two sisters, two of whom, David and Dennis, survive him. During Mr. Mowry's long service as town clerk, he made lots of friends. He was ever kind, courteous and obliging to all, and of him naught but good can be said. Thirty-six years is an unusual length of time for one person to hold an elective office, and it illustrates how firm a hold the deceased had upon the affections of the citizens of the town. Funeral services were held from the Berean Baptist Church Wednesday at one o'clock, and were attended by a large number of relatives and friends. Interment was at Riverside Cemetery.

Electric Lights for Harrisville
January 12, 1902

The operating committee of the Pascoag Fire District believe that it would be expedient to extend the lighting system to Harrisville. At the last annual meeting, the voters in the district left the matter in the hands of the committee to be disposed of, and it is an assured fact that the metropolis of Northwestern Rhode Island will soon be shedding light in a practical manner upon her smaller sister.

During the past few weeks, Superintendent Crosbie has been diligently engaged in making inquiries among the residents of Harrisville, and the result of his labor has been most gratifying. Many of the progressive citizens including Ernest W. Tinkham, John S. Walling, William Inman, and others are preparing to wire their residences, and the leading business houses have declared in favor of the lights. There is at present little indication that the street lights will be installed, but many predict that the time is not far distant when arc lights will be erected as in Pascoag.

Sanatorium Inspected
November 20, 1903

Wednesday morning at 9:35 o'clock a special train of four cars bearing the Governor of the State, members of the Legislature, State officials, physicians, members of the Commission appointed to erect the new Sanatorium, and others, left Providence enroute for this town on a trip of inspection of the State Sanatorium now in course of construction at Wallum Pond. The special stopped at Pascoag, where several more joined the party, and the trip over the extension was commenced, the destination being reached shortly before 11 o'clock.

One Hundred Years Ago in Burrillville by Patricia A. Mehrtens

For the majority of the members of the party, it was their first ride by rail through the northwestern corner of the state, and was in itself a decided novelty. Upon leaving the cars, the party proceeded on foot to the new buildings, which were thoroughly inspected inside and out in a critical manner. The grounds and the adjacent shores of the lake were traversed, and the admirable location received most favorable comment. The visitors seemed pleased with the progress which has been made on the construction and found little to criticize. The buildings are all covered in, and everything is nearly in shape for winter, so that when snow comes it will interfere but little with the progress of the work. Several of the rooms are plastered, and work is being pushed on the heating apparatus so that more can be done in that line.

At 12 o'clock lunch was served by Lyman of Providence in the dining room of the institution, which had been tastefully trimmed with evergreen for the occasion. The lunch was nicely served and was enjoyed with a zest, for the bracing air of Wallum Pond had whetted the appetites of all to almost a ravenous degree. Just previous to the lunch, Governor Garvin was introduced by Chairman Potter of the Commission, and spoke briefly on the need for an institution of this kind in our state. He was followed by Rev. J. J. Woolley of Pawtucket who spoke along the same lines. After lunch, the visitors whiled away the time until the hour of departure, by further inspection of the grounds and buildings, or gathered in groups and discussed weather, politics and what not.

At 2:30 o'clock the special train, which had been backed up from Pascoag, started on the return trip, proceeding with care over the extension and making an express trip to Providence from Pascoag stopping at only a few stations. Considering the raw, cold air of the November day, it was a trip enjoyed thoroughly by all, and will long be remembered by the participants.

June Town Meeting
June 9, 1905

Since the year 1806 when Burrillville was first incorporated as a town, town elections have made their annual appearance, and each has brought its separate feuds and surprises. The first town election was held at the Russell Aldrich farm about a mile above Harrisville on the Round Top road in 1806, and Mr. Aldrich is said to have given $50 to the town for having the election for town officers held at his farm with the right to sell the voters cider, gingerbread, and such other vote-tempting condiments as he chose. Those were the good old days when the coming voters gathered with the fathers and battled with the ball and bat or in other athletic contests, while their daddies battled with party fealty to do their opponents. The town now owns an apology for a town house, and has its four voting districts. Proceedings appear a bit more dignified. There are those who still sell more refreshments on election day than they do on other days, and the willing candidate is as ready as ever to pay for treats and the expenses of getting the voters to their respective polling places. How much this treating has to do with results, it is hard to say.

As the election day this year dawned clear and mild, there was an unusual chance to get the vote well out. The Republicans captured half the school committee positions, the town sergeant and five of the seven councilmen, while the Democrats secured the first three offices, the three assessors of taxes, overseer of poor, and one member of the school committee with the two remaining councilmen. The Democrats may really be said to be the victors, for they have the majority of the positions and those that are very important. On the other hand, the Republican councilmen, being in a good majority and unusually able and well-posted men of affairs, will be very apt to make their Democratic brother officers do their full duty to the best advantage of the town, for it must be remembered that the town council is really the board of censure and removal of all town officers in the absence of town meetings. This fact makes the honors nearly even, and while a few Republicans may have lost the party votes by the introduction of the acts for a new voting district, and the election of tax assessors for three years, yet those were both needed improvements and will not hurt the party in the years to come.

State Census for 1905
October 20, 1905

The state census for 1905 taken last June, in part shows that Burrillville had a population of 7425 showing a gain of 1108 over the previous Federal returns of 1900. There are but three towns in the state showing a greater population, while there are nine that have lost in the number of its inhabitants since the last census returns. As the area of our town has in round numbers 72 square miles of territory, it shows it averages over 100 to the

One Hundred Years Ago in Burrillville by Patricia A. Mehrtens

square mile. For a town starting out its corporate life under as unfavorable surroundings as encompassed our town at the time of its taking upon itself the independent control of its own affairs, it has met with a success in its increase of population and its accumulation of wealth, that gives us no occasions for regret.

Being twenty miles distant from tide-water with no market for our produce, timber, etc. nearer than Providence, it was a long haul for the ox teams of that period to make the journey to market and return with freight each way. The custom was to start with their teams at sunset, arriving at Providence in the morning, care for their teams—frequently three yoke of oxen, or one yoke of oxen and three yokes of partially broken steers—deliver their freight and load for the return trip, starting again at sunset and arriving home in the morning. To give some idea of the class of goods that went to Providence and the class brought back to the town, the testimony of a witness in a suit between a party and the town as defendant would be as explicit as any language one could use today. The witness was asked what kind of freight was carried over a certain road in the town. The answer was principally hoop-poles. What kind of freight was teamed from Providence over this certain road in Burrillville? Answer: Principally codfish and West India rum.

While Burrillville was the laughing stock for the people of other towns of the state for many years, the conditions are changed today. With a sparse population and no wealth, but land with plenty of rocks, our town started out one hundred years ago next October in the race for existence fully realizing that to the strongest the victory belonged. Today we are far ahead in population and accumulated wealth of the other towns that have had a much longer corporate existence. Our facilities for business enterprises are equal to any town in the state. We have frequent and rapid communication by steam and electric roads with the seaports on the Atlantic, also with the commercial West. The telephone is not only connected with business offices but with many private residences. Seventeen manufacturing establishments are in full operation, yet the water power is not wholly utilized.

The outlook for the future was never brighter. With a healthy climate, excellent water and the low cost of living, surely the future ought to more fully develop our yet undeveloped resources that should redown to the interest of those who wish for the advancement of our town in its business prosperity and good citizenship. Francis M. Wood.

One Hundred Years Ago in Burrillville by Patricia A. Mehrtens

SPORTS

Rooster Fighting on a Sunday
May 13, 1881

Last Sunday was a fine day, and one which should have encouraged all men to abstain from wicked and worldly pursuits and devote wholly to religious service. But the devil goeth about like a roaring lion. He entered into a young man's heart about two or three o'clock Sunday and induced him to seize and capture a rooster from its home on the street which runneth out of Pascoag in the direction of Chepachet, and carry said biped to the bluff which is easterly of the Main Street, Pascoag.

Now others with no more fear of doing wrong than is possessed by the average mortal when he is "elevated" with "benzine" had captured a bird of similar species. When they were placed contiguous to each other, behold they did fight and claw each other in a terrific manner. Many were those who were in attendance at this contest, and several there were who did seek for bets on the bird they had staked their hopes upon. All of which is contrary to the law of the State, the moral law and, we have a faint hope, the law of Burrillville. It is perhaps needless to add that most of those present at this interesting and elevating entertainment were thoroughly warmed up with "bug juice" which must have been purchased the preceding day, for, verily there is none sold on the Sabbath day in Burrillville. We omit the names of the owners of the roosters, the referees and the betters, first, because we have no positive information as to who they were and second, because the affair is being investigated by a Pascoag detective.

Pascoag Trotting Park
1885

July 31, 1885 - Considerable interest seems to be

awakened recently in trying the speed of some of our fast horses, and the old half mile track between Pascoag and Chepachet is to undergo repairs. A fund of over $60 has already been subscribed for this purpose, and it is expected that sufficient will be raised to put the track in pretty fair shape. We have not as yet learned of any matches between horses being made, but several are talked of. Several pretty good steppers are owned in the town, and if not able to reduce the lowest mile record, considerable sport is anticipated.

August 21, 1885 - To lovers of horse flesh and what pertains thereto, a chance was given for fun in the several brushes taking place last Saturday afternoon at the half-mile track. The largest number of teams and people including many ladies were on the grounds last Saturday than at any time before this season. The first brush was expected between Ernest W. Tinkham's black mare and a gray stallion from Webster, but Tillinghast did not arrive with his horse. Not willing to get skunked, a race was arranged between Tinkham's horse and Seneca Smith's mare. The last named mare won the half-mile heat in 1:31 1/2. Mr. Everett B. Sherman was asked if he would take a round, and he promptly said yes. The horse of Sherman's was a blooded one but nothing was known of its capabilities as a trotter. When he pulled away in fine style without a skip or a break from Tinkham's mare, the crowd present was surprised. The half mile was made easily in 1:31 1/2. A second heat was trotted with a similar result, Sherman's horse reducing the time three seconds and appeared to do it very easily.

September 4, 1885 - Considerable sport was enjoyed at the track last Saturday by about three hundred people in witnessing scrimmages between various horses. The first spurt was between Dr. Wilcox's bay mare and Pliny Harriman's mare. After the usual amount of scoring "go" was heard, the bay mare came out best. No time given. Two heats were next trotted between a chestnut mare owned in Harrisville and a bay mare owned by C. Tillinghast of Webster. Tillinghast's mare won the first heat in 3:2 3/4 seconds. The second heat was also won by the mare from Webster, time 3:00 3/4. The next on the program was a bout between the bay mare of Dr. Wilcox's, L. E. Miller's sorrel horse, and Pliny Harriman's horse, driven by Fred White. Only one heat was trotted and it was easily won by Doctor Wilcox's mare in 3:15. Fred White was thrown from his carriage by the axle breaking but escaped with only a few scratches.

One Hundred Years Ago in Burrillville by Patricia A. Mehrtens

Local Baseball Teams
September 17, 1886

Last year, the most interest in any sport manifested itself in trials of speed at the half-mile track of horses owned mostly by native residents. There was more or less skirmishing and considerably more talk than downright square trials. The same feeling is noticeably exhibited this season in baseball, namely, Harrisvilles vs. Pascoags, and it seems a great deal like boys' play. It is perfectly natural and proper that Harrisville people should take a more lively and absorbing interest in the welfare of the Harrisville club, and the same of Pascoag people and the Pascoag club. This should not, however, develop into any other feelings than friendly rivalry. So much betting and putting up money to play for, is a species of gambling, and those that indulge in it stand on a lower plane, morally, than they should, for all such things tend to degrade rather than elevate.

The Pascoag team is a fine team and all its members save Stafford and Beauregard have lived here for years. The Harrisville team is also a strong team and has for members several phenomenally reliable players, nearly all of whom work in the Harrisville mill. But many of them have been of the migrating kind having been attracted here because of the great interest in baseball, as well as good pecuniary situations proffered them. The ultimatum now desired by the people is to see a game of ball played between these two clubs, and when one club says they have no time to play they say this, "We are afraid." The idea of going to Providence to play is foolish. When that is done many people who have interested themselves in the two clubs will have no more to do with them. So much interest is now centered on the two teams that a series of games between them would draw crowds and help towards the expense of maintaining them. Put foolishness aside and play ball. Striker up.

A Grand Regatta
September 9, 1887

A boat race is to come off tomorrow that will interest many who like a good time at the Harrisville Pond at Harrisville. A purse of $15 divided into the prizes of $7, $5 and $3 is offered by the Regatta Association. There are at the present time ten entrees to compete for the prizes, and no doubt each boat will be put in the best shape possible and each oarsman do the best to take first prize. The following is a list of those entering the race,

One Hundred Years Ago in Burrillville by Patricia A. Mehrtens

also the names of the shells: John McGinnis - J. eye C. William Pierce - I No. Ferdinand Thornton - Water Lilly. Eli Baker - River Belle. Charles Griffin - Never Tired. Elias Humes - Never Sink. Samuel McCortney - Slippery. John Crotts - Dolphin. William Ryan - Hard to Beat. James McCormick - Thistle.

The course is from the dam, up stream around a stake boat and return, a distance of about one half mile. The start will be made promptly at one o'clock in the afternoon in season. If the wind is good, those attending this the greatest regatta match ever held in town may have plenty of time to witness other amusements of the day. Edgar A. Mathewson and James Murphy are the referees.

Petition Found on Highway
November 11, 1887

The following petition was found in the highway near Elisha Mathewson's this morning and as the matters referred to require immediate attendance, I forward it to the *Burrillville Gazette* so it may be presented immediately where it will do the most good. ie: To his Excellency Honest John W. Davis, Governor, Captain, General, Commander in Chief, etc., etc., etc.

We are residents of Sucker Brook running from Sucker Pond in Burrillville to Spachet and by reason of the Damming of said brook by the Bloated Aristocrats, otherwise called manufacturers, we are without water. Some of us who have tails to shed are prepared to shed them now, but are unable to do so because of the severe drought in our extremities. Others of us have come to a realizing sense of that sensation of a fish out of water, and we are all in fact in a very dry, if not tight place. The remedy is that the Superintendent of Dams forthwith proceed and remove the dam above us like Georgiaville or run a 1/4 inch pipe round said dam to supply us with water. Should you adopt the pipe, we would suggest that a very fine strainer be placed over the end in the pond to prevent the Burrillville democracy from coming through the hole, not on account of the clogging the pipe, (as there is not enough of them for that), but simply because we don't want their company. We would further suggest that Judge Bradley be appointed Consulting Engineer as we see by the returns that he has gone out of the *Fostering* business and is a gentleman at large with plenty of spare time—and as in duty bound will ever, pray.

Signed: Whale, Bass, Pickerel, Kiver, Sucker, Frog, Tadpole, Minnow. Burrillville & Spachet, Nov. '87.

One Hundred Years Ago in Burrillville by Patricia A. Mehrtens

Cockfight near Joe Mowry's
February 22, 1889

Between three and four hundred gathered near the Massachusetts line last Sunday to witness a day of cock fighting. It was a great day for the sports, and a large number of fights took place. Nearly every battle taking place was a battle to the death, some being fought in less time than others. One battle between two evenly matched gamesters took three quarters of a hour to settle who was cock of the walk. The story was first set afloat that the fight would take place in Massachusetts, but this was simply a guy to throw the officers and people here off their guard. The report was in circulation that one of our officers was present at the fight and bet on the battles. But this report we believe unfounded, as it was not verified by asking several who were present if this was so. They avowed they saw no Burrillville officer there. Betting ran rampant, sports being plenty from Waterford, Whitinsville, Southbridge and this place, and a large amount of money changed hands. Probably a dozen battles took place between cocks and a regular sporting day was had. We are unable to give the details of the battles as we were not present, therefore our readers must excuse us. But if an invitation is extended to the next one so we can go, it shall be written up in lurid colors giving all the names of the cock owners and their cocks taking part in the show.

Horse Racing at the Trotting Park
July 12, 1889

Last Saturday, no little sport was had at the Trotting Park occasioned by a race, best three in five, between a Whitinsville horse owned by Daniel Kennedy, a Chepachet horse owned by Louis Houghton, Seneca Smith's horse of Mapleville, and Hugh McCaffrey's of Uxbridge. The judges were Warren Potter, Jerry Sheldon of Chepachet, and Oscar Brown of Burrillville. The winner was to have thirty bushels of oats and the second best twenty bushels, thus it was called an "Oat Race." An entry fee of $5 was charged. The day was fine and the track never was in better condition for trotting. Considerable enthusiasm among the crowd was noticeable and each one wished their favorite would win.

Prince was assigned the pole, Charlie second, Lewis third, and Frank Fourth. At 3:45 the excitement began, and the quartet was off. The first heat was won by the white gelding of

Chepachet in 2.51 1/4, which was the fastest time made during the race. The second heat was taken in 2.53, the third in 2.58 1/4, and the fourth in 2.58 1/2, by Prince, the Whitinsville gelding driven by Dr. Robert Wilcox, who showed himself quite a horseman and an excellent handler. The Chepachet horse came in first the first heat and second in others, and was awarded the second prize, twenty bushels of oats. The Doctor, of course, getting the first prize, thirty bushels.

There were numerous teams at the Park and a good attendance, and an interesting contest was had. Some labor has been done on the track and the course is not to be sneezed at. After the regular race, several tried the mettle of their horses in friendly contests much to the amusement of the owners of the horses and spectators. Many hope this is but the beginning of more contests in horse flesh, as a little excitement and amusement is beneficial to those participating. Dr. Wilcox is said to have the leading spirit in getting up the oat race and is to be congratulated upon its entire success under his management.

Complaint about Baseball Players
October 11, 1889

The young men of this town had another ball game October 5th and as usual they had a night of it. It disgraces this place every time there is a ball game. The whole night is passed in drinking and fighting, and it is not safe to be out after dark. If there is an officer in this town, it is a shame and a disgrace for him to allow such wretched drunkards on the street and not make a move to stop it. This swearing and fighting resembles "Hell on Earth." These little rum hells—for they are nothing but that—sell and fill these young men with rum till they are no longer men but wild beasts. I am afraid that God in His just anger will crush them out.

Why are they allowed to behave so? Has no one authority sufficient to put a stop to this nuisance? Is the town too poor to have an officer who will do his duty? I think it would be an improvement. Oh, the misery and destruction of this place. The poor Christian people have to suffer for this hideous evil. We cannot have peace even in our houses, but must be kept awake all night on their account. I don't think there is another little place in the United States that conducts itself as this does, and no authority to stop it. Signed: A Plaint from a Resident of Main Street, Pascoag.

One Hundred Years Ago in Burrillville by Patricia A. Mehrtens

Pascoag Driving Park
1890

May 9, 1890 - More life and animation seems to attract itself to the Driving Park this spring than for several years past. Mr. Sheldon at one time had a controlling interest, but now Mr. D. C. Remington, Jr., has the largest number of shares. A strip of land has been purchased on the opposite side from the judges stand, and the park will be enlarged and track widened. It is intended to place the judges stand on this side where the track will be wide enough to give plenty of room for scoring. C. T. Brigg, the photographer, has leased the house and barn located at the park and has a general oversight of the premises. Tickets at $5 each are issued giving the holder the use of the track during the season for training of horses. A fence is to be erected in the near future, and other improvements will follow as soon as the way is made clear for them. The center of the park should be leveled and laid out for baseball. With a grandstand and the best half mile track in Rhode Island, no better place could be had for holding a cattle fair.

August 22, 1890 - The Park presented an animated scene last Saturday, the attendance being nearly 500. The waits between the heats were very tiresome, especially to those who had no place to sit unless improving mother earth for a seat as many did. Those having teams are fortunate in two ways, of riding over instead of walking, and of having a seat after getting there. The knoll opposite the judges stand is a very nice place for teams to stand for the occupants to see the races, and it would be an elegant place to build a grandstand. We believe it would be much appreciated and patronized if one was built. Many would be glad to pay a nickel or even a dime to have a seat during the afternoon. Another thing much needed is a water cart to sprinkle the track, as the dust was so dense at times as to obscure the horses. A stranger made a barrel answer for a stand and sold chances on various horses, but he was told to stop business as it was not allowed on the grounds. Dolbeare had Walter Smith and another clerk to help him at his booth and they were busy most of the afternoon selling light drinks, candy and cigars.

Allum Pond Cockfight
March 7, 1890

A cockfight or rather several cockfights came off in the

Allum Pond region last Sunday, and was better attended than most of the churches. It was not known until late Saturday night just where the pit would be made, and many who were anxious to see the fun did not go to bed that night for fear the tide would move without them. As early as five o'clock Sunday morning, some of the village residents were awakened by the heavy rumbling of carriages over the frozen ground, containing parties bound for the scene of action. The objective point was close to the residence of John Riley, and during the forenoon in the vicinity of 200 assembled. The fight was known of in Woonsocket, Millville, Uxbridge, Whitinsville and other places among the sporting men, with teams from these places were present. Laurel Hill had representatives present, and also a cock for fighting, and but few villages were unrepresented.

Five fights or more occurred, and the crowd became very enthusiastic not only with the sport but by imbibing something to keep them warm. Sandwiches were plenty, and no one needed to go hungry who had any money. Considerable betting on the various cocks was indulged in, and while some lost, others won, of course. It is said one Pascoag man made a couple of hundred dollars on bets. The advent of Donahue with his half breed caused some derision, but when his bird won two fights, the laugh was the other way. A more profane and vulgar crowd it would be hard to get together, but people liking this kind of amusement are most generally of that stripe.

Baseball Meeting
April 24, 1891

A meeting was held at the Pascoag Hotel Thursday evening to discuss baseball matters. There was not a large number present, but those were very enthusiastic. At a previous meeting, papers had been drawn up and given to individuals to circulate for money subscriptions. For the short time they had been in circulation, the result was considered to be very satisfactory indeed, $90 being the result. A new element in baseball has sprung up since 1889, and those present included only a few of the old members of the Association. No doubt, with the new timber and the help which the old members will accord the move, a respectable team may be run. The sentiment seemed to run an inexpensive team and to have more games at home than when the state league was in existence in '89.

There are plenty of good clubs in the edge of Massachusetts and Rhode Island with which dates can be made.

In 1888 when an inexpensive club was run, the interest in the games was much greater than in '89. This can be accounted for by several reasons. The first of the season in 1889, it rained several Saturdays when games were scheduled for Pascoag, and thus three weeks would elapse between games. By this, people lost their interest. A moderately expensive team can be run and not be a burden to those willing to join the association to make backing for the club.

The ground is in better condition than ever before. The grandstand, which was erected in 1889, is non est as all such things go to ruin when not cared for. The wire screening which prevented the ball at first base from going into the swamp cannot be found. It is conjectured that someone used it to help build a hen coop. The bat, mask and chest protector have been used up by local aspirants, and a new lot of material will be a necessity. New uniforms are needed, too. It was voted to meet next Monday evening at the rooms of the Pascoag T. A. & L. Association on Sayles Avenue to complete arrangements.

July Fourth Amusements
June 26, 1891

People of this town surely have a chance to spend their money according to their taste on July fourth. The New York & New England gives two very cheap excursions on that day; one to Boston, round trip $1; one to Providence round, trip 75 cents. The Harrisville Athletic Association gives a picnic, to which all will be welcomed—beside the railroad track a little out of Harrisville. A game of baseball is on the list of amusements as well as dancing. A clam dinner will be served. Wheelbarrow races and other sports will fill in a day of pleasure. At the baseball grounds, two games of ball can be seen, one in the forenoon and one in the afternoon at 3:30. The team to play is a good trade team from Boston, who have been putting up a good game. Refreshments will be sold on the grounds, and lovers of baseball can have a day of it. The admission is only 15 cents to each game.

At the Driving Park, Dolbeare has arranged for a lot of fun in the forenoon by giving various sports, and will furnish a bang-up clam dinner with all the fixings. Warner, who was stated would superintend the bake, has given it up, and it will be in charge of John Clayton. If the bakes and dinners he has been giving at Page's Island is any criterion, the dinner will not suffer a particle by the change, but on the other hand be better. In fact, he has been in the business since camping out with his friends, and those partaking of his bakes say they are delicious. He will do his best, and with Dolbeare's aid there will be plenty to eat. Horse racing in the afternoon is creating considerable interest, especially the colt race by Burrillville colts.

The barge of Moore's will leave Pascoag square at 10 o'clock in the morning in season for the sports and dinner. It will leave again at 12:30 p.m. The Methodist Society will give a bake in Sayles' Grove, which is a convenient and pleasant place. Most of the stores will close all day.

That Fish
April 23, 1892

As the *Herald* reporter was going the rounds for news Thursday morning, he called on R. A. Buxton for an item or two. Whether his face wore too dull an expression to indicate having found news plenty or prompted more from thoughts of sympathy for the profession we do not know, but suffice to say that Mrs. Buxton determined to visit the Clear River back of the shoddy mill. With this estimable lady, to determine is to act, so we next saw her by the river's bank gazing intently at a large fish that was sporting in one of the pools of water left by the raising of the flash boards at the dam. Suddenly she reached forth and grasped the finny creature by its tail. He was her's!—no, he slipped through her fingers and dropped again into the stream. Nothing daunted, Mrs. Buxton rushed forward and again seized the fish, this time securing him in her apron. She came to the house and joyfully deposited her prize in a large bread pan. Water was brought, and the fish straightened himself, much to the delight of the sightseers who found him to be a large river sucker measuring over twenty-one inches in length. Mr. Buxton remarked that his wife should do the fishing hereafter.

Excitement in Burrillville
June 1, 1894

The officers of the S.P.C.A. spoiled the fun of a large body of sports Wednesday when they raided a cock fight in the woods near the Elisha Bartlett place in Burrillville near Ironstone and Slatersville They captured two birds, eleven men, a large quantity of sandwiches and liquor and twelve teams. Deputy Sheriff Inman of Burrillville received news of the affairs last week and notified prosecuting officer Nickerson of the society.

Together they made the arrangements. Wednesday, Officer Nickerson of Providence, Constable Place and Town Sergeant Green of Slatersville, Deputy Sheriff Inman, Town Sergeant Fairfield, and Constable Mowry of Burrillville, Constable Smith of Johnston, Agent Brown and Constable Newton of Woonsocket made a descent on the men catching them in the act.

About 75 men were gathered around the birds when the officers arrived, and for a little while there was a lively time. A number of the men showed a disposition to fight, and it was necessary for the officers to fire their revolvers in the air to intimidate them. Eleven men were captured, and with the prisoners handcuffed together and the wagons abandoned by the fleeing men in tow, the officers started for Harrisville where the prisoners who hailed from Uxbridge, Blackstone, Woonsocket and Slatersville, were deposited in the lockup.

Later in the day they were arraigned. Several pleaded guilty and were fined $10 and costs while the others were bound over. The birds came from Pascoag and Blackstone. All afternoon livery stable men were calling for the captured teams and Burrillville had more excitement than it has had before for years. The crowd was well prepared for a stay, as one wagon contained quantities of sandwiches, seven kegs of beer, bottles of whiskey and other liquors.

Pugilistic Contest at Herring Pond
September 28, 1896

Yesterday morning a party of sports from Worcester arrived in town on the 10 o'clock train from Woonsocket, and word was immediately disseminated that there was to be a pugilistic contest in the vicinity of Herring Pond. This intelligence caused the Worcester party to be augmented by the sporting fraternity of this place. By one o'clock, between one and two hundred had gathered to witness the fight. The place selected for the bout was on the Cherry Farm between Harrisville and Herring Pond on the road leading to the Ira Bishop place. It was a secluded spot, and so safe from molestation was the spot considered that a ring was built and arrangements made to have the contest *a la mode*. After the preliminaries were completed, it was found that the gloves had been left behind, and a team was sent post haste to Woonsocket to procure those of the necessary accouterments.

This delay was fatal to the sportsmen, for while the messenger was on his way, Officer Fairfield having learned of the affair was on his way to the Cherry Farm and arrived before the passenger returned. He promptly ordered the ring leveled down and the fighters and the spectators to disperse. Both of these orders were obeyed with a promptness that showed that none of those present cared to become personally acquainted with the working of Rhode Island law. Officer Fairfield remained on the grounds until all semblance of a fighting arena was gone, and the party had agreed to go over the line into Massachusetts to settle the bout.

Mr. Fairfield deserves to be commended for his prompt action in this matter. If out-of-town parties think there is no danger of being molested in Burrillville no matter how flagrant a breach of the law is attempted, this will teach them differently. It is earnestly hoped the lesson will be remembered. The coming into town in broad daylight and advertising a prize fight and then arranging to pull it off at midday almost within gunshot of a village, shows a boldness seldom seen in these parts. Burrillville doesn't want and, what is more, won't have such visitors. It is reported the fighters afterwards met and finished the fight in three rounds. The smaller man easily winning the $800 purse.

Sunday Baseball Playing
August 17, 1900

The Sunday ball player after just a year's sleep has again made his appearance in the villages and caused unfavorable comments from both press and the public. The games were commenced in Harrisville about a month ago, and at first were conducted as orderly as could be expected. Soon after the Pascoag association began to play on the first day of the week, but as soon as they learned of the objections among the larger portion of the citizens in the lower villages, they decided to drop the matter at once. The game last Sunday is the last the Pascoag men will play. The sport on Sunday, no matter how conducted, is unlawful and as it has been conducted, is nothing less than a nuisance.

The citizens in Glendale and Nasonville complain that their lives are jeopardized by racing horses and their peace disturbed from early evening until late at night by so called "hoodlums" who go yelling through the villages. Nor is this the worst or most objectionable feature. If the game is started early in the afternoon, the visitors are able to leave town on the early evening train. But in instances where the game is not begun until 4 o'clock or later, the sun throws its last rays upon an unfinished contest. The gangs of players begin to arrive soon after dinner and congregate along the streets and about the saloons until the game is called. During the contests, which in many cases are attended by ladies and children, profane language and obscene talk is freely indulged in and the performance is anything but edifying. The loud cheering and yelling disturbs those who reside nearby and is heard a long distance. After the games have been finished, the crowd pours into the public streets and congregates along the highways. They spend the evening and oftimes a large part of the night lounging about, making unpleasant remarks and in a general way conduct themselves as they would not dare do in their own town.

Only a short time ago, the barge in which the crowd came stood in front of a saloon on Chapel Street, Harrisville, until a late hour. The visitors were scattered about and even came into the dooryards of some of the homes and became so obnoxious they were ordered out. The games are not conducted by the youths of the town but are fostered and played for the personal benefit of the manager who goes out of the village and virtually hires two nines to come in, he realizing on the gate receipts. None of the players have anything at stake. It is merely a matter of dollars and cents whether they win or lose and the disgrace is dumped upon the village.

The matter has been going from bad to worse, and the promoters have defiantly stated that the games would be continued. Last Sunday afternoon, a citizen was told point blank the games would be played in spite of anything that could be done. The larger part of the residents of the town appear to be unanimous in quelling the nuisance. Acting under legal advice, a complaint will be lodged and warrants issued against all the players who take part in the game advertised for next Sunday.

Old Time Fishing
June 26, 1903

"No," said an old resident of this town the other day, "we don't have such fishing nowadays as we used to. I well remember a haul of fish made over forty years ago in Cook's Pond which has never since been equaled. "Cook's Pond, you know, was at the head of the present Pascoag Reservoir. A saw mill was located there years ago before the present reservoir was built. Hearing that Cook's Pond was low, three Pascoag men went up there to try their luck fishing. They carried two strings on which to bring back their finny spoils. They found the water very low, and seeing no one to interfere, they placed a net over the end of the flume and raised the gates expecting to get their net full of fish. Fish, however, have a tendency to swim against the current instead of with it, and not a one did they get.

"After the pond had been drawn down as low as possible, they noticed considerable commotion in the shallow water and the mud, and investigation showed that the bed of the pond was literally alive with fish. The two strings which they had taken to bring home their spoils were woefully inadequate for the purpose. Two of the men remained at the pond, and the third went back to Pascoag and secured a lumber wagon. When he returned, the wagon body was filled until there was not room for a single more fish, and the wagon had sideboards of generous height, too. It is unnecessary to say that when the three men returned to Pascoag with their load there was considerable excitement caused by the unusual sight of a wagon load of fish. Almost everybody in Pascoag shared in the catch, and fish dinners were the order of things in about every family for a day or two." "This story," said the old inhabitant, "is strictly true and could be proven by a number of old timers who well remember the great haul."

SALOONS, ETC.

Gazza "Bipeds"
January 28, 1881

Three "featherless bipeds" from Gazza, slightly stimulated by the—the weather, tried to procure a team at Kingsley's stable at Harrisville Sunday. Upon the hostler, a man by the name of Williams, refusing them, they attacked him in a savage manner, knocking him down, and causing him to feel anything but happy. They then started towards Pascoag, hammering on doors and performing several other like capers, since which time they have not appeared to the public. Williams went for an officer to arrest his assaulters, but for some reason he failed in his quest, and there have been no arrests.

Liquor Seizure in Harrisville
September 9, 1887

Although considerable liquor has been brought into town in the day time and not particularly under cover, much has been brought here in the dead of night upon teams hailing from different localities. One of these teams, owned by Fred Barrett of Millville, Massachusetts, perhaps did the largest business of any of this kind. The *modus operandi* has been for Mr. Barrett to drive up here during the day, interview the liquor dealers, and take orders from them for the different kinds of beer, ale and hard stuff wanted. He then returns home, puts up the orders, loads up and, in the evening under the cover of darkness, starts from Millville to deliver the illegal stuff. This way of conducting business has been carried on for some time and has continually increased.

Officers Inman and Mowry, getting on to the racket, concluded they would try their hands in the business. As they were green at it, they delivered the wet goods all at one place instead of to the parties expecting them, contrary to the wishes of the drivers of the two loaded teams. In order to do this, they employed some cunning and strategy. Being pretty certain Tuesday night the beer team would invade the town, the two valiant, reliable and daring officers started down the road to meet them. The officers were not mistaken in their surmise, for after waiting some little time in ambush, patience was rewarded by a two horse team and a one horse team heaving in sight, each with a driver on the box.

The two officers cautiously followed in the wake of the two teams and saw the drivers deliver the stuff to a few parties on the way to Harrisville. A suspicious looking jug was left at the house of a good temperance man in the edge of the town, but of course nobody knows what was in it. When Harrisville was reached, the clock on the new Universalist Church said 11:30 p.m. The officers pounced upon the drivers of the teams and conducted them to the little jail by the Harrisville Railroad Station, and locked them up.

Thomas Smith, the proprietor of the Harrisville Hotel, was routed up. The wagons after being unloaded were drawn to the hotel barn by the horses attached. Inman now asked Smith if he would not help take samples and label the stuff seized for analysis, even hinting that he (Smith) was used to such business and would be a great help. It seems that Inman's flattery worked upon the susceptible nature of Smith to the extent of his shouldering a three-quarter inch bit and starting for the scene of deluge, as it proved to be upon tapping some of the large beer barrels. The sampling was satisfactorily done, and the demijon's labeled.

The liquor seized consisted of four barrels of Jones' XXX ale, three kegs of lager beer, and eight jugs of intoxicating liquors of various kinds such as rum, brandy, whiskey, gin, etc. When the liquor had been stowed away in the lockup, the constables retired to their domiciles and rested serenely until morning, probably dreaming of more conquests in the future. Mixing liquors did not seem to effect the officers who came into court Wednesday straight and smiling with not even a smell of liquor about them. Judge Harris was sent for, and came to Harrisville on the morning train Wednesday. Fred Barrett, the owner of the confiscated property, made his appearance by team a little earlier.

On the arrival of Judge Harris, the two drivers of hard stuff were arraigned. Each pleaded guilty of transporting liquor contrary to law, and each was fined $20 and $3.80 costs making $47.60. This amount was promptly paid by their employer, Mr. Barrett, who came with plenty of the filthy lucre prepared for just such an emergency, much to the relief of the men on trial. Both are young men between 30 and 40 years of age. One relieved his mind by saying he should give up his job immediately as he didn't like to be locked up. They were arrested on a warrant charging them with the illegal transit of intoxicating liquors into the state with reasonable cause to believe that said liquors were intended to be sold in the State to some other person, thus violating Section 596 of the Public Statutes of the State of Rhode Island.

Arrest of Itinerants
February 3, 1888

The most excitement seen here for a long time was caused by the arrest at Chepachet of a large family of itinerants. O. A. Inman, with the assistance of other officers, muckled on to the gang at Chepachet while the court was in session on the Ham trial. O. A. Inman never looked more fatherly than he did carrying a young one in each arm through the streets of that village. The whole arrest included twelve human beings from a baby up to old age, two bears of good size, three monkeys, two dogs, and a horse and wagon. The horse was not so poor as the testimony showed Deputy Ham's horse to be, but was in fair condition and had a cow bell attached to him probably to prevent losing him.

The carriage, if it may be called so, was used as a place to stay in. The body was not over eight feet in length and covered with enameled cloth stretched over some low ribs extending ovally from side to side. A view inside revealed boots, both large and small, crusts of bread, dirt, parts of apparel, hay, straw and the general conglomeration of articles necessary for an expedition. In the forward corner, a small stove was wired in place, the funnel projecting through towards the left flank of the horse. Access was gained to this hole by a little door in the front, and the whole team seemed to be in a dilapidated condition. The vehicle would remind one of a horizontal street sprinkler on a small scale. A rack containing canvas for camping out in the woods, and a bundle of hay, were attached to the rear of this odd and unique affair. The children were very poorly clad and must, we should suppose, suffer by this mode of living.

The whole lot was taken to Harrisville and incarcerated in

the dungeon, not without a little trouble with one of the bears and his master, who did not seem inclined to go into the lock-up. Finally, after hitting one bear over the head two or three times, they were safe. Judge Harris came directly from the trial at Glocester, and the parties were arraigned as vagrants and given six months each in the House of Correction. They were taken to Cranston Thursday morning by a mule team of three, driven by Jerry Lawrence and accompanied by O. A. Inman, Esq. The two bears and the three monkeys were in the lock-up Thursday. Looking into the window, one of the monkeys was seen to be feeding the two bears who were in the cells, with crackers left them in a paper bag. The horse was quietly feeding in the Central Hotel stable and the carriage was under the shed. One dog laid tied under the rollinghouse, and the other stayed around the stable with the horse. What will be done with this collection is hardly known. When the people were taken away Thursday morning, tears and cries were in style at leaving their pets behind.

Saloons Raided Tuesday Last
June 15, 1888

Warrants were issued about three weeks ago for searches in this town for liquor. Several of the dealers became a little suspicious about that time and have been very careful about keeping much liquor on hand. In fact, one or two closed up entirely not caring to run the risk of getting pulled. Officer William Esten of Providence came to town Monday afternoon, and Tuesday morning at seven o'clock he, with Officer H. F. Mowry of Harrisville, started in a team on their raiding expedition. The saloon of Alexander Brough was first visited, but the place was locked, Mr. Brough being at his barn. Bosquet across the way had his weather eye out and, taking in the situation at once, did some hustling. The raiders, however, kept on to Pascoag.

Hoey's place was the next one, but here as at Brough's the door was securely fastened. Haniver's place was also locked, so the officers took the next building in which is a saloon kept by Eugene Griffith. This place was found open, and a thorough search was made without revealing anything but some light drinks and cigars. Frank Fagan's place was next raided, but nothing contraband was found, although the rattling of glass bottles as they were hustled out of the window had a look that there might have been enough to have wet one's whistle. The news soon spread to Hanover's place, and lo and behold, not a

One Hundred Years Ago in Burrillville by Patricia A. Mehrtens

whit could be found, although some jugs and bottles were just seen disappearing over the brow of the hill in strong arms that put the precious tonic into a safe hiding place.

A return was now made to Harrisville, and the saloon of Louis Bosquet showed no sign of anything spirituous. The billiard table stood in the center of the room as usual, the glass case holding cigars stood upon the counter and racks of spruce beer, tonic and other light drinks adorned the room, and all seemed to say - "Why this intrusion? Nothing hard is sold here and never was." The scene was not quite so serene at Brough's across the way, and when the beer pump was tried it sucked terribly and failed to send forth only the dregs of a beer barrel. To see why this was, the cellar was visited, and the barrel was found to have been stove in and the beer spilled upon the cellar bottom.

Foiled again, the officers continued their journey to Terrence Smith's place. They found him complacently sweeping the floor and not a muscle in his face betrayed surprise. A good look around the premises failed to unearth the demijohn of fire water. The news of the raids spread like wildfire, and when the officers reached Oakland, they found someone had been before them. McCabe at Glendale, when hearing that the officers were on their way to his place, pulled the spigots and let the beer run to waste. An advance courier was seen by the officers as they were driving towards Lynch's place, and they, concluding it a waste of time to go there, turned around for home. The horse used to inform the dealers was driven very hard indeed. It was hired of Mr. Stewart of Harrisville, who little knew the mission it was about to perform.

Havoc Raised in Pascoag
August 31, 1888

Zavier Tatro and a man named Morrissey started out on a little picnic last Thursday night, and the bent of their desires seemed to be the destruction of property and pure devilishness. It is more than presumable that both men had steamed up with firewater before starting in, as no sane men would have attempted to run such a rig. The tobacco sign on the grocery of Foreman & Fagan was torn from its fastenings and thrown bodily through a window in the yellow block. A similar sign was taken from the corner of the building where Frank Fagan carries on business and was afterwards found in Denigan City. Sayles Avenue, however, seemed to catch the brunt of the battle. Several panes of glass were broken at the shop of Wm. H. Sheldon, and about two thousand shingles were carried to the river and dumped in, floating downstream. A store wagon, belonging to Walter Adams which was left standing by Wm. H. Bowen's blacksmith shop for repairs, was run through the mill yard over a sand hill and turned upside down off the bank into the water. Not satisfied with this, a wheel was poised in the air and dashed through the window of James Polk's blacksmith shop, knocking glass, sash and all into ruins. A plank was run endwise through the small window of Brigg's photograph gallery. The window happened to be open and escaped injury, but the window blind was stove into kindling wood. The end of the plank did some damage by breaking several negatives placed on a shelf inside. Several panes of glass in the building adjoining were broken by stones, also windows in the paint shop of Mr. Wilson. A large chain was pitched into the reading room of the Pascoag T. A. & L. Society's rooms, smashing sash and glass. The officers soon got on track of the marauders, but on a plea of settling they were not locked up. Saturday, however, they came up missing, and no doubt will keep away for some time.

Buck Hill Raid by RI and CT
August 31, 1891

Sheriff O. A. Inman, in conjunction with Sheriff Park of Putnam, Connecticut, raided the place of John Baker over Buck Hill way last Sunday morning. The house where Baker lives is partly in the Nutmeg state and partly in Rhode Island. It has been difficult to get hold of the law breakers here as when officers of this state would attempt to arrest the parties they would go to the Connecticut side of the house, and as you might say, thumb their noses at the officers and vice versa. But this time it did not work so well, as when Baker came to the Rhode Island side of the house to escape from the clutches of the Connecticut officers he landed right into the arms of Sheriff Inman who was ready for him.

It was said that Baker took it quite coolly, and scratching his head made the remark that he hardly knew which side of the house to take. Sheriff Inman told him he guessed it would make but little difference as he had a warrant for his arrest in his pocket. While this talk was going, on a search of the premises was being made. A small amount of intoxicants was found which an inmate there claimed belonged to him. The Officers took Baker in their charge.

One Hundred Years Ago in Burrillville by Patricia A. Mehrtens

Cowboy dupes Townspeople
August 31, 1891

Last Monday evening will be remembered by several persons as long as they live, but whether it will serve as a lesson for them not to get taken in, is a question. "You can fool all the people once, you can fool some of the people a second time; but you can't fool all the people all the time." In the village there is little for excitement, and when anything unusual happens of an evening, there is no trouble to find a crowd. This was found to be so when a man dressed as a cowboy, with belt holding knives and revolvers strapped around him and wearing a broad brimmed hat, lighted his torch and begun his harangue from a carriage in which he was standing.

After giving a few slight-of-hand exhibitions, he began his story of discovering a mine of metal nearly like gold, only lighter in weight. He said he was advertising for a jewelry firm and received $6 a day. He did business a little different from most men and in a peculiar way, as he threw handfuls of finger rings into the crowd. He showed some watch chains and stated he did not sell the chains but only the business card attached to it. Some bought for $1, and were surprised to find that he rolled the money up with the chain and returned both to the purchaser. From this he went to watches, asking $5 for them. As people bought, he placed their purchase into an envelope and sealed it, requesting they not open it for a while.

When the ripe time had come and the crowd was getting a little uneasy, he whipped up his horse and made tracks towards Woonsocket taking about $100 with him, and leaving some worthless jewelry behind. The watches placed in the envelopes were simply cheap cases with a paper dial. It is said the man would not sell to minors or women and did not misrepresent things. If this is the case, it seems queer that some of our most prominent citizens should bite at such bait. One person said that the watches made first rate playthings for the children. In his hurry, the man collided with a team and lost some of his jewelry, torch and hat near Steere's blacksmith shop. What seems more peculiar is that there is no law that will hold him.

Terrible Fright of Two Women
April 12, 1892

About 5 o'clock last Friday a hatless, hard-featured man with bloody face and hands staggered into a house on the road to

One Hundred Years Ago in Burrillville by Patricia A. Mehrtens

Round Top. His bleared eyes, battered nose and tattered garments told all too clearly of some terrible struggle. As his looks forbade all thoughts of peace, the women of the house at once began strategic operations to secure the housing of their children. The older of the two finally plucked up courage and asked the unwelcome intruder his desire. He averred that he had had a terrible fight and got licked—yes, "all pounded to stuffing and I called at Shang Bailey's and he only laughed at me," said this hacked-up specimen of humanity. "But I am hatless! I must have a hat. Any old thing will do and I will pay for it," at which he produced a large roll of bills. The sight of the bills and the apparent honesty of their caller so reassured the women that one of them soon found her husband's old hat, and the other a much-desired glass of milk, with which they regaled their visitor, who after settling the bill, soon placed his face toward Harrisville and was lost to sight.

Savage Assault at Round Top
June 17, 1892

A party of young men from Harrisville went to Round Top for divertisement last Sunday, and one of them met with rough usage at the hands of Fred Bailey who keeps a house of ill fame. The party of three sat in the barn at Bailey's and quaffed at intervals whiskey bought at Germain's across the road. The purchasing of liquor of another party did not seem to suit Bailey, and this was made evident from remarks made by the proprietor of the place. The differences on this point seemed to have been amicably settled, and good nature and good will again prevailed. Towards evening, the sitting room in which there was a piano was occupied by the Harrisville party and others. Patsy Smith was presiding at the piano, and William Clark, the shortstop for the Harrisville nine, was entertaining them with songs.

Without any warning, Bailey came up behind Clark and dealt him several blows over the head with a double lager beer bottle several times. Mr. Clark staggered from the room in a dazed condition and those present scattered in all directions. Clark's scalp was cut open an inch and a half and blood flowed freely. He, with his friends went to Germain's where his wound was washed and cared for as well as possible, then the party returned home. Dr. Boucher was obliged to take several stitches to close the wound. Clark carries also a bad looking nose upon which one blow was received. The case was placed in Lawyer Gannon's care and a settlement asked. Mrs. Bailey saw the assaulted party Wednesday and offered $25, lawyer's fees and doctor's bill, in settlement but was refused. She stated that Mr. Bailey was ill in bed.

Advertisement for Round Top
January 13, 1893

There was a grand dance and oyster supper advertised and given by Herbert L. Sherman at Round Top last Saturday evening. The *News-Gazette* doesn't know whether it was a brilliantly successful social affair or not—presumably it was—but what this paper wishes to say is this. That the spirit of modern progress has at last invaded the one hallowed spot in town where the necessity of advertising was heretofore entirely unknown. For many years the advantages, natural or otherwise, of Round Top needed not the flamboyant embellishments of the printer's art to attract people to its marts. Up to this time, the merits of the wares sold there were known almost by intuition to the town resident and to the stranger within our gates. The road to Round Top was so broad that even the livery horses traveled it without guidance from the reinsman's hand. It was the one spot on earth about whose traffic posters on the wall seemed superfluous. But all has changed. Like any common place Round Top has called in the aid of the advertising agent, and the possibilities this fact calls up causes the imagination to stand aghast. Suppose all the dealers up that way adopt the realistic style of advertising now in vogue and adorn the billboards with pictorial representations of their stock in trade. Suppose in the fury of competition prices are lowered, how the "cut rate" figures would stand out on fences and rock. Suppose—but these drafts on the imagination are useless. If Round Top really goes into advertising in earnest, the bare truths portrayed will outshine the most vivid pictures that fancy can evolve.

Tramps in Town
January 27, 1893

We don't know whether it is owing to atmospheric attractions, the soft hearts of bartenders, or the lenient eyes of officers, but every tramp out of jail seems in duty to bound to make Burrillville his headquarters. The town has attained a unique distinction that it would be fervently glad to get rid of. Last Tuesday morning there assembled on the doorsteps of a Harrisville gin palace a congregation of chaff that broke the record for general appearance. Twelve ragged, dirty, unkempt, frowsy, miserable looking bummers were holding a business meeting. The door was locked (and it may easily be imagined that it must be a pretty tough crowd that would force a Harrisville saloonkeeper to close his doors), so the consultation was of necessity held on steps and sidewalk. Every bum in the gang had stamped on his face that historic motto of Barney Gill of Federal hill, "I never worked, and I never will" and the debate was a prolonged one. Finally the crowd separated into couples and "worked" the village for an hour or two. All were back at the rendezvous at ten o'clock, some with bread, some with additional clothing, and some bearing unmistakable evidence that they had been reasonably successful in getting their petition "Sweet Spirit, hear my prayer," granted.

After another consultation, the gang adopted guerrilla tactics, every man foraging on his own hook, and they're still at it all over town. Our highways are full of gaping holes and our land is covered with boulders waiting to be crushed. There is dynamic force enough in the muscles of these sturdy beggars to do the work, but no one seems to have legal knowledge sufficient to get these three elements into close, if not loving, communion.

Two Questionable Women visit Town
August 5, 1893

A carriage containing two well-dressed if not gaudily attired young women entered Pascoag on Wednesday morning. From their passports it was evident the young women were taking an outing from the nearby town of Uxbridge, Mass. Their mission here was to procure spirituous fluids for the dry, parched throats of those whom they had left behind. Soon after their arrival, they drove up to one of our most prominent saloons, alighted, had their empty bottles filled with alleged port wine and unmistakable whiskey.

One of the women paid from the deep recesses of her nigh stocking into which she thrust her hand in such a reckless manner as to "call the blush to the cheek of modesty"—the bartender and the loungers furnishing the "modesty"—with which article they appeared to be overstocked. These incursions from the neighboring hamlet of Uxbridge must be stopped. Otherwise, the time may come when certain residents of Pascoag will have to face a whiskey famine and go to bed at night grievously athurst.

Great Little Invention
September 14, 1894

One of the neatest inventions of the age is that lately perfected by our former fellow townsman, Mr. N. S. Cary now of Greenville, R. I. It is an automatic beer tap, and is the best thing of the kind ever shown. The device is a marvel of simplicity and is destined to prove indispensable to all who handle malt or other "heady" liquids. Everybody knows the trouble, vexation and losses that attend the ordinary methods of tapping malt liquors. Mr. Cary has now made the operation so simple that a boy 10 years old can do the work in half a minute with absolutely no risk whatever.

The very simplicity of the device makes a description difficult, but a moment's inspection of the tap itself makes one wonder that it was not thought of before. It is operated as follows: A hole is bored into the head of any barrel and into this a socket is screwed. This socket contains a little solid rubber ball like a small marble and this plays freely in its chamber. When the barrel is filled, the pressure forces the ball against the shoulder of the socket and not a particle of air or liquid can escape. The tap is then inserted in the socket until its end touches the ball. A smart blow with the palm of the hand sends the tap into place and there it stays. No hammering nor turning of the tap is required, and not a drop of the liquid is ever lost. The tap can be removed instantly by simply grasping it with the hand, giving it a turn or two, right and left, and then it comes out easily. The rubber ball is pressed into place again and the barrel is perfectly tight.

A barrel can be tapped and the tap removed twenty times in a minute without loss. Experiments have conclusively shown that a pressure of over 300 pounds is required to blow out the faucet. It is a wonderful little thing, and Mr. Cary will undoubtedly reap a substantial financial reward for his invention. Most of the saloon keepers here have adopted it and all give it unqualified praise. Its adoption by all the brewers in the country is only a question of time, for when simplicity, quickness, durability, cheapness and absolute safety are combined, as they are in this device, its recognition is certain.

Flutter in a Dove Cote
October 26, 1894

On Thursday evening of last week Deputy Sheriff William Bates and grand juror Thomas Ryan with a party of volunteer yeomanry from Thompson, Conn. made a descent on the Buck Hill Tavern now run by Nellie Wright. The raiding party succeeded in capturing two of the lady boarders also the bartender who is Mrs. Wright's brother. On Friday morning the prisoners were arraigned before Judge Tourtellotte. They all pleaded guilty and paid fines and costs amounting to $135 in all.

Buck Hill Tavern Fire
July 12, 1895

The far-famed Buck Hill tavern is no more. It has gone up. Parties occupying it moved away last week and Tuesday the structure, perhaps from loneliness or perhaps from abject despair, burned to the ground. Such is the fate of many good hotels and, incidentally, of others. The Buck Hill Tavern was built many years ago and has had a varied and rather a racy history. In early years, it was a most convenient place for moistening parched throats and quenching the devouring thirst of the residents of Connecticut and Massachusetts, both states being then under stringently enforced prohibitory laws. In later years, the history of the place, though unwritten, will be borne sufficiently well in the minds of Burrillville people without being recapitulated here.

Fatality at Saloon in Pascoag
August 28, 1903

Last Saturday afternoon between 5 and 6 o'clock Main Street was the scene of a distressing fatality, when James Nolan lost his life by being thrown or pushed against and into one of the large plate glass windows in Thomas Trimble's saloon. Immediately after the occurrence, Henry Cruise was arrested by Police Constable John Nash as being the responsible party. From the testimony of those who witnessed the affair, it seems that Cruise and Nolan had had some words in the saloon, and that the former had been ejected from the saloon three times by the bartender. After he had been ejected the third time, he was standing on the sidewalk near the steps and was facing Nolan as he came out of the saloon. The two men clinched and some blows were exchanged when Nolan was seen to fall heavily against the window, striking it with his left shoulder and breaking the glass. His head went into the opening and the left side of his neck came across the broken glass. Nolan quickly arose and made a pass for Cruise, but the two men were separated. It was seen that the former was severely injured, and he was assisted into the saloon and medical assistance summoned.

The glass had inflicted several wounds in the side of his neck and head, the most serious being in his neck, where several arteries and the external jugular vein had been severed, and he was bleeding profusely. Dr. E. N. Granger quickly arrived and saw that the man's injuries were fatal, and ordered his removal. Nolan was taken to his home where he expired almost immediately. Cruise was taken to the lockup, and the following morning was arraigned before Assistant Justice Frank F. Davis on the charge of being responsible for Nolan's death. He pleaded not guilty, and in default of $10,000 bonds, was committed to Cranston to await a hearing which will be held tomorrow at Harrisville. Sunday morning Medical Examiner Robert Wilcox, M. D. held an autopsy and ordered an inquest.

One Hundred Years Ago in Burrillville by Patricia A. Mehrtens

HORSES, STEALING, & ROBBERIES

Excitement in Harrisville
March 26, 1880

Mr. Thomas Cunningham keeps the saloon in Harrisville next to the livery stable and lives overhead. About one o'clock Tuesday morning his wife awoke feeling thirsty and got up for a glass of water. She thought she detected strange noises below and nudged her husband. He arose, slipped quietly into his clothes, and went out to reconnoiter. He saw a man in an out-building, and called sharply to know who he was and what he wanted. The stranger in a mildly insinuating voice replied, "Come here a minute; I want to speak to you." But Mr. C. was not to be caught with chaff and raised the cry of "burglars!" "robbers!" etc.

This roused the neighborhood. Sashes flew up and heads poked anxiously out to ask "What's all the row about?" It also disturbed the burglars, two of whom were operating inside while their "pal" kept watch without. They made a threatening demonstration and Cunningham retired in good order to Granger & Smith's drug store, where he procured a revolver and returned to the attack. In the excitement of the moment, two or three honest citizens narrowly escaped being shot at for burglars, but the real culprits vamoosed in the midst of the hubbub.

Sheriff Steere and Constable Smith at once went to work on the case. The robbers first tried to get into the saloon through the back basement door, but failing this went in the window. They rummaged around considerably inside, but their only booty was a box of cigars and about 60 cents taken from the till. Just outside the door was found a kit of carpenter's tools and an overcoat which had been taken from A. A. Steere's wheelwright shop. Later, it was found that the robbers had also broken into Nelson Steere's barn and disappeared with his horse and light wagon. Where they are gone at this writing nobody knows.

One Hundred Years Ago in Burrillville by Patricia A. Mehrtens

More Horse Thefts in Town
August 13, 1880

For the past two or three months Burrillville has enjoyed tolerable immunity from the attentions of burglars and horse-thieves. But the great success of the previous operations of these gentry in our midst will embolden them to repeat the game until somebody is finally caught and something done. Our people were not at all surprised to learn that the barn of Elisha Mathewson, who lives on the road between Harrisville and Glendale, was raided on during the storm of Tuesday night and his horse and wagon taken off. That a part of the same old gang was in this latest enterprise is pretty evident from the fact that they operated in precisely the same way as on previous occasions.

Two men visited Mr. Mathewson's house on Tuesday and asked for food. None of the men folks were about the house, but Mrs. M. said they appeared to be young fellows about twenty to twenty-three years old and apparently both Yankees. They were also observed by a man, prowling about the barn and sheds on the place, evidently getting the "lay of the land." Mr. Mathewson heard a slight barking from his dog during the night but took no particular notice of it. In the morning he found his horse gone from the barn and a wagon from one of the sheds. The harnesses were in still another building and could not be found by the rogues. They pulled the wagon down to Mr. Chas. Lapham's fully a half mile distant, where they obtained the necessary equipment and started off.

Mr. Mathewson set chase after the thieves Wednesday morning. Taking it for granted they would pursue the same old track as before, he drove directly towards Woonsocket and found the missing property at the "Branch" between Forestdale and Union Village. The horse had been abandoned near that place and was taken in charge by the watchman of the mill. It was considerably blown and badly chafed in the hind legs by being driven in a short breeching, but otherwise the property was all right when recovered. Mr. Mathewson is quite eager to have the fellows caught and convicted. It is hoped that their depredations will soon be brought to an end.

Runaway Horses in Pascoag
August 14, 1885

The horses of Pascoag seemed to have entered into a conspiracy last Friday, for there were two runaways, something we

One Hundred Years Ago in Burrillville by Patricia A. Mehrtens

are not often called upon to chronicle. Fred Esten, while on his route, left his horse to go into William Sherman's with some baker's bread. While inside, for some cause unknown the horse started and ran by Bailey's store, the M. E. Church, down towards J. O. Inman's Mill. In descending the hill, the body of the cart became detached from the forward wheels by bouncing over a water bar, and landed in front of James O. Inman's office in a somewhat wrecked condition. The horse continued with the fore wheels down through Turkeyville across the P. & S. R.R. track, and came near the door of the bakery. Mr. Esten stood in the door and thought the horse would stop, but he kept on towards the barn. Instead of going into the barn as expected, he leaped the fence for the woods. In jumping the fence, the horse came down astride the thill, thus impeding his progress so that he was caught. Strange to say no one was injured in the horse's long run. The front part of the cart was somewhat broken and the hide was knocked off one of the hind legs of the horse.

 Just before this, the mettled animal in the store team of Eddy & Schofield was left standing in front of George W. Esten's bakery by Elmer Schofield while he went upstairs with some goods. The horse suddenly started and, making a circle, just grazed a telephone pole on the right side of the road and one on the left side near Adams' grocery store. Then he struck a clothes rack, knocking it into kindling wood. At this time he became entangled in a coil of wire and fell. Help soon was on the spot, and got the horse out of his sad predicament. The top of the team was pretty well smashed and the wheels were racked out of shape in the overturning. The load of groceries was somewhat scattered and disarranged. On the whole, the damage was lighter in both cases than one would think.

Horse Trader Arrested
May 28, 1886

 William Carter, quite an old resident living in a secluded place not far from the Town Farm in the neighborhood commonly known as Round Top, was arrested Sunday night last and brought before Trial Justice O. A. Inman on Monday. The warrant for his arrest charged him with "fraudulently receiving one bay horse of the value of $30; one brown mare, value $30; one black horse, value $60; one brown mare, value $50; one dark horse, value $50; four carriages valued at $50 each, of Christopher Carter, knowing the same to have been stolen."

 Carter was also arraigned on another complaint of aiding,

assisting, abetting, counseling and procuring his wife, Naomi Carter, to burn the barn of said Carter to obliterate traces of crime. Naomi Carter, who by the way is considerably younger than her husband, was also brought before the bar to answer to a charge of willfully burning the barn of her husband. On the first complaint of fraudulently receiving and disposing of property knowing them to have been stolen, Carter stated that he had the horse flesh and chattels of his brother, Christopher. On this complaint he was bound over to the June term of Court of Common Pleas in the sum of $1,000. On the second complaint of abetting with his wife in burning his barn, when asked if guilty or not guilty, he hardly knew what to say, but finally as much as admitted his guilt by saying that he got into a hard fix and did not know what to do.

Naomi Carter was sworn, and testified that her husband told her he was in a bad fix and did not know whether to destroy everything or not. She set the barn on fire between twelve and one o'clock Sunday morning by throwing a lighted match into the hay mow near the ladder, and then immediately left. This being sufficient evidence, the Court bound Carter over in the sum of $1,000. His wife, Naomi, on being arraigned on complaint of willfully burning the barn, pleaded guilty at once, and the bail was fixed in the same sum, $1,000. They were unable to find bail and both were committed to jail. The sudden and overwhelming evidence just brought to light of the criminal actions of Wm. Carter is quite a shock to many of our people. Our officers, however, have for sometime suspected that some of the transactions of Carter were illegitimate, although nothing occurred before this to give sufficient grounds for his arrest. William Carter is below medium height, about 64 years old, and has been employed in the capacity of night watchman at James O. Inman & Son for the past fifteen years. His character was considered, as a rule, an average one.

Christopher Carter, a brother of William, seems to have been the principal in the nefarious business, the *modus operandi* being to steal almost anything when opportunity offered and run it into Burrillville to be disposed of. From information gained, this business has been carried on for several years, which is remarkable in this day of rapid communication. Carter's residence is in rather an "out of the way place" and he having always dealt in horses and having the reputation of being a trading man, the opportunity for illegal disposition of stolen property was very favorable. So closely was Carter watched the last two or three days of last week that he stuffed several harnesses into the stoves and burned them, but the half peck of buckles and other metallic substances used in building harnesses found in the ashes gave the thing away. The barn and the house in which he lived were owned by him. Christopher Carter has operated mostly in Vermont and New Hampshire, running stolen property from that section in this town. He is now languishing in jail in New Hampshire, being apprehended in trying to get away with a fine span of horses.

Beware of Tramps
July 25, 1886

The readers of the *Gazette* are familiar with the name of Joseph K. Temple as an advertiser for the past year as blacksmith and horseshoer at Harrisville. Perhaps a short history of his doings might not be uninteresting. When first known, he came to Oakland as a tramp. Nathaniel G. Carey gave him work in his blacksmith shop where he gave good satisfaction shoeing horses. He worked for Mr. Carey until a change in the business, and no further employment. He came to Harrisville and hired the shop on Chapel street, and by close attention to business built up a good trade. When Temple first came here he had no money and no credit, and some of the residents here helped him. Mr. Carey lent him some tools to start with, and other parties guaranteed his bills in Providence. Had he attended to business he might have done well. But like a good many others, he could not bear prosperity. In fact it killed him, and he got into bad habits and neglected his business. As a final windup he got into debt as much as he could, raised all the money possible by mortgaging his tools and stock, took what part of his effects he could carry off, and Arab-like folded his tent in the night and silently stole away, having previously sent away his wife and child with what goods his wife could get away with without exciting suspicion. He left town a week ago last Saturday, leaving behind him what property he could not conveniently dispose of and the reputation of a rascal. It is fair to suppose that the places here that knew him once will know him no more. The moral of this short history is—beware of tramps.

Burglaries at Harrisville and Pascoag
June 8, 1888

A burglar or burglars made their presence felt late Tuesday night visiting the store of William Carpenter and the

One Hundred Years Ago in Burrillville by Patricia A. Mehrtens

Harrisville Railroad Station. At Mr. Carpenter's store, an attempt was made to force the front door with a chisel some inch and a half wide, but the blade failed to reach the lock. A side window was next tried which was fastened with a large screw. The window was raised a few inches, when the attempt was abandoned as the large head of the screw embedded itself in the window frame and made further progress impossible without making a noise and arousing the neighbors. The rear of the store was then visited and another window tried with better success, and the store was entered. Several drawers were ransacked, but the thieves had little success, only securing about $1.25, money taken by him for the Harrisville Library and kept in a drawer by itself. This, with about twenty-five or thirty cigars taken from a glass show case, was all that was taken so far as Mr. Carpenter was able to find.

The burglars had better luck at the station. Here they entered the waiting room by raising a window. The door between the office and the waiting room was unlocked in some way without damage. Once inside, the chisel was again brought into play in breaking the lock to the cash and ticket stand where several dollars, probably between six and seven, were taken. No railroad tickets, it is thought, were taken. Two drawers in the desk were forced open, and some three or four dollars taken. Mr. Smith, the station agent, found the doors all locked as usual on Wednesday morning, but found the drawers open and papers on the desk strewn around on the floor.

Probably the same parties who committed the burglaries here entered the hardware store of James H. Smith the same evening by forcing the lock of the front door with a chisel. That chisel and other tools were stolen from James Geer's wheelwright shop on Sayles Avenue, the parties gaining an entrance through a window of Polk's blacksmith shop, then opening the slide door between the two shops. Mr. Geer stated he had missed a good bit stock, bit and two chisels so far, but did not know if there were more tools missing. None of the tools have been found as yet. They were probably thrown into the pond, hid, or carried away.

The till was opened, but although forty cents in pennies were there, they were not disturbed. The amount of plunder secured seemed rather small for the risk run. Two or three persons are suspected but not sufficient grounds exist for the arrest of any of them. It is believed someone entered these places who were pretty well acquainted with the surroundings. The inside door at the depot was either opened by a regular key or a skeleton key, for it was found locked and all right in the morning.

One Hundred Years Ago in Burrillville by Patricia A. Mehrtens

Horse Thief Caught
February 8, 1889

The horse stolen from Mr. Tourtelotte, who resides in Thompson, Conn., some two weeks ago, was found by Sheriff W. N. Bates of that town last week in Coldbrook Springs 17 miles above Worcester. The man arrested was Solomon A. Sherman. He drove the horse to Worcester, got it clipped, and sold her in the auction stable of A. O. Kelly and signed the book in his own name. He was arrested at the house of a man by the name of Del Ward in East Thompson. The officer knocked at the door, opened it and walked in, overturning a table and two chairs which were placed against the door, found Ward, a colored man, and this Sherman. The officer placed his hand on Sherman's shoulder saying, "You are my prisoner!" Sherman wilted and allowed the handcuffs to be placed around his wrists and was led away by the officer. He was tried Saturday, Feb. 2nd. in Thompson. As he could not get bonds, he was taken to Brooklyn jail there to await his trial at the May term of Court.

Wars and Rumors of War
September 18, 1891

Harrisville had its share of excitement last week, and of such a kind it is hoped that may not occur again very soon. John Bodman is a stone mason, and was arrested by Inman and Timmons in Pascoag in a perfectly helpless condition Saturday morning. He had wandered around all the previous night endeavoring to find a place of refuge, and awakened several of the citizens in Pascoag by pounding and rattling around their houses. Mr. Bodman was fined $2 and costs for drunkenness and was released upon a friend of his paying it. Before the officers had turned from the courthouse, a messenger informed them there was a terrible row up at Creighton's house near Graniteville Bridge. Inman, McDermott, and Timmons took a team and started for the scene of carnage, and upon entering found a sickening sight of two brothers—we believe twin brothers—with blood covering them so as to be hardly recognizable. When the officers entered the house, the combatants ceased fighting. The weapons used were a handsaw and hatchet. The head of Thomas was pretty well scarred up with the saw and his left wrist showed where he had received a rasping. Owen bled profusely from a wound over the right eye, and a shovel and broom were used in removing the blood from the house floor. Inman took Thomas

Creighton to the lockup, and McDermott and Timmons turned their attention to Owen who resisted the officers and swore he would not go, but with help they placed the kicking man into a team and safely landed him in the station. The two men remained in the lockup over Sunday, also receiving a doctor's attention.

Monday morning Mrs. Creighton brought a clean shirt down to her husband before his going to court, the one taken off being saturated with blood. Judge Harris arrived on the morning train to hear their case. Thomas walked promptly into court, but Owen claimed to be weak from loss of blood and unable to stand. A team was procured, and he was lugged by the officers into a room adjoining the courtroom and pleaded not guilty to the charge of assault, while lying prostrate on the floor with simply a pillow under his head. He was bound over under bonds of $200. He did not obtain bail and was not taken down to Cranston until Tuesday on account of his condition. Thomas pleaded not guilty and was placed under $500 bonds. He was taken to Cranston the same day.

Mad Dog Bites Horse
May 13, 1892

Trying events have transpired at the residence of Luther C. Angell on the Wallum Pond road which Mr. Angell or anyone connected would not care to have repeated. The cause of all the trouble was a very pretty little pug dog having a yellow ribbon tied in its collar and supposed to have been somebody's pet. It was impossible to trace the origin of the pug or the direction he came from, as stories conflict. Some claim that it came from Massachusetts, while it is also said that it was first seen or noticed in the vicinity of Harmony. Ed. Walling of this place saw the pug and made something of it,, but it acted strangely, snapping at things, and he pelted it with stones driving it away. Finally, the residence of Mr. Angell was reached by his canineship and was taken in. It acted so strangely that it was tied in the barn. While there, a horse in the barn floor was bitten on the lip as the horse reached to the floor for a nibble of hay. No particular scar was made or blood drawn. The pug became so snappish in the presence of Peter Jarvis, a near neighbor, that he took a stick and killed it. This all happened a little over three weeks ago.

Last Friday, Mr. Angell hitched the horse that had been bitten beside another horse. They plowed together in the forenoon and nothing unusual transpired, although Mr. Angell said the horse had seemed for a few days previous to have been more irritable and cross than usual. In the afternoon he used his team to draw logs to have sawed into shingles, when he noticed the horse shudder and tremble as if not feeling well. He acted strangely, and bit the other horse on the neck. Mr. Angell started for the barn with his team as it became apparent that something was wrong. The horse was placed in a stall, and by spells when spasms came on, thrashed around terribly, biting and kicking. He set his teeth into the oak manger with such force as to break them out, and when his teeth were all gone continued with all venom to bite until his jaws were all pulpy and bleeding and finally broke his jaw. The stall was broken, and as it was evident nothing could be done to save him, he was knocked on the head by James Riley.

We hardly think a case as violent as this, especially in a horse, has ever occurred in town before, and people now feel that the law should be enforced thoroughly as to muzzling dogs. The officers have been very lax in carrying out the provisions of the ordinance in regard to muzzling dogs which was recently passed by the Town Council, and so far as they have been concerned, the law has been a dead letter.

Eldridge's Mad Cow
July 13, 1892

Hearing there was a mad cow at Mason Eldridge's near the building formerly used as a creamery on the Douglas Road, the reporter made a trip there Wednesday morning in company with Everett B. Sherman. Mr. Sherman called at the house and at first received no response but, finally, a child in answer to questions said his father was away but his mother was at the back of the house doing the family washing in the shade of some pine trees. After the usual greeting she was asked if they had a sick cow to which she replied, "yes, I guess it is mad." She led the way to the edge of the forest not far from the house, where it lay extended on its left side among the stones, and tied to a small sapling with a stout rope. At times, the cow would kick and struggle then again raise its head only to lay it down again upon the sward or stones. The grass was all trampled up within a short radius of where the animal lay and the trees were denuded of their bark.

We were informed that the cow was bitten last May 7th by a dog which came running along through that section and that the cow had not appeared right for a number of days. Dr. Bruce advised the family not to use the milk. For three or four days the animal has refused to eat or to drink, and when water was placed before it a few days previous to the visit, it seemed to infuriate the animal. The cow became so violent and ugly that Mr. Eldridge tied it where it was, fearing to handle it. Deputy Sheriff Inman visited the place Wednesday morning and saw the condition of things. He consulted the president of the council, and just before noon shot the animal to relieve it of misery.

Mr. Eldridge said they slept but little the previous night because of the bellowing and noise of the maddened bovine. This case excites considerable interest among stockholders, and many visited the scene as soon as the facts became known. The cow is black mostly with white spots and looked some like the Jersey breed. The cow was considered to be an extra good one by Mr. Eldridge. The scene was not pleasant to look upon as she plunged about, and as she became so weak was unable to stand and thrashed around lying on her side.

Attempted Robbery
September 30, 1892

Monday afternoon Mrs. Mary Slattery made a friendly call upon a neighbor close by, and at about 4 o'clock returned. As she reached the yard, she noticed a veil on the grass which looked like her daughter's. Upon getting to the rear what was her surprise to see shoes and a fur cape coming through a slit in the screen at one of the windows. Around the end of the house she found some articles laid out upon the grass from the window, which is nearer the ground than those at the rear. She spied a man inside, and was not long in getting inside and collaring him.

Word was sent to Officer Fairfield who went and took the marauder to the lockup. His name is Duquette, married and lives at Graniteville. Entrance was gained by a window at the end of the house by pulling a wire screen out. The window being up, an easy entrance was gained. He was arraigned, and for lack of $1000 bonds was taken down to Cranston await trial Saturday. The above information was gleaned from Mrs. Slattery who also said that the intruder was intoxicated. When confronted, he disgorged freely all he had taken and did not offer to harm her.

Elopement In Pascoag
April 7, 1893

At 7:30 o'clock Monday night, Johnny McNamee hitched up Andy Higgins' gray horse, went to Pascoag, and into the wagon jumped George Burke. Back to Cemetery Hill came

One Hundred Years Ago in Burrillville by Patricia A. Mehrtens

the pair and, as they passed the house of James Davis, Burke jingled a sleigh bell and out came Davis' young daughter, Bertha. Into the wagon she climbed, and at shortly after 9 o'clock the horse was pulled up in front of a well, if not favorably, known resort in Woonsocket. Burke and the girl got out and engaged accommodations for the night, and McNamee drove away. At 11 o'clock, Mr. Davis became thoroughly alarmed at the prolonged absence of his daughter, and in the course of his search came to Harrisville. At 11:30 o'clock Town Sergeants McDermott and Higgins were on their way to Woonsocket.

At 1:00 o'clock a.m. they found the birds in the aforesaid resort. They were occupying separate apartments—at least they were at the instant they were found, but there were other indications. At 3 o'clock a.m. the captured but still happy young couple were ensconced in the Harrisville lock-up, and there they remained until 2:30 p.m. Tuesday. Judge Harris came up but found the case was out of his jurisdiction, as the law had been violated in Woonsocket. Back to Woonsocket on the 3:40 p.m. train went the youngsters under official guard. Burke was arraigned under the statute that provides for the punishment of "a male of over eighteen years of age having unlawful carnal intercourse with a female under the age of eighteen years." The maximum punishment for this offense is five years imprisonment. Bertha came home with her parents about 5:30 no case being brought against her. Burke will be 21 years of age today; Bertha will be 14 years old next September. Such is a resume of the facts in a case that created more than a ripple of excitement on the quietness of the daily routine of life in Burrillville.

Saved by a "J" - April 14, 1893 - George Burke, who took 14-year old Bertha Davis from Pascoag to Woonsocket on the night of April 4th was tried for the offense in Woonsocket Monday. The case against him was brought under chapter 730 of the public laws of Rhode Island. The girl herself was the principal witness and she testified in a straight-forward manner about going to Woonsocket with Burke, occupying the same room, etc. Burke's chances of going to jail appeared most excellent, but his keen-eyed attorney had discovered a fatal defect in the warrant. In his plea he said: "Your Honor will see that this warrant charges George Burke with having intercourse with Bertha Davis. This girl swears her name is Bertha J. Davis. Now if your Honor sentences Burke on this case, there is nothing to prevent Bertha J. Davis from bringing a case in her name thus putting the prisoner in jeopardy twice for the same offense, which is clearly against the law. I hold that Bertha Davis and Bertha J. Davis, are, in the eyes of the law, two separate and distinct persons." Judge Lee acknowledged the justness of the claim and promptly discharged Burke. Another suit may be brought by Bertha J. Davis if it is deemed advisable, but we have heard of no steps being taken as yet.

Bold Daylight Robbery
June 13, 1893

The residence of Frank Paine in Pascoag was entered last Tuesday afternoon by one of the boldest and most adroit sneak thieves that ever worked in this town. Mr. Paine lives in one of the Frank Sprague houses on the hill near the Pascoag station. About half past three o'clock Tuesday afternoon Mrs. Paine stood in the driveway in front of her house conversing with Mrs. F. F. Arnold, who was in her carriage. Mrs. Paine's son, Mrs. C. S. Aldrich, and Mr. Frank Sprague were also present.

A rather well dressed man came along and passed near the party. There was nothing specially unprepossessing in his appearance, still, the ladies kept a watch on him. He finally escaped their observation, sneaked behind Mr. Paine's house, and removed a sliding screen from a bedroom window. He placed it carefully under the piazza, crawled in, and from a bureau stole two gold watches and nearly $100 in bills. He made his exit in the same way and fled.

Mrs. Paine, soon after, went into the bedroom for her gloves and discovered the loss and at once notified her husband. Deputy Sheriff Inman and Town Sergeant McDermott were soon at work on the case. Thanks to the keen eyes of the ladies, a very full and particular description of the man was obtained, and his identity was at once established. He was about 30 years old, 5 feet 6 inches tall, red complexion though dark skinned, black hair and moustache, derby hat and tan shoes. This minute detail spotted him at once as Louis, or Henry Jendron who is well known throughout the town having worked in various mills here.

The officers searched all the afternoon and evening, and early Wednesday morning went to Greenville where they searched several houses. On Wednesday, John T. Fiske, Jr., took a quiet trip to Webster, ostensibly to hire a barber—really to capture a sneak thief. Mr. Fiske worked his clues in good shape and finally ran his man to earth. Sheriff Maurice P. Clare collared Mr. Jendron, telephoned Deputy Sheriff Inman, who went to Webster instantly and soon after six o'clock p.m. Wednesday Jendron was in a cell in the Harrisville lockup.

Both watches and $80 in money were found on his person, he having spent only $10 or $15. On Thursday morning, Jendron was arraigned before Judge Harris, pleaded not guilty and was bound over in the sum of $500 to the September term of Common Pleas. He was committed to jail. Jendron is sometimes known as Louis, sometimes Henry, and sometimes Albert, and is an old offender, having served several terms in Massachusetts. There have been several houses entered lately in this vicinity and probably Jendron did the work. Our local officers worked energetically in this affair, and Mr. Fiske deserves great credit for his skillful handling of the case. It is probable that when Jendron's record is read in court, he will get the full extent of the law, and he undoubtedly deserves it.

Sedgwick's Store Robbed
December 29, 1905

At an early hour last Friday morning, the cigar and confectionery store of Frank E. Sedgwick at Bridgeton, which was to have been opened for business for the first time that day, was entered, and the greater portion of the stock was taken. Entrance was effected by breaking one of the windows. The building was a new one having been recently erected for Mr. Sedgwick's use, and the goods taken were practically all in the original packages and had not been unpacked. Mr. Sedgwick consulted Deputy Sheriff Roscoe S. Wood. The following day, a search warrant was obtained, and the house occupied by J. William Bamford in Bridgeton was thoroughly searched.

No trace of the stolen property was found on the main floor of the house. But in the attic, entrance to which was gained by means of a ladder through a scuttle, all of the goods were found hidden under old books and papers. Bamford admitted his connection with the affair and said he was not alone. After a while he divulged the names of his associates—William B. Morrissey and James O'Mara. Sheriff Wood took Bamford to the lockup in Harrisville for safe keeping and then found Morrissey and O'Mara, who he gave quarters in an adjacent cell.

The following day, all three of the parties were arraigned in the District Court on charges of breaking and entering in the night time. All three waived examination and were bound over to the March Grand Jury under $500 bonds each. The trio were committed Monday in default of bail. Bamford and Morrissey were also charged with breaking and entering J. H. Smith's store in Pascoag on December 19th. They waived examination and were held under $500 bonds for their appearance before the Grand Jury. While the arrests occasioned considerable surprise, there is a feeling of satisfaction, for it is believed that there will now be an end of the petty burglaries in this section. If there were others implicated, they will be taught a lesson by the apprehension and arrest of these parties.

Triple Burglary
May 31, 1907

At an early hour Wednesday morning, burglars entered the general store and post office of Arnold W. Clarke in Mapleville, the general store and post office of C. M. & F. W. Mitchell at Oakland, and the saloon of Fred Charest, also in Oakland. Save in the latter place the visitors were unrewarded by securing any booty. It is supposed Mr. Clarke's store was the first to be visited. Since the post office was burglarized several months ago and the safe blown open, Mr. Clarke has not locked his safe and has kept nothing of value in the store overnight. Wednesday morning the safe was opened and its contents examined. Finding nothing of value, the visitors proceeded to draw on the proprietor's stock of canned goods and fruit for a nocturnal lunch. After satisfying the wants of the inner men, they left without taking anything so far as could be learned. Entrance was effected by forcing a door with a chisel.

The front door of the store at Oakland was also forced open with a bar or chisel, and the place thoroughly ransacked. Except for a few postage stamps and possibly a few pennies, nothing was taken at this place. On the opposite side of the railroad track is the saloon of Fred Charest. Here the burglars showed evidence of belonging to the profession by forcing open the safe with nitroglycerine, following the usual method of soaping the cracks around the door. Inside the safe they found four two and one-half dollar gold pieces and a quantity of old coin. Had they ransacked the place more thoroughly, they would have found $20 in change under a coat lying on top of the safe, which was left for the use of the clerk who opens the establishment in the morning. There was also some money in the desk near the safe. This, too, was unmolested. Thus, for all the hazard attending breaking into three places, a total amount of booty of less than $15 was secured which was seemingly "hardly worth the candle."

One Hundred Years Ago in Burrillville by Patricia A. Mehrtens

ACCIDENTS & DEATHS

Lifeless Body of Woman Found
April 1, 1881

    At about 6 o'clock last Monday morning, what appeared to be the lifeless body of a woman was found at the foot of the hill on the Griffin new road in Pascoag. Officer John Moore was notified and identified her as Bridget Gaines, daughter of Katherine Gaines, and putting her into a buggy, conveyed her to her house. She had been missing from home, and Mr. Moore had been searching for her sometime before she was found. At just what hour she commenced her wanderings is not known, but it was sometime after 10 o'clock. She was very thinly clad having on a dress and a light shawl. Life was not quite extinct when she was first taken up, but she survived only a few moments. There were no marks of violence, and the general appearance was that the cause of her decease was freezing by exposure in such insufficient covering. An inquest was deemed unnecessary, and she was given in charge of her family.
    Miss Gaines was a native of County West Meath, Ireland, and ever since the sickness, death and burial of her father which occurred on the passage to America, she has been partially deranged and has been carefully watched by her mother to prevent her from wandering away from the house. Her age was thirty-eight years, her mental condition hopeless, and it is well she is now safe from the anguish and trouble of this world.

Dead in a Well in Mapleville
December 8, 1882

    Last Friday night the body of a man was discovered in the well of John Slater Colwell near Mapleville. The authorities were notified, and there being no regular coroner in town, O. A.

Inman, acting by virtue of his power as Justice of the Peace, called together a jury and an inquest was held.

Three witnesses were examined. Joseph Taylor, who was with the victim a short time before his death, Ben Gibson, one of whose boarders the man was, and the man who discovered the body. The victim's name was John Somerville, a Scotchman, and he was without relation or friends in this country. On Friday accompanied by Joseph Taylor, he went to Harrisville where both became somewhat intoxicated. Taking one or more drinks at every dispensary they passed, they were very drunk and became separated before reaching the scene of the fatality. Somerville went on alone, and doubtless in attempting to draw some water at the place where he was found, his feet slipped from under him. He pitched head foremost into the well, striking his head on the stones, making a long gash. Taylor, after losing his companion on the road between Harrisville and Stott's store, went on to Gazza arriving there at 8:30 Thursday evening. The body was not discovered until about 7 p.m. Friday.

The body was taken to Harrisville and buried by the town. Facts gained from a member of the jury after the above was written show that the deceased was a native of Glasgow, Scotland, where he has a wife and several children. He was a member of the Masonic order and since residing in this town had worked at Gazzaville. The jury returned a verdict of death by misfortune.

Frozen to Death
February 12, 1883

James Fletcher, an employee of the Gazzaville Mill, was frozen to death on Saturday night, while under the influence of liquor. On Saturday evening about 11:15 o'clock, Constable John Moore's attention was called to four drunken men who were creating a disturbance on the streets of Pascoag. Mr. Moore induced them to get into their wagon and start for home. It seems they must have stopped before they were far from the village and filled up again, for very early Sunday morning two of the party were again in Pascoag hunting for some liquor, saying they had a comrade down on the railroad who was numb and needed stimulants.

The men had apparently been out all night, as they were covered with snow and very cold. They procured some liquor, and can give no intelligent account of themselves until they arrived in Gazza, where one of them was at last accounts quite sick from the effects of the exposure. A little after noon on Sunday the body of a man covered with snow was discovered beside the railroad track near Carson's Grove. Upon being brought to the Pascoag depot, he was identified as Fletcher by Constable Moore. He was not dead when found. Dr. Lace was called, and adopted every known method for bringing the unconscious man back to life, but without result. Death ensued about two hours after he was discovered. There was no inquest held, as death was evidently caused by exposure and not by any injuries inflicted, although it is quite probable that there had been some dispute among the party and possibly some blows. The body was suitably dressed, a coffin procured, and after consultation by telegraph, forwarded to his mother at Auburn, New York.

From letters on his person and from friends in Gazza, it appears the deceased was to have returned to Auburn on Monday, where his mother had promised him an opportunity to inherit her property on condition of his being at home during the remainder of her life. Fletcher is spoken of as being ordinarily steady and industrious, and had a credit of $30 at Gazza for undrawn pay. He went to Pascoag Saturday to buy some clothing, and falling in with his companions went on a "final racket" which has so unfortunately proved to be absolutely final with him. The hopes of his mother, his own good prospects, and a happy and easy fortune, all destroyed for the sake of going on a spree. How many more will have to be sacrificed before young men will learn to avoid the rum bottle?

Sleigh Accident in Mapleville
March 6, 1885

George A. Suffa, a resident of Smithfield, appeared before the Council and related how on Monday evening last past he was in a sleigh with others and was driving at a moderate pace down the hill, which is in the village of Mapleville, when the runner of his sleigh came into violent collision with a stone at the corner of the two roads, which are on either side of the residence of James Legg. The shock broke his sleigh into several pieces, and caused the sudden and entirely unintentional leaving of the sleigh by its occupants, resulting in two or more pains in the body of the driver and a sore elbow and disturbed mind on the part of the other occupant.

Mr. Suffa went on to say that his sleigh was in process of repair and the "total damages by the collision" were $18. He intimated that he would give a receipt in full for all breakage, aches and pains, if the Council would allow him that sum. He also intimated that in case of their failure so to do, he should take other measures and should place his damages much higher, by just what process of computation he did not state. The stone against which Mr. Suffa directed his sleigh is a perfectly proper and necessary feature of the landscape in the vicinity of Mapleville, and keeps people from going into the ditch, and there would seem to be no need for any driver to run into a stone by the side of the road when he had seventy-five feet, or thereabouts, of space in which he might have driven. The Council took no action, and the Suffa—ing gentleman from Smithfield took his departure after a couple of hours tarry in the presence of Burrillvillians.

Drowning in White Mill Pond
March 6, 1885

After many days, the mystery of James Scott's disappearance has been explained. On Sunday afternoon last, a body was discovered in the White Mill Pond, and was found on examination to be that of "Scotty." The town authorities were notified. The body was placed in a box and held at the pond to await the arrival of Medical Examiner Smith. Mr. Smith was present Monday morning, and after looking at the remains, which were especially in the face badly decomposed, decided no inquest was necessary. Mrs. Scott, the deceased wife, was also notified by telegraph and arrived at Pascoag on the Tuesday noon train. The funeral took place on the afternoon of that day, the interment being in the Catholic cemetery.

"Scotty" had been missing eleven weeks, and when last seen alive was very much intoxicated. In all probability he fell into the river, perhaps from the bridge on Warner's Lane. There is no particular reason for supposing he committed suicide, and still less that he was the victim of foul play. There are some who think one of these was the case, and who have many arguments to prove their theory. The deceased was certainly not a valuable member of society and was at times, when intoxicated, somewhat uncomfortable to get along with, but all who knew him regret that he should have come to his death in such a distressing manner. His faithful dog still haunts the place where his master lived, relying on the neighbors for food.

One Hundred Years Ago in Burrillville by Patricia A. Mehrtens

Accident in Pascoag
June 12, 1885

Tuesday at about seven o'clock in the morning, L. D. Salisbury, who was working with Orrin Taylor shingling the Manufacturer's Hotel barn, met with a serious mishap, which fortunately did not result in instant death. Mr. Salisbury started from the staging with an armful of shingles, a hammer and a saw to carry them on to the roof. Just as he was stepping on to a ladder lying on the roof, he struck the toe of his boot against the end of a board, which threw him over the edge of the staging. Before he could recover himself., he fell, striking on his side on the roof of an outhouse four feet below, rolled off and struck on a lot of old shingles, sixteen feet further down, striking his knee against a bank wall in his descent. Strange to say he arose, came around, and into the front door of the hotel before Mr. Taylor could descend from the roof and inform the people inside of the accident. A wound on his head was bleeding profusely, strengthening cordials were instantly given, and Dr. Lace sent for. Being unable to find the doctor, Dr. Granger of Harrisville was telephoned for and made his appearance a half hour later. Dr. Granger made a thorough examination of his patient, but found no bones broken, which was remarkable.

A reporter of the *Gazette* visited Mr. Salisbury Wednesday afternoon and found him propped up in bed as comfortable as possible. He said the cut on his head did not trouble him much or the bruised left limb, but across the stomach and back he was very sore. Circumstances point to a speedy recovery, but it is as yet impossible to state beyond a doubt. His striking on two feet of old shingles in all probability saved his life, as they made a cushion. After looking at the place of accident, the wonder is that he was not killed outright. His many friends hope he may soon be able to finish the job partially completed.

Death of Lydia Phetteplace
October 1, 1886

Monday morning at about five o'clock, Lydia Phetteplace, who was sentenced twenty-six years ago to prison for life for killing her husband with an axe, died at the Cranston jail. She was tried for the murder in Providence just before the breaking out of the war in 1860. The deed was committed here in Burrillville, and many who have resided here for a quarter of a century will distinctly remember the circumstances of the case.

One Hundred Years Ago in Burrillville by Patricia A. Mehrtens

The family was not possessed of the highest intelligence, and the husband was very much addicted to drink. When intoxicated, he would cruelly beat and maltreat Lydia. Patience, however, ceased to be a virtue in her case, and she made up her mind she would put a stop to it when the opportunity arrived. One day her husband was exceedingly ugly and misused her, but finally turned a chair on the floor so the back made an inclined plane, and laid on it in a drunken stupor. She stole out and got the axe, which he had sharpened the day before to chop wood with, and cut his head nearly from his body. She then dragged his body out of the house across the yard, and left him under an apple tree. Her boy, who was lying sick upstairs, heard the noise, and coming down wished to know what the matter was. At this time, Mrs. Phetteplace was washing up the blood covering the floor. It soon was known, and she was arrested for the deed, but did not seem to realize the enormity of the act. She said, "If I had known there would have been so much fuss about it, I guess I would not have done it, but I thought everyone would be glad to get rid of the old cuss." After fifteen years of prison life in the old building, her mind gave way, and she became hopelessly insane. After being transferred to the new prison at Cranston, her insanity became more violent, until her death.

Body of Baby Found in Mill Trench
April 25, 1890

The principal theme of conversation for several days has been the finding of the body of a baby in the trench at the Harrisville mill about four o'clock Saturday afternoon. The babe was a well developed male child and weighed eight pounds. It was found tied up in a meal bag bearing the name of D. C. Remington, being one of a lot of bags stenciled more than twenty years ago. The sack containing the babe was found by Ernest W. Tinkham, who with James P. Flannigan was clearing the rack in the trench of refuse accumulated there, preventing the ready flow of water. Mr. Tinkham, it is needless to say, was surprised when he brought the sack to the surface and found what it contained.

Deputy Sheriff O. A. Inman was immediately notified, and he in turn notified Dr. George R. Smith of Woonsocket who is medical examiner of this district. A hydrostatic test was made by the doctor, who found indications of air in the lungs, showing that the child had breathed after birth. It was plainly a case of infanticide. Monday, a more thorough examination of the vital organs took place, and the body of the child was buried. The

Medical Examiner found sufficient grounds for an inquest, and has ordered the Coroner, Dr. Robert Wilcox, to have one. Dr. Wilcox at the present time is considerably indisposed, and it is not known today (Thursday) when the inquest will take place. There are plenty of rumors concerning the matter, and in an article in a Providence daily last Monday, suspicion was directed in the direction of a certain unmarried girl, which was entirely unjust as has been clearly proven. We prefer to await the Coroner's inquest before speaking of suspicion in any direction.

Lost Four Days in Woods of Douglas
July 9, 1892

Probably there is nothing that has startled the good people of Douglas and Burrillville as the wandering away from the Douglas Town Farm last Friday of Ellen Thayer, who while out in the pasture, is supposed to have had a fit. Coming out of it dazed, she wandered into the woods towards Douglas Pike where for four days without food or shelter she was allowed to remain until the selectmen of the town on Tuesday of this week offered a reward of $25 for her recovery and organized a search party.

This party, starting from the town farm at one o'clock Tuesday twenty feet apart, soon became scattered through the woods. About three o'clock, the southern end of it came upon the prostrate form of Ellen behind a knoll where she had doubtless laid down to die. She was much exhausted, having had no food or drink for four days and nights, but managed to answer their calls. They came to her aid and brought her to the highway, where a passing carriage brought her to the town farm.

Fully two hundred men and boys had gathered to witness her return, among whom was her brother, Smith Thayer, and family. When asked if she was not afraid to stay so long alone in the woods, Ellen said "No," but she admitted that she had felt rather hungry at times, though the severe rain on Sunday did not trouble her. A much closer guard should be kept upon her in the future, as this is the second time she has wandered away and she is not able to see far ahead on account of defective eyesight. Moreover, her tendency to fits makes it almost necessary that she have a constant attendant. Miss Thayer will be better known to our readers, perhaps, as the daughter of "Joe Tige Thayer" and Prussia Arnold who upon their death left her and her brother a fair income that has since been disposed of without much benefit to Ellen.

One Hundred Years Ago in Burrillville by Patricia A. Mehrtens

Sudden Death in Glendale
June 8, 1894

    Mrs. George H. Darling died suddenly Tuesday morning in the Glendale depot while waiting to take the 8 o'clock train for Woonsocket. As the first train for Woonsocket stopped at Glendale, the passengers were somewhat startled at seeing the station agent, Mr. Smith, fanning Mrs. Darling with a newspaper. She sat pale, speechless and limp in a chair close to the depot entrance. Dr. Wilcox, who was on the train, placed her in a reclining position upon the floor, and a hasty examination convinced him that life was fast going and nothing could save her. In a few minutes after the train left, she was dead. Mr. Smith, the station agent, said he was busy in the inner room when Mrs. Darling came in, he heard her cough considerably, then she remarked she did not feel well and that she never felt so queer before in her life. She repeated this, and asked Mr. Smith to fan her. He asked her if she would not like to sit in the doorway, and she said yes, and this was the position she was in when the train arrived. Mrs. Darling intended a trip to Providence to visit her sister, Mrs. Joseph Bell, and little knew how near death she was.
    Her husband, who was peddling milk in the village, was sent for and arrived before her death. She was unconscious and unable to speak. Mr. Smith summoned help from the houses through Miss Mabel Orrell who came to take the train, and all that was possible was done. The body was removed to her home in Mr. McQuades carriage, and friends notified of this sudden bereavement. The direct cause of death is uncertain, although a rupture of a blood vessel in coughing or apoplexy are possible causes as well as heart failure.

Who Shot the Man?
June 2, 1895

    A fairly well dressed, smart appearing stranger, apparently about 30 years old, was seen wandering around about the break of day Wednesday in Mapleville. He entered George Plumb's yard, and asked Mr. Plumb to carry him to the Rhode Island Hospital, saying he had been shot during the night. Mr. Plumb endeavored to ascertain who the man was and where he had received the wound, but the stranger, who was covered with fresh blood, was evasive in his replies. Finally Mr. Plumb took him to the boarding house, and seeing he was suffering severe pain, sent for Deputy Sheriff Inman.

The officer was soon at hand, but the stranger declined to tell him where the trouble occurred. Inman finally took him to the town farm and summoned Dr. Bruce. An examination revealed the fact that the man had been shot just above the right knee, the ball apparently of about 32 caliber ranging upward. The probe was inserted about five inches, but no bullet was touched, and the supposition is that it has lodged in the muscle near the leg bone. The stranger now gave his name as Michael Donahue and said his father, James Donahue, lived in Great Barrington, Mass. He is a tall, powerfully built man with red dish mustache, and says he is a weaver and had worked in the town years ago. There were no signs of liquor about him, and he would not tell how he came to be shot. He had lost so much blood that Dr. Bruce thought it best not to make further search for the bullet, and yesterday morning Sheriff Inman conveyed him to the hospital at Cranston.

It is a mysterious case, as from the course of the ball Donahue must have been lying down when shot or in the act of getting in or out of a window. Although weak from loss of blood, Donahue appears in no immediate danger. The authorities at Cranston may learn something more about the case, but this fellow is very close mouthed about the matter.

Martin Mowry Sentenced
July 21, 1899

Saturday morning, Martin Mowry, the recluse of Sweet's Hill, who was tried and convicted of the murder of Abbie Jane Reynolds and who also killed her husband, Edwin Reynolds, and adopted daughter Savilla, was brought before Judge Wilbur for sentence last Saturday. Mowry persisted in saying that he was innocent and was a victim of prejudice. Martin appeared in court attired in a black suit, and looked as if his time in prison had not affected him unfavorably. When asked if he had anything to say before sentence was pronounced, Martin started an address. He spoke of the Gordon hanging, the last in the state and insisted on his innocence. Judge Wilbur said, "There is only one sentence that can be imposed in this state for this crime, that is imprisonment in the Cranston jail for his natural life at hard labor. Mr. Clerk, you will impose the sentence." This was done, and apparently had little effect on the prisoner, who was then taken back to Cranston by Deputy Sheriff Viall.

The deed for which Mowry was convicted was one that made those who heard the news of it shudder at its atrocity. On

One Hundred Years Ago in Burrillville by Patricia A. Mehrtens

April 14, 1897 about 2:30 o'clock in the morning, the old homestead of Elisha Mathewson on Sweet's Hill was discovered to be in flames. Upon investigation, the neighbors made known the details of a most horrible crime. The house and its contents were sprinkled with oil, and in numerous places flames were fast wiping out the traces of one of the most diabolical deeds in the history of the state. The body of Mrs. Reynolds was removed from the burning structure gasping for breath. She had been frightfully hacked, and died shortly after being brought into the open air. No sign of Mr. Reynolds or the girl Savilla was seen, until the burned and charred remains were pulled from the ruins the next day. Mowry was missing and was found near Ironstone the next morning. He had a 22-calibre bullet in his head, and told a story most absurd. Mowry was tried, convicted, denied a new trial by the appellate division and, unless pardoned by some future governor, will spend the rest of his natural life at Cranston jail.

Dynamite Explosion near Box Turtle
April 20, 1900

Jonas Williams of Harrisville and Thomas Prue of Woonsocket were badly injured in an explosion of dynamite at a farm owned by Louis Methieu near Box Turtle last Saturday forenoon, and it was almost miraculous that they were not blown to atoms. They have been engaged for some time in digging a well on Methieu's farm. Last Thursday, they placed a charge of dynamite in the ledge. Because of water in the bottom of the well, the fuse did not ignite to explode the dynamite. Saturday morning, the two men endeavored to remove the charge. They both went down into the well, which was about twenty feet deep, and began to remove the packing with a drill, when without warning, the dynamite exploded. Both men were thrown against the sides of the well. The left side of William's face was ground almost to a pulp, his left eye destroyed and he sustained a large cut extending from the temple over the top of the head. His left hand was badly mangled and he was otherwise injured about the body. Prue was not injured nearly as badly as his companion. His injuries were confined to his face and legs.

Prue, who is about 32 years old, was conveyed to his home in Woonsocket and will probably recover in a short time. Williams, who is 60 years of age, was conveyed to his home on East Avenue in Harrisville, and was attended by Dr. Robert Wilcox of Pascoag.

Wagon Accident on Buck Hill
October 19, 1900

Last Sunday, a sad accident happened to a party of young folks on the Buck Hill Road. The party was from Webster, and was made of the conventional number—two. He was a newspaperman, and his companion was of a more gentle mold—in short, a poem in ruffles and laces. Neither had been over the rugged road between this place and their home, and their initial drive was of more than passing interest to them. He bubbled over the autumn woods and the bracing air, and ever and anon a squirrel or chipmunk startled them and beat a hasty retreat at their approach. It was during one of the anons that a snapping, grating noise caused her to interrupt his heavenly trend of thought and turn his attention to matters of a more earthly nature. They alighted, and both peered under the vehicle, only to find that the forward axle had become hopelessly detached from the wagon. A long walk to the nearest farmhouse, an impromptu repair with ropes and strings, and a ride extending far into the glimmering gloam formed the program of the remainder of a "pleasant" drive. The scribe was disturbed in his sleep by visions of the many "vehicular accidents" which he had unfeelingly written, and when these were interspread with visions of the aforesaid model of simplicity, he awoke in a cold sweat. It is safe to predict that in the future, the humble residents of the Bay State will be treated with more consideration in matters of this kind.

Charles A. Stoddard Suicide
April 4, 1902

Monday night, a well dressed and gentlemanly appearing man fifty years of age arrived in this village on the 7:40 train from Providence. He seemed to be well acquainted with the village and proceeded directly to the Manufacturers' Hotel on South Main Street, where he sought lodging for the night. Mr. Francis, the proprietor of the hotel, was not on the premises, and his wife expressed her regret at having nothing but a small side room to offer her guest. Upon looking at the room, the man said it would do very nicely as he was to remain in Pascoag only one night, and the small room would answer just as well as a larger one.

He left his belongings in the room and soon afterwards went to the smoking room, where he remained the rest of the evening. He went to the desk and spent some time writing, and then played cards and talked with the other guests, proving to be a very entertaining man. During the evening he drew a legal looking document from his pocket and said it was his will which he neglected to sign before leaving Providence. Three gentlemen were sitting close to the man, and he asked them to witness his signature and sign the instrument as witnesses.

The man retired about 10:30, but did not leave any instructions as to the time he wished to be called. Tuesday morning, the people at the hotel, believing their guest a traveling salesman, called him at 7:30. He did not respond, and was again called at 9:30. Just before noon, Mrs. Francis noticed the man had not left his room and she sent Bernard Dailey to ascertain the cause. He came back and said that the man was still in bed, but that he had his eyes wide open and did not answer his calls. Other messengers were sent to the room and found the stranger cold in death. His arms were stretched downward by his sides, his fingers tightly clinched, and the bedclothes were drawn up close to his throat. He looked as though death had come to him easily and that he had passed away without a struggle.

Special Officer Robert J. Haniver was notified and quickly responded. He looked upon the man as a suicide and gave orders to have the room closed until the arrival of the medical examiner. Dr. Robert Wilcox arrived about 2 o'clock and pronounced it a case of suicide. When the man was found in his room, a small table stood close to the bed. A tumbler, which probably held the fatal draught, stood upon one corner where it had evidently been placed after the man had drunk the mixture. Under the tumbler was a letter addressed to Mrs. Charles A. Stoddard and a note. The note requested those who might find the man not to send for his wife, as he had already notified her of his deed. It further requested that the letter be held until Mrs. Stoddard arrived, and in the meantime to notify Albert Taft of Bridgeton of the man's death, and to turn the remains over to Undertaker Waterman. These instructions were carried out.

As far as can be learned, no cause is given for the man's act. His friends know of no domestic trouble and speak very highly of Mrs. Stoddard. His business relations appear to be in a satisfactory condition, and it is supposed that a weariness of life and an act committed on the impulse of the moment are responsible. When the room was searched, a revolver was found beneath his pillow. Some believe that had the drug failed in carrying out the desired end, the revolver would be used to complete the deed. The funeral took place from Waterman's undertaking rooms Wednesday afternoon. A very simple service, consisting of prayer by a local clergyman, was offered, and the remains were then laid at rest at the side of immediate relatives in the Pascoag Cemetery.

Discovery of Injured Man
June 13, 1902

Monday afternoon at a late hour, Joseph Smith, a lumberman, was working near a saw mill near the old John Paine place when he discovered a man lying behind a large pine log. The man appeared to be trying to conceal himself, and Mr. Smith tried to drive him away. When the man left the shelter of the log, he walked about in a circle, and taking a paper from his pocket kept mumbling to himself the number of a street which he said was in New York. The lumberman saw the man was evidently not in his right mind, and sent to Mapleville for an officer. Frank L. Phetteplace responded, and placed the eccentric stranger under arrest. The front of the man's clothing was covered with blood, and his waistcoat and trousers were cut in several places. On the way to the bridewell in the village of Harrisville, the man told the officer his name was John Taylor of Crompton, R. I. He said he was forty-eight years of age, unmarried, and had no relatives in the country. About ten days or two weeks before his arrest, he said he left Blackstone to go to Providence. He had seen his name in some paper the Sunday previous, and the paper said that John Taylor was going to be arrested.

On the train from Blackstone to Providence, everyone on the train, Taylor says, kept saying "John Taylor will be arrested when he reaches Providence." Taylor said he was pursued by men who wanted to kill him, and when he got to Pawtucket, he left the train and went to the officers and offered to give himself up. He could find no officers in that city who would place him under arrest, and started to walk back to Manville. Somewhere on the road, he could not remember where, he was overtaken by the men who were following him. He tried to escape, but they caught him and gathered a number of sticks, poured oil over them, and made preparations to burn him at the stake. Taylor said that he was suffering very much, and when he saw he could not escape, he took his jackknife and stabbed himself. He was not sure what became of the men, as he seemed to have no further knowledge of what happened until he found himself in the officer's clutches.

Officer Phetteplace brought the man to Harrisville and locked him up. On his person was found a number of cuts evidently self inflicted. He had a jackknife in his pocket, which was covered with blood, and he also had a surgeon's lance with three blades. Dr. Alfred Poirier was called and examined the wounds. He dressed them and made Taylor as comfortable as possible. Taylor told about the same story to the doctor and to those who were in the lockup, and he seemed to be raving about some woman whose name he could not remember or did not know. He was examined by Dr. Poirier and Dr. E. V. Granger Tuesday afternoon and, in their opinion, he was not of sound mind. He was arraigned before Assistant Justice Lace Tuesday afternoon, and sentenced to the State Asylum for the Insane.

Bridgeton Fountain Accident
August 22, 1902

Wednesday afternoon, Samuel Mellor and his son, George, were driving a spirited horse in the vicinity of the fountain at Bridgeton. The animal became frightened at an automobile which was near William H. Prendergast's office, and turned between the old boarding house and the dwelling next to it. As the horse turned, one of the reins fell upon its legs, and with a mighty plunge the animal went toward the river almost reaching the embankment, but turned away sharply. The quick turn overthrew the wagon, and also threw Mr. Mellor and his son down the steep bank. He fell heavily, striking his left shoulder on the ground with such force as to stun him. The carriage, which was a fine pneumatic tire runabout, overturned. The body was wrenched off, and with the upturned running gear, the horse ran at headlong speed down Church and Main streets to Harrisville. Passing through that village to the railroad, it cleared itself from the running gear, and being diverted from the highway by a freight train at the crossing, ran down the tracks until it reached a bridge, where it was secured.

In the meantime, Mr. Mellor had been carried into Mr. Prendergast's office where he was cared for until he was carried home. Dr. Bruce came and found Mr. Mellor had sustained a dislocation of the left shoulder and was also badly shaken up by the fall. Ether was administered and the dislocation reduced. Master Fred was uninjured save for a few scratches. Mr. Mellor was as comfortable yesterday as could be expected. He was feeling the effects of the shock and his shoulder pained him considerably. His many friends hope for him a speedy recovery.

One Hundred Years Ago in Burrillville by Patricia A. Mehrtens

Fatal Shooting at Graniteville
January 30, 1903

Last Friday afternoon shortly after 4 o'clock, Michael Angelo de Palma shot Robert Lyons, Sr., killing him almost instantly, and fired several shots at Robert Lyons, Jr., all of which took effect but none proved serious. The shooting occurred in the store room in the rear of the dyehouse at Anchor Mills in Graniteville, where all of the men were employed. The three men were engaged in emptying alkali from the large bags in which it is received at the mill into barrels. The elder Lyons and de Palma were lifting one of the bags, and the latter was not able to raise his end of the bag so high as his companion, for which remissness it is said the elder Lyons upbraided him. A few heated words followed, and it is claimed Lyons then seized de Palma by the throat and struck him. De Palma says he feared that a threat, which had been previously made to injure him, was about to be carried out, and so for self protection he drew his revolver and fired two shots at his assailant, one of which entered his mouth and another through the side of his head.

The younger Lyons sprang to his father's assistance, and de Palma turned upon him, firing three shots in rapid succession. His aim this time was less effective. One of the bullets penetrated the young man's shoulder, another plowed a furrow through the flesh just over the clavicle bone, and the third gouged a piece out under the chin. After emptying the five chambers in the revolver, de Palma rushed through the finishing room of the mill and out of the mill, closely pursued by young Lyons who had secured the empty revolver. News of the affair spread like wild fire through the mill, and ere the smoke had cleared away, fellow operatives in the dyeing department had rushed to the side of the man who was mortally wounded. When they arrived, he had breathed his last.

Special Constable Roscoe S. Wood was immediately notified of the shooting and started in immediate pursuit of de Palma. At the same time, de Palma left his sister's house where he had gone directly from the mill to give himself up to the officers. De Palma disclaimed having any ill feelings toward either of the men whom he shot, but admitted having had trouble with the younger man some time ago causing him to fear danger from them since. In the altercation between the two men at that time, de Palma had his arm slightly scalded in a dye kettle. He claimed that the Lyons men had threatened to throw him into a hot kettle. De Palma has only been here a short time, the greater portion of which he had been employed in the Anchor Mills. He is about 18 years of age and was born in Italy.

Robert Lyons had not been a resident of this village for a much longer time than de Palma, having come here from Glendale late in the fall. He was a native of Roscommon County, Ireland, and during his early years, was a sailor. Coming to this country he married Miss Mary A. Kenny of Blackstone, and has since worked in the mills in Northern Rhode Island and adjacent parts of Massachusetts. He leaves a widow and seven children, two sons and five daughters.

Sad Fate of Annie Trask
May 6, 1904

Last Friday night shortly before 9 o'clock, two lads who were passing over the bridge near the mill of the Laurel Hill Yarn Co. found a ladies' pocketbook and umbrella beside the highway near the bridge. Investigation showed them to be the property of Miss Annie Trask, daughter of the late Abel and Mrs. Trask of Bridgeton. The articles were taken to the home of Miss Trask's brother-in-law, Durwood D. Bailey, and the whereabouts of Miss Trask were immediately sought. It was found she had left the home of William A. Inman where she was employed, early in the evening, presumably to visit Dr. Bruce who was her physician, and under whose care she had been for several weeks. A hasty inquiry made at Dr. Bruce's revealed the fact she had not visited his office that evening. Grave apprehensions for her safety were then felt by her people who feared that she had lost her life in the mill pond beside which her pocketbook and umbrella were found.

The assistance of friends and neighbors was at hand, and a search was instituted. A boat was secured, and the pond was dragged late into the night. Work was resumed soon after light and continued all day without result. While many felt that the search was fruitless, others were more sanguine, and Sunday morning the pond was drawn off. Eager eyes scanned the bottom of the pond as the water went down. When there was but a small stream running over the bed of the pond, the body was discerned about forty feet from the bridge. The body was taken from its resting place and tenderly carried to Mr. Bailey's home, where it was later viewed by Medical Examiner Wilcox and permission given for its burial.

Several theories have been advanced as the cause of the sad fatality, yet whether it was accidental or done in a moment of temporary insanity can never be known. Miss Trask was a most estimable young lady and had a wide circle of friends. Her home surroundings were of the most pleasant nature, and the grief stricken family have the most sincere and kindest sympathy of all in their deep bereavement.

Depot Square Accident
September 20, 1905

An accident which came very near terminating fatally occurred on Depot Square Saturday morning. Mrs. Abram Tourtellotte and a lady friend had stopped in front of the Pascoag Bakery, the former going inside. Just then, the Woonsocket train came in, and the horse, becoming uneasy, commenced backing and turned so that the carriage, occupant, and horse all went over the high embankment between the bakery and the small building nearby. The embankment is abrupt, being formed by a perpendicular stone wall about ten feet high. Over this the carriage, a phaeton buggy, went. The horse struggling frantically was carried clear over the vehicle and struck on its back with such force as to stun it for a few moments. The carriage was completely overturned and badly wrecked.

Assistance came quickly, and while some held the horse down others assisted the lady from her precarious position in the wreck. Beyond a severe shaking up, she was uninjured, and walked to a nearby carriage which conveyed the two ladies away from the scene. The horse was disentangled from the harness and seemed but little the worse for his mishap. The carriage did not pass through the accident so well, for when it was righted it bore but little resemblance to the handsome phaeton which a few moments before stood on the street. The embankment, totally unprotected by a rail or fence of any kind, has long been looked upon as a dangerous place, and should be given immediately the attention which has so long been needed.

Accident at Wilson's
October 8, 1909

Alonzo A. S. Mills is able to be at work again, having recovered from the effects of a severe fall which he sustained week before last. On Thursday of that week, Mr. Mills was returning from work at George W. Sly's and stopped on the dam at Wilson's Reservoir to converse with a friend. While talking, he leaned against a fence on the edge of a high bank wall and the fence being of a frail nature gave away and precipitated Mr. Mills to the bottom of the bank wall. He was considerably bruised and shaken up by the fall, but fortunately escaped without serious injury.

Snake Hill's Mystery
August 25, 1911

While out in quest of berries last Sunday forenoon, James Gervais and Lyman Rondeau, two young men of Mapleville, found the skeleton of a human being partially covered with earth and concealed in the cleft of a large rock in the woods on Snake Hill, a short distance from the village of Mapleville. The young men sat down on the edge of the rock and were cursorily moving the accumulation of leaves on the ground nearby. Their attention was attracted by a white object underneath a covering of leaves. Examination showed it to be a human skull, and a further investigation revealed an entire human skeleton.

The skeleton was covered with a few inches of earth and was, with the exception of the skull, well in the crevice in the big rock. Several fragments of what was once a woolen dress were discovered beside the skeleton, and at the foot were the soles of two shoes and the remains of a pair of overshoes. Judging by the soles, the shoes were about a size three for woman's wear. On the bones of the hand were two gold rings, unmarked, and several buttons were found which evidently were on a woman's dress. Locks of brown hair were discovered in the dirt where the skull was found.

Those who first saw the skull stated that there was a clearly defined and sharply cut bullet hole in the forehead and that after the skull had been handled by several people, the bones crumbled or fell apart, so that all traces of the hole were gone when the skull was examined afterwards. As soon as the young men ascertained the nature of their find, they hastened to Mapleville and reported their discovery to Dr. George W. Ashton, who in turn notified Dr. Richard L. Shea, medical examiner of Glocester, medical examiner Robert Wilcox, M. D. of this town being away on a vacation. The two physicians made a careful examination of the skeleton and pronounced it as being unmistakably that of a woman of average size and probably under 50 years of age.

The spot where the skeleton was found is about ten feet from a path leading into the Snake Hill Woods across the railroad track from the "Piggery" house and is some twenty feet from the edge of the woods. From the location of the remains it is evident that the body must have been pushed into the crevice in the rocks feet foremost, and then lightly covered with earth, after which a good-sized stone was moved toward the crevice to partially conceal the freshly moved earth. If the assertion of the early visitors to the scene last Sunday morning is true that there was a bullet hole in the skull, it seems probable that the woman was taken to the spot and there murdered. If the deed was committed in cool weather, the noise of a firearm in the woods would be unnoticed as that section is frequented in the hunting season. The hair, the rings, the buttons and possibly the texture of the remnants of the dress are all the clues which are at hand to prove the identity of the woman, and it is felt that the find of last Sunday morning will ever be the "mystery of Snake Hill."

One Hundred Years Ago in Burrillville by Patricia A. Mehrtens

MEMORIES

William Rhodes & Rhodesville
February 26, 1886

It may be of interest to many of the present generation to know that the Rhodesville referred to in last week's *Gazette* is now the village of Harrisville, and the family of Rhodes was many years ago buried on what was then called the Plain, adjoining the Harris burying ground. The ancient headstones mark their last resting place, but few of the old settlers remain who remember the family. The late Andrew Harris bought the property from them, and its present name, Harrisville, is for him. There is no male member of his family living at the present time. Albert L. Harris, the last male heir, was buried in the old family burial lot last July.

Some may remember William Rhodes, an old inhabitant of this town. When a boy he was poor. He learned the cooper's trade and went to the West India Isles to work. In his frequent voyages he learned the art of navigation and, engaging in the more lucrative occupation of a privateer, intercepted many English vessels on their way to the West Indies laden with sugar and molasses. He covered the wharves at Providence with his cargoes, and at one time felt so rich he "didn't care for John Brown, Clark and Nightingale, nor the d—l." He bought land at Harrisville, then called Rhodesville, built the large house on the corner, and owned the Othniel Young farm, the Smith Wood farm, and much land besides. He used to ride to the city on horseback, and often took a trip to South Carolina where he owned a store. They tell of his standing upon a stick of timber thirty feet long and going the length of it at three hops. He sold his prizes for Continental money, and his wife urged him to invest it in real estate, but he refused. It became almost worthless. Capt. R. said it was the only time he thought his wife knew more than he did.

218

One Hundred Years Ago in Burrillville by Patricia A. Mehrtens

Old Town House
March 18, 1887

In the *Providence Journal* Thursday, March 10th, a history of the Old Town House is given in which several errors appear. The correspondent states "that for more than eighty years the Old Town House has stood solitary and alone except on election days." The facts are, that during that time the building had been occupied by various religious and other societies. Rev. Maxey Burlingame, a popular and well-known Freewill Baptist denomination, held many services within its sacred walls. Among other societies, the Universalists held services there for several years, which were conducted by many able ministers of that faith among whom was the late Rev. John Boyden, whose memory is greatly revered. The Methodists also held services within its ancient walls conducted by Elder Taylor. The Roman Catholics also held a few meetings there before they had a church to worship in, and once performed the marriage ceremony in the presence of a large congregation. Many temperance meetings and lectures by popular speakers of the times were held there. Also, anti-slavery advocates ably expounded the unrighteousness of slavery in the South from its lofty pulpit from time to time.

    The funeral services of many respected citizens were held there as they departed from life, all of which have occurred within the last forty years. It was frequently used for various purposes—in fact it was the only building in the center of the town for many years which was suitable for public use. A memorable event took place there in the year of 1856 when the semi-centennial celebration of the organization of the Town was held in this ancient edifice. The occasion was honored by the presence of the Governor of the State Hon. William Warner Hoppin and other distinguished state officials, which was an occasion of great interest at the time and drew a large number of people together.

    The language describing the removal of the pews as being "axed up" to warm the voters, partakes of the sacrilegious. The pews in the body of the house were removed for the convenience of the voters, and many have been used for fuel in after years. No vandal's hand with a spirit of discretion removed them, and sweet memories still linger in the breasts of some of the older residents who were wont to worship in this ancient temple, dedicated as the first Freewill Baptist meeting house in Rhode Island. The old citizens, who formerly assembled there to worship, are entitled to more respectful consideration than the title of the "Old Guard," would seem to imply, for among them are represented some of the best and most respected families of the town. Let us then reverence the old building where so much instruction has been given to the people of the town in the years past, and let no dishonorable reflections be cast upon its time-honored walls. It should also be noted that Episcopal services were held there conducted by the late Rev. James H. Evans, D. D. This resulted in the building of the Episcopal Chapel in Harrisville, from which Chapel Street took its name. It was one of the first buildings on the new street opened as a highway. Let the Old Town House have all the credit it so justly deserves, to be honored in the years to come as in the past.

Two New Houses in Pascoag
February 24, 1888

The new houses to be occupied by Rep. Albert H. Sayles and Mr. Arthur Waterhouse are nearly completed. Both are nicely arranged inside and their exteriors are tasteful and elegant ornaments to the village. The residence of Rep. Sayles is some larger than the other building, and the arrangement of rooms and finish is also different. Mr. Sayles' house has an excellent cellar under it, a portion of which is bricked off for the steam furnace which heats the house. Another part is set off as a laundry, with set kettles and all conveniences for that kind of work. The kitchen is convenient, and is finished in white wood, natural finish. The floor is laid with narrow maple boards and oiled. Off the kitchen is a good sized pantry with sink, faucets and pump, and nearby is a china closet. The dining room, sitting room and parlor are large, airy rooms and connected by rolling doors. The dining room is finished off a little darker than the kitchen and has a bow window.

The sitting room is finished in cherry, and has an ornamental and unique open grate or fireplace with a hearth of prettily colored tiles. The parlor is somewhat similarly finished, and has a bay window. The hall, if it can be so called, is nearly as large as any room in the house, has an open fireplace, and is finished in quartered oak. The reflection of light through the five colored glass windows gives this hall an enchanting halo that makes one feel this to be the prettiest room in the house. A stairway leads from this hall to the five beautiful sleeping rooms above, and the rail is finely carved. Before entering this hall from the outside, a vestibule is entered off of which is a toilet room with a wash basin supplied with hot and cold water. There are five rooms, each with a good clothes closet and a bathroom on the second floor. Two stairways lead from this floor, one directly to the kitchen, the other to the lower hall and sitting rooms. The workmanship shows that good carpenters have been employed in its construction, and the mitered work came together like a single piece.

The house of Mr. Waterhouse is not quite as far advanced towards completion, and the carpenters have been delayed by the non-arrival of the stair rail. More paint has also been used in finishing the rooms Mr. Waterhouse preferring it. Both of these fine residences were built under the direction of the contractor, Mr. E. L. Foskett of Warren, Mass. The architect was John G. Skipper of Warren, Mass.

"Blowing-Out Ball" of 1852
March 30, 1888

The celebration of the night of March 20th by holding balls and parties is almost obsolete. They were called "blowing out" balls as that was the date when manufacturers ceased to light up for evening work. We recall with mingled pleasure and sadness the "blowing out" ball of 1852 given in the old hall at Harrisville. The proprietor at that time has lain under the daisies for more than a quarter of a century. Many others who threaded the mazes of the dance that night to the inspiring music of violin, harp and cornet "have joined the innumerable caravan." Four from one family who actively participated in the festivities Nelson, Simeon, Alice and Mowry Steere are silent on earth forever. A cousin "Varnus" as he was called, whose agile feet would perform a *pirouette* at the first note from Joe Greene's bugle, has also "passed on."

Andrew F., Albert B. and Lydia Harris, guests at that evening's entertainment, lie in the old graveyard at Harrisville. Matilda, wife of O. A. Inman, is listening to sweeter strains than ever came from earthly harps. Malvina, daughter of David Richardson, passed away in young womanhood, leaving husband and children to mourn her loss. Joseph O. Clarke, whose presence seemed to hold in check turbulent spirits by his calm self-possession, sleeps in the hillside cemetery at Harrisville. Another whose enthusiasm in all wholesome amusements was almost youthful, whose presence was an inspiration among the ball players of the time, and whose sterling integrity no man dared question, was Smith R. Arnold. His resting place with that of his companion is near J. O. Clarke's on the hill side. Brown

Richardson and wife, Miss Ellen Arnold, sister of the wife of Mayor Robbins, Mrs. John Arnold, Willard Marshall and Sarah Walling, Charles and George Whipple, Miss Maria Sayles, James Olney, whose presence was indispensable as floor manager, the Misses Emma and Marcella Arnold, with many others who made the banqueting hall merry with jests and laughter that night, lie with hushed lips and hands quietly folded.

Through the shadowy years we see them as they moved to the sound of delicious music evolved from the instruments of "Greene & Brown's Quadrille Band." No incandescent light displayed the wrinkles and crowsfeet, making it extremely unwise for any but those in the first purple flush of life's morning to stand under the chandeliers. Light emanated from lamps whose supply was furnished by the waters of the North Pacific. Although not as radiant as more modern "glims," it sufficed to light faces and forms of women whose claims to personal attractions were far above the average. Burrillville, at one time claimed the banner girl of the state, and we think that there are many who would conscientiously endorse the claim. But this review of the past is getting lengthy—may be taking too much valuable space, but the scenes and incidents of that time were so fresh in our memory today, its anniversary, that we could not forbear this tribute to their memory. -W

Memories of Central Pascoag
January 31, 1890

Dear *Gazette* - I feel it would not be amiss to go back 55 years and compare the times then to now, relative to a business sort of view to bring forward persons who were our strong men then in affluence and influence, who gave us their help, temporarily, financially and personally, in all business matters. We will commence with Major Arnold Hunt who lived at that time where A. L. Sayles now lives. He owned a great tract of land what was then called Buck Hill and had men work the year round by the month, men with families and without. He kept a store in the brick basement across the street. He kept rum, tobacco, codfish and more rum, calico, hats, caps, boots and shoes and paid his men out of the store. Your reporter well remembers that every Thanksgiving and Christmas he would go out south where is now A. L. Sayles' barn and put up turkeys a certain number of yards, and charge so much a shot. If the marksman hit the turkey he had it. If not—shoot as long as he wanted to pay the price named. He had great influence on town elections by treating the voters. He had the first bank in his house called the Pascoag bank, his son Dennis was cashier.

One day we heard the alarm of fire, and we ran to see what it was. The bank was on fire, but was soon put out. A great many of the bills were picked up, some half burned and some less. The next day the cashier was missing, and some thought he was seen in the woods east the village and made fun of us boys to go and help find the lost man. Two days search brought no tidings from the lost. Some suggested he might be in the pond, and a cannon was brought out and fired with no success. Some said he would raise in nine days. He did, but not out of the pond. Where he died and how he died we leave for future reference. What is now Laurel Hill was once named after him, Huntsville. After the fire, the bank was kept in an ell room adjoining where the bank is now. Upstairs James S. Cook, cashier; Whipple Walling assistant, until it was moved where it is now. Pascoag Savings Bank was considered safer than to have the money in your own pocket, and it was until its termination.

The next man was James Harris, Esq., brother-in-law of Hardin Sayles. He was a tanner and currier. The bark mill where he ground bark was where A. L. Sayles' dye house now stands. His tan vats were where the bridge now is with a large two story shop back, basement for stock, and upstairs a shoemakers' shop. He kept a shoemaker the year round. If we could get a suit of clothes made from Hardin Sayles' double and twisted cloth, and a pair of James Harris' square-toed shoes, we were rigged out to go and see our best girl if we had one, if not, we would go and see the next best one. - L.D.S.

More Central Pascoag by L.D.S
February 28, 1890

Dear *Gazette*: We will commence with the Kimball Estate that was burned at the lower village abut 25 or 30 years prior to our first date. There was an old forge where Arnold Sayles carried on the business that boomed until it came to an end. Peter Place bought the privilege and all concerned, and built a saw mill and grist mill and a tobacco factory and figured largely in business—and that had an end. Soon after this Peter Place and Lyman Copeland made coarse satinettes, and this company dissolved and Place & Copeland sold out to Benjamin and Mason Hathaway, brothers. Peter Place still doing outside business for this firm as he had capital experience in connecting Providence and Pascoag together. About this time, some imagined that

One Hundred Years Ago in Burrillville by Patricia A. Mehrtens

Providence and Pascoag did about all the business of this small State. Royal Chapin and John Waterman were very important men in those times—with their money and influence they were stocking and giving help to most all the factories in the state. At that time, the writer well remembers of working for the Hathaways, and Mr. Chapin coming up to bring the money to pay the help and his saying to me, "Stick to your work and learn all you can, maybe you will run a factory sometime."

After the Hathaway's had their day, they sold to Jason and Stephen Emerson, brothers from Uxbridge, Mass. They enlarged the mill, floors were laid, and made great improvements; made a better class of goods. Every year they gained. Jason left and Stephen still ran and made money, being honest and industrious and using the old farmers motto: "If you by your business would thrive, you must either hold, or drive." He left the mill with a competency, showing to his successors, making your business your own business and attending to it, you will always succeed.

Lafayette Reynolds, buying the estate, took down the old mill which was wood, and put up a very handsome and strong stone factory which he ran and made still more improvements. As years passed, knowledge increased, war times came on, and there was a great call for army goods. Everyone who ever saw a factory went at manufacturing and some, yes a great many, were made extremely rich in the raise of prices and make what they had a mind to make. They would say the government is able to pay, he had his day. Horace Kimball came in next, and being a monied man managed his own business until the mill burned down, and now we have the satisfaction of looking on the ruins the fire made.

I will now give you a little insight into our preaching in those days. Our preaching cost nothing and it was well worth it. Peter Place was a pious man and a Sunday School superintendent, keeping the Sunday School in the old schoolhouse on the corner of the road as you turn to go up the Reservoir Road. Peter Place could and did preach to us. Many a time he has been to Providence on business with his horse called "Railroad," starting early in the morning attending to his business and, turning towards home would go to sleep, sleeping all the way. His horse would drive himself under the shed across the road from where the furniture shop now is and the family hearing the horse come, would go out and wake him up. After eating his supper he would preach in his own home. Our choir, consisting of twenty voices, would sing, and then we would disperse for our homes.

One Hundred Years Ago in Burrillville by Patricia A. Mehrtens

Mapleville & Daniel Cooper's House
July 24, 1891

A trip to Mapleville found business good at the mill and with good prospect for fall business. This village shows more thrift of late, which is easily discernible by an experienced eye than for several years past. The buildings were looking tidier and better kept. The road leading up the hill has lots of small stones lying loose, and is not in as good shape as it should be but, in time it is expected that they will receive proper attention. Carey at Oakland has been crowded with work ever since he built his capacious new shop, and Mr. Allen overhead has the best facilities for painting carriages of anyone in town, and does first-class work.

One survey made for a track to connect the Woonsocket road with the P. & S. branch cuts the fine field back of Mr. Salisbury's house right in two. Another survey has been below the silk mill along the edge of the water. This would connect with the P. & S. branch some ways below the Oakland station across the stream. It is not known yet where they will locate. The Y track would be a great convenience here in transferring Boston freight from the Woonsocket road to the Providence road, and vice versa. Speaking of crossing Mr. Salisbury's land, some of the older residents might get a better idea if we should say it crossed the land in the rear of the old Daniel Cooper house. Mr. David S. Salisbury, an old resident of Burrillville, but who has for many years been in the west, bought this place two years ago and the house has been newly fitted and renovated throughout. The house was built in the beginning of this century (1800's) by Mr. Daniel Cooper and was built according to his own liking. There were peculiarities about Mr. Cooper, and it is not strange that there were some peculiarities about the construction of the house.

We do not expect nowadays to see houses built the same as they were 100 years ago. In those days they believed in using plenty of timber, and most of it was hewn. Not having the machinery to get out finish with, it was done by hand work, and, consequently, much slower work to build a house. One peculiar feature in connection with this house is a large tunnel leading from the cellar under ground thirty or forty feet to the outside. The covering of this tunnel are huge flat stones. The floor is of stone and also the sides. It is exceedingly well built, and the joints are very close, so much so that nothing of the vermin kind could ever find entrance. An idea of the size of this square tunnel is given when we say Mr. Cooper drove his ox team through to the cellar. The floor of the cellar under the house is also laid with large flat stone, and so closely that it is impossible to run a case knife between the joints. At the front door, huge flat stone door steps are found, which goes to show that an immense amount of labor for those times must have been bestowed upon the stone work. The cellar stairs were very steep indeed, and made of solid triangular blocks of wood placed upon huge stringers.

After building the front stairs, it is said they did not suit Mr. Cooper, and he drove the oxen to the front door, hooked a logging chain to them, and yanked them out. The chimney was very large, as was customary in those days, in order to have fireplaces for the various rooms. The amount of brick used in some of the chimneys would build a half dozen of the modern pattern. About midway between the first and second stories and to which entrance can be gained only by a door from in the wall located half way up the stairs in the front entry, is a smoke place for meat and also a place to hang meat to keep it from the flies. A look inside with a light showed it to be very grimmy. In the other was noticed an old fashioned cradle which formerly belonged to Joseph Mowry of Smithfield, and had done the "lulla-by" act for several generations of the Mowrys. What would our ancestors have said if one of our modern "rock-a-by's" could have been seen in that primitive age? Welcome Mathewson, father of David Mathewson, made the door latches and Rufus Williams the hinges used in the house of Mr. Cooper. Many of these ancient things can be seen now about the house, which Mr. Salisbury in his remodeling, did not destroy, although the general appearance of the inside has been entirely changed.

Retrospective & Prospective
August 16, 1895

The growth of a village appears slow to the ordinary individual, but to one who in former years resided within its borders, and who after having spent years away returns to his native town, the changes seem more pronounced. Take our own village for example. Quite often we hear some impatient individual exclaim, "Pascoag grows very slow." Otis Eddy, a native of this village who returned to the town a few weeks ago after years of residence in the west, did not so express himself. From his ninety odd years of knowledge, erect form and bright memory, he drew sketch after sketch of the early history of the

One Hundred Years Ago in Burrillville by Patricia A. Mehrtens

town. He could remember Pascoag with only four houses, and gave the names of each occupant. Well he remembered the first mill, where No. 2 now stands; the first store was also depicted. Mr. Eddy and his brother built the first hotel where Potter & Salisbury's store now is. The first church, the Free Baptist, the first bank, its trials, etc., also came in for a short history. All the men and women, boys and girls he knew then are gone.

The village now has railroads, electric lights, telegraph and telephones, five churches, a mission, nine or ten schools, streets by the score where only cowpaths or forests existed then. There are eleven mills clattering away, only a sawmill then represented our industry. We have seventy odd stores and offices, houses by the hundreds, and almost all of this growth has come since 1850. Should the same pro rate growth keep on that has blessed us since 1850, we shall, by the time our citizens who are now in their forties reach the age of Mr. Eddy have become a city with 90,000 population. This would be at the rate of from 100 people in 1840, to 100,000 people in 1940, or one hundred years later. Ought not that to be satisfactory?

The secret of a sure growth is the fostering of every local industry small or great. Bid each welcome, and so far as you can, give them your support. Each laborer, clerk or proprietor counts one not only for himself but for his family and those who minister to them. Consider him or them only common enemies who, living outside our village, hold idle property in our midst or who try to divert industry from the town. There is no excuse for them. Let them pay the full tax rate, and our people who labor for the growth of the village or town be the ones to gain our consideration. Be ready for improvements, and there is no reason why the next twenty years shall not see us looking quite citified with as well located a village as there is in New England.

How to Pat the Juba
4/19/1907

When the ordinary boy has reached the age of from twelve to fourteen years, he has usually developed into the most awkward appearing animal on earth. A girl will grow from babyhood to old age and do it gracefully through the whole journey. But a boy, while he starts out with as much grace as his sister, and having reached his maturity has about recovered his lost ground, there are a few years when he finds himself sadly in the lurch. His legs have lengthened out a little too fast for the plumpness they have taken on, and the knee joints and ankles have been all ready for two or three years to receive the plumpness that may come later, while the feet are the most progressive part of his anatomy. As for hands and arms, no boy about to go into a room with company present ever knew what to do with them.

Now, Otis Wood was an ordinary boy, a little accentuated. Yet there were occasions when awkwardness or the appearance of awkwardness was no part of his attributes. As a boy he was a fine dancer, and at that time to be a good dancer was to possess an accomplishment to be desired. In the cotillion, every movement was a graceful accompaniment to the music that set his feet in motion, while the stirring strains of "Money, Musk" or "Soldiers' Joy" would send him through the mazy dance with the lightness that an autumn breeze would send a thistle-down awhirling. But to see him dance the Juba breakdown was to see great things. I wonder if anyone nowadays would know what a Juba breakdown was like. Maybe everyone knows but I don't believe I have heard the name in fifty years. Lest there should be some who do not know what it is like, I will try to explain it. The dance requires two, one to pat the Juba and other to dance it.

To pat the Juba, one must stand with the weight of the body mostly on one foot, the other foot being slightly advanced, with the toe of the advanced foot beat a sharp steady beat while with both hands using the advanced knee as a sort of drum head keep up a continual patting between the beats of the toe producing crescendos and diminuendos ad libitum as the case seems to require. Artists competent to pat the Juba are born so, never made.

At noontime one winter day after dinner had been eaten, Harley Smith (who having been born a Juba patter was a competent artist) commenced to pat the Juba for any boy who wished to dance. The sound of dancing feet soon called Otis from outside. As he entered the room he caught sight of the teacher's shoes which had been discarded for boots while going to dinner. Pulling them on over his cowhide boots with a whirl and a dash and a clatter, he threw himself into the breakdown with all the vim that the added weight of the shoes to his already heavy boots could give.

His long legs had well developed muscle, and the way that shoe leather was thrashed and stamped and shuffled and kicked was a sight. While Harley, responding to the magnetism of the flying feet, redoubled his efforts in the patting accompaniment. The wild whirl and clatter went on with wilder clatter and whirl wholly unmindful of the awful figure out on the street who, helped by a strong wind, was rapidly bearing down on the old school house, the long cloak in as violent agitation as though a modern hay tedder was in active operation beneath their folds. The door flies open and the face of "Old Keep" with the under lip protruding with mighty displeasure appears.

Harley, who stands with his back to the door unconscious of the apparition, bends his energy to the beat and adds the sharp cry of hi! hi! hi! to quicken the wild measure to greater speed. While Otis, who has caught a glimpse of the face, gives a light, quick sweep of the foot, and one shoe goes zip against the door. A returning sweep and the other shoe has followed its mate, passing through the open door to the entry beyond. Otis, properly clad in cowhide boots only, innocently walks off to his seat, and Harley, executing a beautiful diminuendo movement, brings the entertainment to a stately close, leaving the teacher with nothing to do but to enter on the tablets of his memory on the debtor side a good large sum to be liquidated at some future time with interest properly added.

Pascoag in 1872
May 23, 1908

(The following article on Pascoag was taken from a newspaper printed about 1872 and will doubtless be of interest to many of our readers. Editor, *Herald*) We made our annual pilgrimage to Pascoag and vicinity on Monday, and was pleased to notice evidences of improvement and prosperity. The village has a new public house, the "Manufacturers Hotel" erected during the past year by Albert L. Sayles, Esq., and well kept by T. M. Baker & Son. The house is eligibly situated with pleasant surroundings, and has the modern improvements. When built, its dimensions were thought ample for the locality, but its popular landlords already find its rooms too few in number for the public demand. Mr. Sayles is remodeling the old hotel and will convert it into stores and tenements.

The Pascoag National Bank and the new Savings Bank have recently been located in new, elegant and convenient quarters on the first floor in the building next west of the old location. The old plan of a deep vault and barred shutters has been abandoned. The rooms are peculiar for being nearly all windows, and the massive safe stands in broad daylight. The cashier, Jas. S. Cook, Esq., (an olden time Woonsocketer) entertains the idea that the valuables of a bank are safer in such premises in a village or town street than those shut from public view—an opinion which we endorse. Many banks, after an entrance is obtained, enable the robbers to perform their work in perfect security. The new Savings Bank is a gratifying success, the deposits already amounting to over half a million. In the west end of the bank building, Messrs. H. Sayles & Son have fitted up a very handsome counting room. They are the most extensive and most successful manufacturers in Pascoag.

Two of the village mills are standing idle, having been stopped several weeks for repairs—those of Mr. Kimball and Fiske & Sayles. The new railroad to Providence, whose western terminus—for the present at least—will be Pascoag, has so far advanced as to be regarded as a fixed fact. It will enter the village at the valley at the east end where the roadbed is already completed. This enterprise has given new business hope and prospect to the villagers. They would have preferred the completion of the half-built railroad to Woonsocket, as that offered direct routes to Boston and Worcester as well as to Providence; but we are not surprised that the mismanagement and delay on this line finally turned their efforts to another route. Woonsocket is now likely to lose an important business from the northwestern section of the State.

Midway between Pascoag and Laurel Ridge is the cassimere mill of James O. Inman, which turns out weekly 3,800 pieces of first quality goods equal to those made anywhere in the country. Still higher up on the Clear River are the woolen mills of T. E. Hopkins and J. A. Walden and the spindle manufactory of A. S. Hopkins. Spindles have been made here for forty years, and they enjoy a high reputation. The hard-working farmers of Burrillville have the gratifying prospect of good crops. The hay harvest is much better than last year. Corn, potatoes and other vegetables look exceedingly promising.

Remarkable Caves in Pascoag
July 17, 1908

Everybody familiar with the natural curiosities of Pascoag has noticed the peculiar caves in the ledges on the south side of the Reservoir Road at a point midway between South Main Street and the old quarry. The caves are peculiar in that they are very low and are apparently supported by water worn columns or pilasters, as carefully placed by nature as they would have been by human ingenuity, to keep the fissure open and the heavy weight of rock above from falling down and closing up the caves. The exterior appearance is familiar to all, and many a Pascoag lad has explored the interior recesses with greater or less trepidation. It is doubtful if ever lads of the present generation have entered the low caves with feelings akin to those felt by a party of boys sixty odd years ago, when they were searching for the body of a man whom it was thought might be found in the furthermost corner.

An official of a bank, which was then located in the village of Pascoag, disappeared suddenly, and the condition of the institution was such that it was feared the man had taken his own life. Acting upon the supposition that he had crawled into the caves in the ledges and there committed suicide, the lads were importuned to crawl into and thoroughly explore the unknown recesses. One of the party of youthful explorers is still a resident of Pascoag, and the other day related his experiences to a *Herald* reporter.

It was with difficulty that the boys were able to enter the caves and progress was very difficult. Every moment they expected to see the body for which they were searching, and were pleasantly disappointed to have their task prove fruitless. Public opinion was then positive that the body was beneath the waters of the Union Mill Pond, and a cannon which had seen service in the Dorr War was brought up from Chepachet, and all day long was fired across the pond with a view to raising the body. This expenditure of gun powder likewise proved unavailing, and the search was given up except in a somewhat desultory manner.

A new clue was gained, and the creditors of the then defunct institution sent a local man to New York in search of the missing official. This, too, proved futile. Some time afterwards, the official returned to Pascoag, and it is said that he immediately went to the spot where he had concealed a quantity of bank bills, only to find them in such condition as to be useless for the purpose of circulation. The hiding place of the bills was said to have been in a drill hole in a rock into which the bills were forced after having been tightly rolled up. The hole had been filled up with earth through which moisture worked and spoiled the money. Some of the books of this old bank now repose in a garret of a house in this town, although the officials and creditors of the institution have long since passed away.

Thus ends our travel through time using the old newspapers of Burrillville. Hope you enjoyed your visit. - P.A.M.

www.ingramcontent.com/pod-product-compliance
Lightning Source LLC
Chambersburg PA
CBHW051045160426
43193CB00010B/1075